UNDERSTANDING MODERN REAL ESTATE TRANSACTIONS

Alex M. Johnson, Jr.

Vice Provost for Faculty Recruitment and Retention
University of Virginia

Mary & Daniel Loughran Professor of Law
University of Virginia School of Law

2001

LEXIS Publishing™

LEXIS®-NEXIS® • MARTINDALE-HUBBELL®
MATTHEW BENDER® • MICHIE™• SHEPARD'S®

QUESTIONS ABOUT THIS PUBLICATION?

For questions about the **Editorial Content** appearing in these volumes or reprint permission, please call:

Adriana Sciortino .... (800) 252-9257 (ext. 2572)

Outside the United States and Canada please call .... (212) 448-2000

For assistance with replacement pages, shipments, billing or other customer service matters, please call:

Customer Services Department at .... (800) 833-9844
Outside the United States and Canada, please call .... (518) 487-3000
Fax number .... (518) 487-3584

For information on other Matthew Bender publications, please call
Your account manager or .... (800) 223-1940
Outside the United States and Canada, please call .... (518) 487-3000

Library of Congress Catalog Card Number 2001089712
ISBN   0820546097

Editorial Offices
2 Park Avenue, New York, NY 10016-5675 (212) 448-2000
201 Mission St., San Francisco, CA 94105-1831 (415) 908-3200
www.lexis.com

(Matthew Bender & Co., Inc.)   (Pub.3127)

TABLE OF CONTENTS

CHAPTER 5   BREACH OF THE PURCHASE AND SALE CONTRACT

CHAPTER 7   VOLUNTARY TRANSFERS OF MORTGAGED PROPERTY

PART 2:   CONDOMINIUMS AND COMMUNAL OWNERSHIP

CHAPTER 11 FORMS OF COMMUNAL OWNERSHIP

PART 1: THE BASIC RESIDENTIAL REAL ESTATE TRANSACTION

There are many variations of the process through which real estate is bought and sold, but at a minimum, real estate transactions typically require: (1) the execution of a contract of sale, (2) the buyer's inspection and acceptance of the seller's title, (3) the buyer's arrangement of financing, (4) the closing or settlement of the deal, and (5) the recording of the deed, given by seller to buyer, and the recordation of any mortgage or other security instrument executed by the buyer.

CHAPTER

1

THE PARTIES TO THE TRANSACTION

SYNOPSIS

[B] Beneficiary

[C] Trustee

§ 1.01 Overview

The first step in learning the basic residential real estate transaction is understanding the parties and terminology involved in the typical transaction. This section provides a capsule look at the parties primarily involved in the basic residential real estate transaction and defines their role therein. As we progress and new parties, i.e. the escrowholder, title insurer, etc., are introduced to the transaction, their roles will similarly be defined and explained. Though initially the focus of this text will be restricted to the residential real estate transaction, later sections will address the issues involved in communal ownership (condominiums) and commercial real estate transactions.

§ 1.02 Vendor

The vendor is the *seller* of the real property. "Vendor" is synonymous with "seller" but is preferred to the generic term "seller" because it connotes a seller of real property, as opposed to personal property. In older cases, and in rare instances today, vendor was used solely to refer to sellers of real property pursuant to an installment land sales contract.[1] Today, vendor is the preferred term used to describe the seller of real property irrespective of the manner of sale and is used herein to describe the seller of real property.

§ 1.03 Vendee

The vendee is the *purchaser* of real property. Though at one time "vendee" was only used to describe a purchaser of real property pursuant to an installment land sales contract, today vendee is the preferred term used to describe the purchaser of real property, irrespective of the manner of purchase, and is used throughout to describe the purchaser of real property.

§ 1.04 Broker

The broker is the party employed by either the vendor or the vendee, although typically the vendor, to arrange the sale or purchase of real property as the agent of the hiring party. In most states, the broker must be licensed by the state in which she acts and operates by passing a written test and satisfying certain prescribed educational requirements. Frequently, the broker is referred to as a realtor, and in many cases "realtor" is synonymous with "broker." However, realtor is a service mark term (similar to a trademark) indicating that the broker is a member of the National Association of Realtors and is qualified to be described as a realtor. Therefore, one may be a broker and not a realtor, but one

---

[1] For a discussion of installment land sales contracts, see *infra* § 3.04.

may not be a realtor without the broker certification. The majority view is that a broker has authority to show, advertise, and market the property, but cannot enter into an actual contract of sale with a prospective purchaser. Another common type of license used in the real estate brokerage industry is the salesperson's license, which is relatively easier to obtain than a broker's license, but requires that the salesperson act under the supervision of a licensed broker.

[A] Listing Broker

The broker selected by the vendor as her agent to sell the real property is frequently referred to as the listing broker. The listing broker is responsible for *"listing the property,"* for example, publicizing its availability for sale by posting notices, placing ads in the newspaper, and, more importantly, registering the property being sold in the local Multiple Listing Service (MLS).[2]

[B] Selling Broker

"Selling broker" evolved as a term of art to specifically designate the broker who is the proximate or procuring cause of sale of the real property listed by the vendor.[3] The selling broker may be, but often is not, the listing broker. As a result, typically two brokers are involved in the sale of a residence.

[C] Middleman

A middleman is someone engaged by the vendor, vendee, or both, to bring the parties together to effectuate the sale of the real property. "Middleman" is not synonymous with "broker" since the middleman's only job is to bring the parties together by identifying, as the case may be, suitable prospective vendors or vendees. The middleman is not in a fiduciary relationship with the party who hired him and plays no role in the negotiation of the transfer of the property unless specifically requested to do so by the parties. The middleman usually earns his fee or commission upon sale of the property and not upon the execution of a contract of sale which the vendor accepts.[4]

§ 1.05   Multiple Listing Service (MLS)

In the listing broker's efforts to market an available property, access to a Multiple Listing Service (MLS) is key. A MLS provides a computerized database of available listings, making listed properties widely accessible to prospective purchasers and other brokers who subscribe to the MLS. In exchange for the opportunity to pool their listings, member-brokers agree to split commissions earned from sales of the listed properties between the listing and the selling brokers according to some predetermined scheme, typically 50/50.[5]

---

[2] For a description and definition of a multiple listing service, see *infra* § 1.05.

[3] For a discussion of the relevance of the proximate or procuring cause of sale as it relates to the payment of the commission owed to the broker by the vendor, see *infra* § 2.03.

[4] For a discussion of when the broker's fee or commission is earned, see *infra* § 2.03.

[5] For a discussion of brokers' commissions in the MLS context, see *infra* § 2.02[E][1].

For example, vendor enters into an agreement allowing broker to list the property with the MLS of the county in which the real property is located. Broker fills out a form provided by the MLS and submits the form to the MLS office. The information on the form is then entered into a central computer which is accessible by any dues-paying member, or any employee of a dues-paying member, of the MLS. More importantly, a book containing descriptions and photographs of all MLS listings, differentiated by location and price, is updated and disseminated to MLS members periodically. Thus, any broker-member of the MLS has access not only to his own listings, but also to all of the other listings that have been submitted to the MLS. Hence, a prospective vendee can be shown both the broker's own listings and any of the other listings appearing in the MLS.

§ 1.06 Mortgagee

A mortgage is a financing device that secures repayment of a debt evidenced by a promissory note. The mortgagee is the entity or party who lends money to the owner of real property and receives, in addition to the promissory note that evidences the debt, a security interest in the borrower's (mortgagor's) ownership interest in the real property. If the debt is not repaid to the mortgagee, the mortgagee is entitled to foreclosure proceedings and may seize the real property in repayment of the debt.[6] The mortgagee is usually, but not exclusively, a bank, savings and loan association, or other financial institution. The mortgagee's security interest in real property, as opposed to personal property, is what differentiates a mortgagee from a personal property secured creditor who is regulated solely by the rules of the Uniform Commercial Code.

One way to clarify the unique rules that have developed regarding real, as opposed to personal, property is to recognize that real property is immobile, unique, and has an infinite life. Hence, many of the rules regulating personal property security interests are inappropriate, unnecessary, or ill-suited for real property. Yet, many efficient rules adopted to regulate the creation, use, and termination of personal property security interests can readily be adapted to regulate real property security interests. One practical theme is whether the maintenance of separate rules for regulating real and personal property is justified or whether it results from historical accident and is no longer useful. Many uniform acts have been passed to address this issue and have begun to integrate the rules governing real and personal property. For example, the Uniform Vendors and Purchasers Risk Act (UVPRA) and, more importantly, the Uniform Land Transactions Act (ULTA), have been promulgated with the goal of modernizing real estate law by eradicating historical anachronisms that serve no purpose and integrating, where warranted, modern developments in the law of personal property into the law of real property.

---

[6] For a discussion of foreclosure proceedings, see *infra* §§ 8.04 and 8.05.

[A]   Purchase Money Mortgagee

A purchase money mortgagee is a mortgagee who provides the vendee with a portion or all of the money to *purchase* the mortgaged property. In certain states, priorities and advantages that are not given to mortgagees generally are given to purchase money mortgagees, such as preferences in the recording system and in obtaining a deficiency judgment.[7]

For example, Buyer wishes to purchase a piece of real property, Blackacre, from O, the owner. Buyer applies to First Bank for a loan of $80,000 and agrees to provide $20,000 of his own money to pay the remainder of the purchase price (the "downpayment"). First Bank agrees to make a loan to Buyer, if it is secured by a first mortgage on Blackacre. To effectuate the title transfer from O to Buyer, Buyer pays O $20,000 and First Bank, in effect, pays O the remainder of the purchase price, or $80,000. Simultaneously with this transfer of title from O to Buyer, or immediately thereafter, First Bank will record its mortgage on Blackacre as the first mortgagee. Hence, First Bank's mortgage is a purchase money mortgage and First Bank is a purchase money mortgagee because the funds lent to Buyer by First Bank were used to actually purchase Blackacre. Any borrowed funds that are utilized by the vendee to purchase an asset are purchase money funds, and the individual or entity that supplies that money is properly designated as a purchase money mortgagee.

To distinguish a purchase money mortgage from other mortgages, assume that five years later Buyer applies to Second Bank for a loan of $10,000 to build an addition on the house situated on Blackacre, and Second Bank approves the loan conditionally upon obtaining a valid mortgage on Blackacre. Once again, Second Bank will record its mortgage on Blackacre simultaneously with, or immediately after, disbursing the proceeds of the loan to Buyer. (As a practical matter, since Buyer is the record owner of Blackacre at the time the loan is made, the Bank may require that the mortgage be filed of record prior to disbursement.) Assuming that the first mortgage has not been paid off, Second Bank will hold a second mortgage on the property because Second Bank's mortgage is second *in time* and, more importantly, second *in priority* due to the operation of the recording system. Second Bank's mortgage, which is used to improve, but not to purchase, the residence is *not* a purchase money mortgage. The fact that the funds are used to improve the value of the residence is irrelevant to the loan's characterization as a purchase money mortgage or non-purchase money mortgage.

[B]   Third Party Purchase Money Mortgagee

Occasionally a distinction is made between a purchase money mortgagee-vendor and a third-party purchase money mortgagee or a non-purchase money mortgagee-vendor. A purchase money mortgagee-vendor is a seller who finances a portion

---

[7] For a discussion of the recording system, see *infra* Chapter 10. For a discussion of deficiency judgments, see *infra* § 8.07.

or all of the purchase price of real property by taking a mortgage in the property sold as security for all or part of the purchase price. Thus, the vendor becomes a mortgagee. Thus, if O, in our hypothetical purchase and sale, accepted a down payment of $20,000 and the vendee's note to pay the remainder of the purchase price ($80,000) secured by a lien on the real property sold, O would be a purchase money mortgagee-vendor. A third party purchase money mortgagee is the holder of any purchase money mortgage who was not the vendor of the property at the time the mortgage was executed. Thus, in the hypothetical above involving First Bank, First Bank is properly characterized as a third party purchase money mortgagee.

§ 1.07 Mortgagor

The mortgagor is almost always the vendee or purchaser of the property.[8] The mortgagor is the debtor in the mortgagee-mortgagor transaction whose debt is secured by a mortgage—for example, a lien on her real property. The mortgagor, like the mortgagee, executes two standard instruments to create a valid mortgage. The first, and most important, instrument is the *promissory note* by which the mortgagor promises to pay off the debt owed to the mortgagee. The second instrument is the *mortgage*, which identifies and establishes the security interest in the real property that secures the debt. It is important to remember that these are two very distinct instruments containing unique rights created when a mortgage is executed.[9]

§ 1.08 Deed of Trust

A deed of trust is a financing device used in the purchase of real property. Pursuant to a deed of trust, the vendor transfers legal title to a trustee who holds title for the benefit of the beneficiary. For various reasons having to do with obtaining a deficiency judgment (largely historical and no longer relevant), in many states a deed of trust is used instead of a mortgage to finance the purchase of real property.[10] If a deed of trust is used, three *seemingly* new characters are introduced to the typical real estate transaction. However, in reality, only one new character is introduced; the other two characters merely change labels to reflect the fact that a trust is used and various equitable interests are created as a result.

---

[8] *But see* Harms v. Sprague, 473 N.E.2d 930 (Ill. 1984) (one joint tenant mortgages his interest in separate commonly-held property in order to purchase another parcel of property, and the mortgage and his property interest in the commonly-held property were extinguished upon his death).

[9] For a discussion of the recording system, see *infra* Chapter 10. For a discussion of deficiency judgments, see *infra* § 8.07. For a more in depth discussion of a mortgage as a financing device, see *infra* Chapter 6.

[10] For a discussion of a deed of trust as a financing device, see *infra* § 6.03.

[A] Trustor

The trustor is the *mortgagor*. Thus, the obligations and identity of the trustor and the mortgagor are, for all intents and purposes, identical. In the arcane language of trusts, the mortgagor is referred to as the trustor, or settlor, because it is she who has the obligation to act (here to make the monthly payment to the trustee for the benefit of the beneficiary) pursuant to the trust.[11]

[B] Beneficiary

For all practical purposes, the beneficiary is the *mortgagee*. Therefore, the obligations and identity of the beneficiary and the mortgagee are, for all intents and purposes, identical. In the arcane language of trusts, the mortgagee is referred to as the beneficiary because she or it gets the benefit of the trust (here, the receipt of the monthly payments made by the trustor/mortgagor).

[C] Trustee

The trustee is the only party introduced by the deed of trust who does not have an analogous counterpart in the typical mortgagee-mortgagor transaction. The trustee is an independent third party bound by the provisions of the trust to act in a fiduciary capacity to both the trustor and the beneficiary of the trust. However, since the trustee's role in the typical real estate transaction is: (1) to collect payments from the trustor and forward them to the beneficiary; and/or (2) upon default to conduct the foreclosure sale to maximize the interest of the beneficiary, the trustee's real interest lies with the mortgagee-beneficiary and, thus, the trustee frequently is, and should always be thought of as, an agent of the mortgagee-beneficiary. Indeed, in most deeds of trust, the trustee is selected by and can be replaced at any time by the beneficiary/mortgagee.

Do not confuse a deed of trust, which is a relatively simple financing technique to secure repayment of a debt, with a Real Estate Investment Trust (REIT), which is an *ownership* vehicle designed to maximize certain tax advantages. (A REIT is a complicated ownership vehicle. Essentially, REITs are organized as real estate investment vehicles that issue shares of stock, debentures, etc., to investors in order to acquire funds for investments in real estate.)[12]

---

[11] For a further discussion of the trustor's obligations, see *infra* § 6.03[A].

[12] *See,* Carol MacMillan Stanley, *The Real Estate Investment Trust: Legal and Economic Aspects,* 24 U. Miami L.Rev. 155 (1969).

(Pub.3127)

CHAPTER

2

BROKER-VENDOR AGREEMENTS

---

§ 2.01 Introduction

The best way to analyze the typical residential real estate transaction is to examine the various steps in the transaction as they would normally occur chronologically. The first significant legal event in the typical residential transaction is the vendor's execution of a listing agreement, which allows a broker to market and sell the vendor's real property.

§ 2.02 The Broker's Listing Agreement

The broker's listing agreement is a contract for the delivery of personal services. The vendor agrees to compensate the broker in exchange for the broker's efforts to sell the vendor's real property. The well-reasoned majority view is that the broker agrees to use his good faith efforts to sell the real property in exchange for a promised commission, although there are still some aberrant decisions in a few states holding otherwise.[1] The minority view entitles the broker to a commission if the property is sold even though the broker has not engaged in good faith efforts to perform. However, such a minority view tends to render the contract one-sided, illusory, and void.

---

[1] *See, e.g.,* George Lefcoe, Real Estate Transactions 28 (2nd ed. 1997).

Although the cases appear to be evenly divided concerning a requirement that the broker's listing agreement be in writing, the better view is that a broker's listing agreement is an agreement to render personal services, and is therefore outside the Statute of Frauds even though the personal services relate to the sale of real property. Hence, the listing agreement need not be in writing to satisfy the Statute of Frauds since the real property is not being conveyed pursuant to the agreement. Although the broker and the vendor may personalize their arrangement, employing a customized or unique agreement that satisfies the standards of contract law to sell the real property, such an arrangement is very rare. Overwhelmingly, brokers' listing agreements typically fall into one of the four types discussed below.

[A]   Open Listing Agreement

Perhaps the rarest but simplest to explain, the Open Listing Agreement grants the broker the non-exclusive right to sell the vendor's real property pursuant to the terms and conditions of the listing agreement. The vendor and any other brokers similarly employed by the vendor also have the right to sell the vendor's real property. If the broker proves that his efforts caused the property to be sold to the vendee, he has fully performed the agreement and is entitled to the compensation set forth in the listing agreement (usually stated as a percentage of the sale price—today 5-7% is the norm).[2]

Open Listing Agreements are rarely used due to problems in subsequently determining who procured the sale. It is also relatively easy for the vendor to circumvent the broker's claim of having caused the property to be sold to the vendee. At the very least, the vendor can bring a strike suit against the broker, tying him up in litigation by claiming that it was the vendor's efforts that precipitated the sale, notwithstanding the fact that the broker arranged the initial contact between the vendor and the vendee. These potential problems, coupled with the fact that the broker will work harder when she is guaranteed a commission on the sale of real property, have led to the obsolescence, if not outright demise, of the Open Listing Agreement.

[B]   Net Listing Agreement

Another rarely used listing agreement, albeit for reasons different from the Open Listing Agreement, is the Net Listing Agreement. In the Net Listing Agreement, the vendor agrees to employ the broker as his exclusive or non-exclusive agent for the sale of the real property. What is different about the Net Listing Agreement is that the parties agree on a *minimum price* for the sale of the property, 100% of which shall be *paid to the vendor*. The broker has the right to sell the real property at or above the minimum price. The broker's

---

[2] For a discussion of the "procuring cause of sale" concept and its importance in determining the broker's entitlement to a commission, see *infra* § 2.03[A].

"commission" is the excess of the sale price of the real property over the minimum price. In other words, the vendor always receives the minimum price.

The use of a Net Listing Agreement guarantees the vendor a price with which he will be satisfied. If the broker produces a vendee who is willing to pay X thousands of dollars in excess of the specified sales price, the X thousands of dollars will belong to the broker as her commission. In one sense, the Net Listing agreement can be conceptualized as an option agreement between the vendor and broker pursuant to which the broker has the option to buy the property at its stated price, sell it to a third party at a higher price, and pocket the profit, without violating his fiduciary relationship with the vendor.

Riddled with ethical problems, the Net Listing Agreement is rarely (almost never) used in a residential real estate transaction and is carefully scrutinized by courts. An unscrupulous broker has the potential to overreach due to her expertise, duping the vendor into accepting a guaranteed price below the fair market value of the property. After all, in most instances, the vendor is relying on the broker's advice in setting the sales price. Thus, if the ultimate sales price is far in excess of the minimum price reserved in a Net Listing Agreement, the tort causes of actions against the broker are almost limitless. Hence, Net Listing Agreements should only be utilized if the parties possess the requisite degree of legal and market sophistication to withstand close court scrutiny.

[C] Exclusive Agency Listing Agreement

Used frequently, the Exclusive Agency Listing Agreement grants the broker the exclusive right to sell the vendor's property on the vendor's behalf pursuant to the terms and conditions set forth in the agreement. The vendor retains the right to sell the property himself on any terms and conditions he deems appropriate. The vendor can, therefore, avoid paying the broker's commission if he sells the property and proves that the broker was not the procuring cause of sale. If the property is sold by anyone other than the vendor on his own behalf, however, the broker is entitled to the commission established in the listing agreement. Hence, the Exclusive Agency Listing Agreement provides the broker with exclusivity and the certainty that if the vendor's real property is sold as a result of any third party's efforts, exclusive of the vendor, the broker will be entitled to a commission. Because this type of listing agreement may still raise factual and legal issues concerning who is the procuring cause of sale when the vendor is involved in selling the property, most brokers prefer to use the Exclusive Right to Sell Listing Agreement.

[D] Exclusive Right To Sell Listing Agreement

This is the most commonly employed listing agreement in the United States. Under an Exclusive Right to Sell Listing Agreement, the broker is entitled to a commission if the property is sold or transferred by *anyone*, including the vendor, during the term of the listing agreement. Typically, "sold or transferred" is defined very broadly in a standard Exclusive Right to Sell Listing Agreement. These generous definitions result in the broker's entitlement to a commission even if any number of non-standard occurrences happen during the term of the listing agreement, including, but not limited to, the condemnation of the property, its destruction by accidental fire or casualty, or the vendor's decision to take the property off the market. Basically, if the real property is transferred, either voluntarily or involuntarily, during the term of the Exclusive Right to Sell Listing Agreement, the broker will have a strong claim to a commission. The benefit the vendor allegedly receives for entering into this apparently one-sided agreement is the broker's "best effort" to sell the real property. The rationale is that since the broker can rest assured that if the property is transferred during the term she will be entitled to a commission, she will put forth her best efforts to sell the property. Note, however, that the broker is under no legal obligation to use her best efforts to sell the property pursuant to an exclusive right to sell or any other sort of listing agreement, but must merely perform the provisions of the contract by exercising good faith.[3]

Whatever listing agreement is used by and between the parties, the law of contracts governs its enforceability and interpretation. Hence, the listing agreement (contract) must be read closely to determine the respective rights and responsibilities of the parties. One fairly common feature of most listing agreements, which frequently results in litigation, is the insertion of a *procuring cause of sale clause* which protects the broker, entitling him to a commission if the vendor's real property that is the subject of the listing agreement is conveyed to anyone procured by the broker within some set period, usually six (6) months to a year, following the expiration of the original listing agreement unless another, subsequent broker is employed by the vendor and that subsequent broker (Broker #2) is owed a commission upon the sale. When a procuring cause of sale clause is present, the listing agreement covers two time periods: the life of the listing agreement and the period following the agreement's expiration set by the procuring cause of sale clause. All the different types of listing agreements discussed above can, and usually do, contain a procuring cause of sale provision.

As an example, assume that Vern Vendor and Bob Broker execute an Exclusive Right to Sell Listing Agreement on January 1, 2000, which expires on May 31, 2000. Pursuant to the listing agreement, Broker attempts to sell the real property by showing it to many prospective purchasers, including Vivian Vendee. On June 15, 2000, Vendee and Vendor execute a standard purchase and sale agreement pursuant to which Vendee agrees to purchase Vendor's property on the exact terms and conditions set forth in the listing agreement. If a typical form listing agreement is used, Broker will be entitled to a commission pursuant to his Exclusive Right to Sell Listing Agreement with Vendor unless Vendor can prove that another, different broker is entitled to a commission from the sale. If Vendor

---

[3] *See supra* § 2.02.

has entered into a listing agreement with another broker, Broker #2, that covers the time period June 1, 2000 through December 31, 2000, and Broker #2 deals with Vendee as Vendor's representative, pursuant to the second exclusive right to sell listing agreement, Broker #2 would be owed a commission. The initial broker, Broker #1, has no claim to a commission even though she may have set up the initial contact between Vendor and the ultimate purchaser. As a practical matter, though Broker #1 may be unhappy that the sale was not consummated while her listing agreement was in effect, she can rest assured that Vendor has not engaged in opportunistic or improper behavior to evade paying a commission, as a commission is due and payable to Broker #2.

This sort of arrangement is an attempt to protect both Vendor's and Broker's rights. It prohibits the vendor and the prospective vendee, who are brought together by the original listing broker, from attempting to eliminate the cost of the broker's commission (the savings of which they will presumably split in some agreed upon fashion) by agreeing to delay the execution of the standard purchase and sale agreement until after the expiration of the original listing agreement. On the other hand, if the vendor is dissatisfied with the performance of the broker, she is free to engage another broker following the termination of the original listing agreement with the knowledge that, if the property is sold during the period covered by the second listing agreement to a vendee who was first tendered during the original listing agreement, she will owe only one commission to one broker: the second broker during whose term the sale took place.

[E] Multiple Listing Service (MLS)

One relatively recent development, which is employed in conjunction with exclusive right to sell and exclusive agency listing agreements, is the vendor's consent to have the property registered with a Multiple Listing Service (MLS) in the location (city or county) in which the real property is located. Although MLS organizations were once exclusively the province of large urban areas, they are now used almost everywhere to list and sell real property.

For example, Vern Vendor enters into an exclusive right to sell agreement which contains a clause allowing Bob Broker to list the property with the MLS of the county in which the real property is located. Broker fills out a form provided by the MLS and submits the form to the MLS office. The information on the form is then entered into a central computer which is accessible by any dues-paying member, or any employee of a dues-paying member, of the MLS. More importantly, a book containing descriptions and photographs of all MLS listings, differentiated by location and price, is updated periodically and disseminated to MLS members. Thus, any broker-member of the MLS has access not only to his own listings, but also to all of the listings that have been submitted to the MLS. Hence, a prospective vendee can be shown both the broker's own listings and any of the other listings appearing in the MLS.

[1] Commission

Of course the engine that drives the MLS is the money generated by commissions on the sale of real property listed therein. Property sold that is listed with MLS is subject to a unique arrangement agreed to ex ante by the brokers. Essentially, the broker who lists the property with the MLS, the *listing broker*, receives one-half the commission if the property is sold during the term of the listing agreement to a vendee who is produced by another broker-member, the *selling broker*.

Continuing our hypothetical, assume the property being sold pursuant to the exclusive right to sell agreement is submitted to the MLS and sold to the vendee at a final price of $100,000, subject to a 7% brokerage commission. Pursuant to the MLS arrangement, the 7% commission or $7000 will be divided equally between the broker who listed the property with the MLS, the listing broker, and the broker who produced the vendee who purchased the property—the selling broker. Obviously, if the listing broker and selling broker are one and the same, in this hypothetical, the broker receives the full 7%. In addition, each broker may have to remit a small portion of his fee to the MLS to maintain the service.

[a] Setting Commission Rates—Antitrust Implications

Serious antitrust questions are raised by the imposition of a recommended or required uniform fee or commission scale by the local MLS, the local board of brokers, or any other professional organization to which the vast majority of brokers belong. As with both voluntary and involuntary bar associations, such organizations cannot set, encourage, or recommend a fee scale without violating antitrust laws.[4] Similarly, brokers who deviate from the "normal" or typical fee cannot be penalized by being denied access to the MLS or other services made available to brokers generally.

Historically, the brokers' industry engaged in price fixing, as local brokers' associations developed price schedules for their commission rates and viewed price-cutting as a violation of the brokers' code of ethics. This practice was prohibited by the Supreme Court in the 1950s,[5] and brokers' associations were further barred from issuing advisory schedules or recommended commission fees. However, even today, there remains a high degree of uniformity among the commission rates quoted by brokers to potential clients. The practice by which brokerage firms follow the pricing practices of their competitors, known as conscious price parallelism,[6] is not per se illegal, though price fixing clearly constitutes an antitrust infraction.

---

[4] Goldfarb v. Virginia State Bar, 421 U.S. 773 (1995).

[5] United States v. National Association of Real Estate Boards, 339 U.S. 485 (1950).

[6] *See*, Donald Turner, *The Definition of Agreement Under the Sherman Act: Conscious Parallelism and Refusals to Deal*, 75 Harv. L. Rev. 655 (1962).

MLS structures are peculiarly suspect as a means of broker price-fixing, as it is easy for member-brokers to detect price-cutting on the part of other members. Since commissions are split between the listing and selling brokers, each MLS member has access to the prices set by other members. Furthermore, MLS organizations are in a unique position to enforce adherence to uniform prices among their members, as members may be reluctant to sell homes listed by brokers known to charge lower commissions.

In order to prevail on a claim of brokerage fee setting, a plaintiff must establish both that there exists a uniform pricing practice and that there is discrimination against those providing a service at a lower price. To date, few plaintiffs have obtained judgments in their favor on these types of claims as it is difficult to provide evidence that brokers whose rates are lower than the norm have sustained damages as a result of alleged boycotting by other member-brokers.[7]

[b] Access to Multiple Listing Services—Antitrust Implications

A majority of multiple listing services have access requirements for brokers. Usually, in order to use the service, a broker must either be a member of the MLS itself, or be a member of the trade association which controls the MLS. As access to the local MLS is often essential to selling a property, this membership requirement creates two antitrust issues. First, is it an antitrust violation to deny non-member brokers access to an MLS? Second, do the membership requirements utilized by the MLS unreasonably restrain trade by unfairly denying brokers membership, and thereby access to the MLS?

For both of these questions, the threshold inquiry is whether the MLS possesses sufficient market power to be charged with an antitrust violation. In other words, is the MLS of "sufficient economic importance that exclusion results in the denial of the opportunity to compete *effectively* on equal terms."[8] Courts review three objective factors to determine the extent of an MLS' market power: (1) the number of brokers in the MLS, (2) the total annual dollar amount of listings sold through the MLS, and (3) the MLS organization's efficiency as a generator of sales (percentage sold out of the total number of listings).[9] In applying these factors, courts have found that ". . .when broker participation is high, the service itself is economically successful, and competition from other services is lacking. . .", the MLS possesses market power and the threshold requirement is met.[10] Analogously, when there are several competing multiple listing services in one market area, the courts tend to find no single MLS possesses sufficient market power. If it is established that an MLS has the requisite market power,

---

[7] Park v. El Paso Board of Realtors, 764 F.2d 1053 (5th Cir.1985).

[8] Austin, *Real Estate Boards and Multiple Listing Systems as Restraints of Trade*, 70 Colum. L. Rev. 1325, 1346 (1970).

[9] United States v. Multi-List, Inc., 629 F.2d 1351, 1373-4 (5th Cir. 1980).

[10] *Id.* at 1374.

the court will address the issues of whether non-members must be given access to the service and, if not, whether the membership requirements in effect constitute an antitrust violation.

[i]   Non-Member Brokers

Courts have held that denying non-members access to an MLS constitutes an unreasonable restraint of trade under both a per se antitrust violation standard and under a rule of reason analysis.[11] However, where a court has ordered that non-member brokers be given access to the MLS, it has also required the non-member brokers to comply with the MLS organization's operational policies (such as submitting all their listings to the MLS).[12]

[ii]   Membership Regulations

The membership regulations of an MLS are evaluated by the courts under a rule of reason standard. Under this standard, "[t]he true test of legality is whether the restraint imposed is such as merely regulates and thereby perhaps promotes competition or whether it is such as may suppress or even destroy competition."[13] In applying this test, courts have reasoned that since a multiple listing service's goal is to create a public market by bringing all brokers and listings into its operation, the adoption of any exclusionary membership criteria must be shown to be justified by the operational needs of the association. Many MLS organizations' membership requirements focus on maintaining a given quality of brokerage services by imposing professional and ethical norms on its members. However, a number of courts considering such membership requirements have held that, "where a state extensively regulates the licensing and business conduct of real estate brokers, an MLS may not impose additional responsibility and competence on those who seek to join."[14]

Hence, multiple listing services are limited by antitrust law in the types of membership requirements that they may impose on brokers. Nonetheless, courts have held membership requirements based on reasonable membership fees, geographical constraints, and the use of exclusive listing agreements only by member brokers are reasonable and, therefore, not a restraint on trade.[15]

[c]   Analysis of Multiple Listing Service and Its Impact on Listing Agreements

The recent prevalence of MLS organizations presents some unique legal problems that have yet to be addressed by the courts or the real estate industry.

---

[11] Marion County Board of Realtors, Inc. v. Palsson, 16 Cal.3d 920, 130 Cal. Rptr. 1, 549 P.2d 833 (1976).

[12] Grillo v. Board of Realtors, 91 N.J. Super. 202, 219 A.2d 635 (1966).

[13] Chicago Board of Trade v. United States, 246 U.S. 231, 38 S.Ct. 242, 62 L.Ed. 683 (1918).

[14] *Multi-List, Inc.*, 629 F.2d at 1377-78.

[15] Guadagno v. Mt. Pleasant Listing Exchange, Inc., 2 CCH Trade Cases 61065 (NY Sup. 1976).

In essence, a listing agreement entered into by and between broker and vendor in which they agree to list the property with an MLS is nothing more than the broker's representation that he has access to an MLS, and the vendor's consent to pay half the commission on the sale of realty on that basis alone. In effect, what looks like an exclusive right to sell or exclusive agency listing agreement becomes an "open listing agreement" when an MLS is used. The benefit of using an MLS, however, when compared to an open listing agreement, is that the brokers have agreed ex ante that the procuring cause of sale concept is irrelevant with respect to the listing broker since the listing broker "found" the vendor and induced the vendor to enter into the listing arrangement employing an MLS. The selling broker, the broker who would otherwise be viewed as the procuring cause of sale, gives up his right to half the commission in order to receive access to the additional properties found in the MLS. In the absence of the MLS, these properties would be marketed exclusively by the listing broker pursuant to an exclusive agency or the exclusive right to sell agreement. Without the employment of an MLS, if one broker were the exclusive listing broker and the selling broker were to prove that he was the procuring cause of sale, either the vendor would be forced to pay two commissions, or the selling broker would receive no commission, since the vendor has already contractually agreed to compensate the listing broker to the exclusion of other brokers.

[i]   Benefit to Vendor

Since access to information is a valuable right, access to an MLS provides a benefit to the vendor in correcting any information asymmetries that may occur and impede the sale of the property. Similarly, the vendor, by allowing her property to be listed with the MLS provides a strong incentive for every member of the MLS, except the listing broker, to sell the property and earn half the commission. Obviously, there is still a strong incentive for the listing broker to sell the property since in doing so, she will be entitled to the entire commission as opposed to having to split it with another broker.

[ii]   Vestpocketing

In order to prohibit MLS member-brokers from submitting only difficult to sell properties with the MLS and retaining their more profitable, more saleable properties, most MLS organizations require their members to submit *all* of their listings within a certain time period (usually 72 hours) upon execution and receipt of a listing agreement. Thus, the MLS member-broker is precluded from a practice known as vestpocketing—holding back submissions or listings from the MLS until the saleability of the property is determined.

[d]   Disadvantage to the Vendor

Although difficult to quantify, there may be a disincentive to the listing broker to be as diligent in her efforts to sell the listed property as she otherwise would be, given the fact that the listing broker will gain only an additional one half of the commission if she produces the person who ultimately purchases the property. Conversely, there will be an increased incentive for brokers to locate saleable property and induce vendors to execute listing agreements that can be entered in the MLS.

In addition, once two brokers are involved, transaction costs may rise to account for the insertion of the second "selling" broker "representing" the vendor in this complicated transaction. One example of this problem is the creation of dual or joint fiduciary duties which are alleged to arise when the vendor engages one broker, the listing broker, to sell his property, and the selling broker is first approached by the vendee for help in finding suitable property. Since the vendor pays the commission to both brokers, is it fair to characterize the selling broker as the agent of the vendor because he is paid by the vendor, with all the legal ramifications attendant to such a determination? By selecting a broker to assist them in locating suitable property for purchase, many vendees may be under the erroneous impression that the selected broker is *their* agent and not, as the law allocates, an agent of the selling vendor.[16]

§ 2.03   The Timing of the Broker's Entitlement to a Commission

A common misconception is that a broker (assume that the listing and selling broker are one and the same) is entitled to her commission only when the real property that is the subject of the listing agreement is sold and transferred to the vendee. Indeed, most vendors expect to pay the broker's commission from the proceeds of the sale of the real property. However, the broker's commission is due and payable in most states when the broker is able to prove that she produced (or *procured*) a vendee who was ready, willing and able to purchase the real property pursuant to the terms and conditions set forth in the listing agreement or other terms acceptable to the vendor. Thus, the broker's entitlement to a commission normally occurs prior to the transfer of the real property and can arise even though the real property is not ultimately sold pursuant to the contract. For example, this occurs when a valid contract is entered into between the vendor and putative vendee, and the vendee subsequently breaches the contract by refusing to consummate the sale.

[A]   Procuring Cause of Sale

If either an open listing agreement or an exclusive agency listing agreement is used, the broker will be entitled to her commission only if she can show that she was the procuring cause of sale. However, if the vendor claims and proves that the vendor (and not the broker) was primarily responsible for causing the property to be sold to the vendee, the broker will not be entitled to a commission. The burden of proof is normally placed on the broker to prove that her efforts were the dominant factor which caused the property to be sold to the vendee.

---

[16] For a discussion of this issue, see *infra* § 3.02[B][1].

Stated another way, if the broker can show that the sale would not have taken place without her efforts, she has established that she was the procuring cause of sale. The procuring cause of sale concept is very similar to the theory of proximate cause utilized in tort law to determine responsibility for wrongs.[17]

The procuring cause of sale concept can be expressly negated by contractual provision. For example, in *Galbraith v. Johnston*,[18] the issue presented was whether a broker is entitled to a commission pursuant to a clause in the listing agreement even though he was not the procuring cause of the sale. In this case, Vendor (defendant) engaged Broker #1 (plaintiff) to list his farm under a non-exclusive listing agreement which stated that if the property was ". . .sold within one year after the expiration of this listing to anyone with whom #1 had negotiated prior to expiration. . .," then Broker #1 was entitled to receive the commission. Contrary to the exclusive listing agreement typically used by brokers, the listing agreement used by Broker #1 did not negate payment of a commission to Broker #1 if the Vendor employed another broker who subsequently consummated the sale. After the expiration of this first non-exclusive listing agreement, the Vendor entered into another non-exclusive listing agreement with a second broker, Broker #2. Broker #2 ultimately sold the property to a prospective vendee with whom Broker #1 had unsuccessfully negotiated. The Vendor paid Broker #2 a 5% commission. Broker #1 then sued the Vendor for the 5% commission pursuant to the express clause in the contract. The jury held that Broker #2 was the procuring cause of sale and found for the Vendor. The Supreme Court of Arizona reversed the lower court's decision and held that the Vendor owed Broker #1 the 5% commission regardless of who was the procuring cause of the sale in light of the clear language of the contract obligating the payment of the commission to Broker #1.

However, the court in *Galbraith* can be criticized for exalting form over substance. Broker #1 and Vendor attempted to change an exclusive listing agreement by amending it into a non-exclusive listing agreement. The parties intended that Broker #1 should earn a commission only if he was the procuring cause of sale. However, because the vendor failed to delete an inappropriate clause in what originally was an exclusive right to sell listing agreement, the vendor expressly contractually obligated himself to pay two commissions.

[1] Impact of Multiple Listing Service on Procuring Cause of Sale

As a practical matter, the procuring cause of sale concept is no longer important given the widespread use of exclusive right to sell listing agreements in conjunction with the advent of the MLS. Further, the contractual language of

---

[17] Mellos v. Silverman, 367 So.2d 1369, 1371 (Ala. 1979) ("[p]rocuring cause refers to a cause originating with a series of events which, without break in their continuity, result in procuring a purchaser ready, willing and able to buy on the owner's terms").

[18] Galbraith v. Johnston, 92 Ariz. 77, 373 P.2d 587 (Sup. Ct. Arizona 1962).

many listing agreements frequently supplants the general procuring cause of sale concept with specific rules requiring that the broker be paid a commission if the property is sold during or shortly after the expiration of the listing agreement.

[B]   Ready, Willing, and Able Buyer

Once the broker establishes she was the proximate or procuring cause in producing a putative vendee to purchase the property, she must next demonstrate that the putative vendee is ready, willing, and able to buy the real property upon the terms set forth in the listing agreement or upon other terms acceptable to the vendor in order to become entitled to the commission. As articulated in the leading case in this area, the current majority view [19] is that "[t]his rule has been construed to mean that once a customer is produced by the broker and accepted by the seller, the commission is earned, *whether or not the sale is actually consummated.* Furthermore, execution of a purchase and sale agreement is usually seen as conclusive evidence of the seller's acceptance of the buyer." [20]

[1]   Rationale

In order to prevent the vendor from evading the payment of a commission when the broker has performed, the majority rule is that the broker has earned her right to a commission—has fully performed pursuant to the contract—when she produces a vendee who agrees to purchase pursuant to the terms set forth in the listing agreement. This view is no doubt influenced by the fact that there are many contingencies in the typical real estate purchase and sale contract, some of which are controlled by the vendor and others controlled by the vendee, which can cause the sale to be canceled subsequent to the execution of the real estate purchase and sale contract which the broker worked to procure. [21] The rationale is that once the broker has produced a putative vendee who is satisfactory to the vendor, the broker has done all that she has promised to do, and her commission should not depend on subsequent events and contingencies over which she has no control. As noted in *Tristram*, the vendor has the right to reject the broker's "tender" of the putative vendee unless the broker can prove that the putative vendee should be satisfactory to the vendor. Upon signing a real estate purchase and sale agreement, the vendor accepts the vendee and waives any possible objections that she might have had to the vendee tendered by the broker. *More importantly, by accepting the vendee, the vendor accepts the risk* that the real estate purchase and sale agreement may not result in the actual sale of the real property even though a commission has been paid on the "sale" of the real property to the broker.

---

[19] Stephen Dean Streiker, *Getting Paid Commissions: A New Power Balance Between Real Estate Brokers, Appraisers and Their Clients Under the Missouri Commercial Real Estate Brokers' and State Certified Real Estate Appraisers' Lien Act*, 63 UMKC L. Rev. 727 (1998).

[20] Tristram's Landing, Inc. v. Wait, 367 Mass. 622, 327 N.E.2d 727, 729 (1975) (emphasis added).

[21] For a discussion of the standard real estate purchase and sale agreement and the contingencies that impact the agreement, see *infra* § 3.02.

As an example, assume that Vern Vendor executes an Exclusive Right to Sell Listing Agreement with Bob Broker's Realty Company granting the company the exclusive right to sell his real property at the price of $125,000 for a period of six months following execution of the listing agreement. Ignoring the financing and other contingencies that might be addressed in the Exclusive Right to Sell Listing Agreement, if Broker produces a vendee who meets all the conditions of the listing agreement (date of closing, etc.) but is willing to pay only $122,500 for the property, Broker has *not* earned her commission because she has not accomplished what the contract requires her to do: produce a buyer-vendee who is ready, willing and able to buy at $125,000. However, if Vendor agrees to accept $122,500, Broker *has* accomplished her task: she has produced a vendee *acceptable* to Vendor and therefore is entitled to her commission. Thus, Vendor determines if the price and the vendee are acceptable.

However, Vendor has the right to reject the vendee proposed by Broker, even if the vendee is willing to pay the price set forth in the listing agreement ($125,000), if Vendor believes that the vendee is not *ready, willing, or able* to purchase the property. In this situation, the law places the burden on Vendor to ascertain and establish the bona fides of the putative vendee. If Vendor accepts the vendee by entering into a real estate purchase and sale agreement with the vendee, the executed purchase agreement serves as evidence that the vendee is acceptable to Vendor notwithstanding the fact that Vendor may know nothing about the vendee except the information gleaned from Broker. In the unlikely event that the putative vendee is rejected by Vendor as not being ready, willing, or able to perform as required in the Exclusive Right to Sell Listing Agreement, the burden then shifts to Broker to prove that the putative vendee is able to perform pursuant to the terms and conditions set forth in the listing agreement.

[2] The Modern Trend—*Tristram's Landing, Inc.*

In *Tristram's Landing Inc.*,[22] the court adopted the rationale first set forth in *Ellsworth Dobbs, Inc. v. Johnson*:[23]

> When a broker is engaged by an owner of property to find a purchaser for it, the broker earns his commission when (a) he produces a purchaser ready, willing, and able to buy on the terms fixed by the owner, (b) the purchaser enters into a binding contract with the owner to do so, *and* (c) *the purchaser completes the transaction by closing the title in accordance with the provisions of the contract.*[24]

The "modern" emerging trend, entitling the broker to her commission only if the purchaser actually *completes* the purchase, is said to be fairer than the common law rule discussed above because it is in accord with the vendor's

---

[22] 367 Mass. 622, 327 N.E.2d 727, 729 (1975).

[23] 50 N.J. 528, 551, 236 A. 2d 843, 855 (1967).

[24] *Id.* (emphasis added).

expectation that the commission is payable only when the purchase is completed. Although the stated rationales of fairness and expectations are somewhat conclusory and circular, the trend can perhaps be justified because it places the risk of loss on the party best able to bear it, the broker. For a number of practical reasons, the broker is in a better position to evaluate the bona fides of the prospective vendee and, due to the nature of the business and the transaction, to spread the risk of vendee failure to perform. After all, the broker is the real estate expert and can assess the qualifications of the putative vendee much more accurately and efficiently than the vendor, who is not in the "business" of selling real estate on a daily basis.

In *Tristram's Landing, Inc.*, the issue was whether a vendor owes a broker a commission when the vendee fails to purchase the property and neither the broker nor the vendor is at fault. The vendor entered into a purchase and sale contract with a prospective vendee who had been procured by his broker. On the date of closing, the vendee refused to perform the contract. The vendor retained the vendee's deposit as damages and refused to pay the broker's commission. The broker then sued the vendor for the commission. Given the language in the purchase and sale contract that made the sale contingent upon the vendee obtaining appropriate bank financing, the court held that the vendee had to complete the purchase by closing title in accordance with the provisions of the contract in order for the broker to earn a commission. Hence, since the vendee failed to perform fully, no commission was earned.

The rationale behind the modern trend that the broker should bear the burden of vendee default is that the broker is better situated than the vendor to know or discover the vendee's ability or inability to perform the contract. Though the parties can contract around this allocation of the burden, such contract provisions which favor the broker or place the risk of loss on the vendor will be strictly scrutinized by the courts because brokers ostensibly possess superior knowledge with respect to contract performance and typically produce the contractual form obligating the vendor to pay the commission.

[C]   Limitation to the Modern Trend

The modern trend limits the vendor's liability to pay a commission only if the vendor can show that the sale was not completed due to the fault or refusal of the *vendee* to perform. In other words, the vendor must himself be ready, willing and able to perform in order to evade his contractual obligation to pay a commission if the purchase is not completed. If the purchase is not completed as a result of actions of the *vendor*, the vendor's contractual obligation to pay the commission is still viable—the broker has the right to the commission called for in the contract.[25]

---

[25] Dworak v. Michals, 211 Neb. 716, 320 N.W.2d 485 (1982).

In *Drake v. Hosley*, the issue was whether a broker is entitled to a commission when he procures an acceptable vendee but the vendor circumvents the sale of the property.[26] In this case, the broker procured prospective vendees who entered into a contract with the vendor to purchase property. During the executory interval between the execution of the contract of sale and the closing, the vendor sold the property to a third party and then refused the initial vendees' offer of payment. The broker sued the vendor for the contracted-for commission. The court adopted the minority rule that the sale must be consummated for the broker to be entitled to a commission, but held that since the vendor's "frustrating conduct" had prevented the sale, the broker nevertheless was entitled to the commission.

Drake v. Hosley demonstrates the limitations of the modern trend which places the risk of loss for nonperformance on the broker, if, and only if, the vendor is not at fault. The vendor's responsibility for nonperformance is often a difficult question given the strategic moves parties make once it appears there may be a problem closing the sale. Thus, the vendor must maintain his ability to perform pursuant to the agreement unless he can prove that such action would be futile because the vendee has already clearly breached, and will not consummate the contract.

[D] Problems and Issues Raised by the Modern Trend

Although the modern trend is simple to apply in cases of vendor breach (commission still owed to broker) and vendee breach (commission not owed to broker), interesting questions are raised regarding the broker's right to recover the commission or damages from a vendee if the vendee breaches the contract when contingencies are written into the real estate purchase and sale contract.

For example, if the vendee was unable to obtain financing to purchase the real property, is the broker entitled to recover her commission from the putative vendee even though the vendee was unable to perform through no "fault" of his own? More importantly, with the advent of MLS organizations, the listing broker presumably is not harmed by the putative vendee's breach if the real property is sold during the term of the listing agreement. But what of the putative selling broker who loses her half of the commission because the real property is ultimately sold to a vendee procured by another broker? Alternatively, should the broker be entitled to quantum merit recovery for her services if she is not entitled to a full commission on a failed purchase? Finally, what if the vendor retained a substantial deposit as liquidated damages resulting from the vendee's failure to perform?[27] If the broker is the vendor's agent, are the broker's rights limited or curtailed by the action of her principal so that the vendor's decision to retain the deposit or, more importantly, the decision not to pursue her remedy of specific performance, limits the broker's recourse against the putative vendee?

---

[26] Drake v. Hosley, 713 P.2d 1203 (Sup. Ct. Alaska 1986).

[27] For a discussion of liquidated damages, see *infra* § 5.04.

Although resolution of these issues is better addressed in classes on contracts and remedies, one suggested solution is an ex ante agreement by and between the parties that specifies the rights and responsibilities of each party in case of breach and, more importantly, the disposition of the deposit and the explicit allocation of the risk of loss in case of default. In states that follow the modern trend, and other states as well, listing agreements increasingly address this question and provide for the forfeiture of the deposit to the vendor and grant the broker the right to pursue the breaching vendee. Other form agreements provide that the vendor will retain the deposit and that the broker's claim to a commission will be limited to recovery against the amount retained by the vendor; however, the broker is usually entitled to no more than 50% of the deposit amount retained by the vendor.

Among the advantages of a shift from the common law rule to the modern trend are the dissemination of information to the vendor regarding the broker's entitlement to a commission and the employment of an express ex ante allocation of the risk of loss in the event of default. Such a shift presumably promotes a more efficient result. Most vendors are unfamiliar with the requirements regarding brokers' entitlement to commissions and are surprised to learn that they owe a commission to a broker although the purchase was not completed, whereas most brokers are aware of the rules and can efficiently convey such information to the vendor. Nonetheless, the current majority view remains that the real estate broker becomes entitled to his commission once he has procured a ready, willing, and able buyer who is accepted by the vendor.[28]

§ 2.04   The Role of the Real Estate Lawyer

Despite the legal complexity and consequences of residential real estate transactions, the parties involved in such transactions are not required by law to obtain the assistance of counsel. However, both parties should retain counsel for the protection of their interests, as the savings in lawyers' fees is not worth the risks involved in proceeding without the guidance of counsel. The importance of the real estate lawyer is paramount in drafting the contract of sale, assessing the status of the seller's title, drafting or reviewing financing documents, and explaining the meaning and ramifications of particular courses of action to the client.

[A]   Lawyers Acting as Brokers

Most states do not require attorneys licensed to practice law in the state to comply with the state's real estate licensing requirements, allowing attorneys to recover commissions for locating a purchaser without having a broker's license.[29] However, states differ considerably as to the scope of the attorney's exemption

---

[28] *See* Streiker, *supra* note 19.

[29] Atlantic Richfield Co. v. Sybert, 295 Md. 347, 456 A.2d 20 (1983).

from real estate licensing requirements.[30] Moreover, conflicts of interest and other professional ethics problems may develop in situations where attorneys act as real estate brokers.[31]

§ 2.05 The Broker's Role in the Transaction

[A] Brokers Acting as Lawyers—Unauthorized Practice of Law

Although many states allow lawyers to act as brokers without broker certification, it is clearly illegal for brokers to engage in the practice of law without being licensed as an attorney. This creates the problem of determining the extent to which brokers may assist in the negotiation and drafting of the sale transaction without engaging in the unauthorized practice of law.

Within the United States, real estate brokers are universally authorized to complete some legal instruments concerning the transaction in which they are participating as brokers, though the extent of this authorization varies from state to state. Earlier courts frequently prohibited brokers from preparing any documents that affect the legal rights of buyers and sellers. More recently, many states have allowed brokers to act as scriveners to fill out "simple" standardized real estate forms, as long as the forms have been approved by a licensed attorney and the broker does not charge for the service or actively provide legal advice in relation to the documents. Some jurisdictions further require that the broker's preparation of such documents be an essential and inherent part of the broker's business, or necessary to allow the broker to complete her services and earn her commission.[32] Over the years there has been substantial debate over where to draw the line for unauthorized practice, and each state has developed its own restrictions on the activities of real estate brokers.[33]

[B] Fiduciary Relationship and Duties

Traditionally, the broker acts as the agent of the vendor who hired her to sell the real property. Thus, the broker and vendor find themselves in a principal/agent relationship with all the attendant duties and responsibilities.

As the vendor's agent, the broker must act in the best interest of the vendor (the principal). The broker owes the vendor the fiduciary duties of good faith, loyalty, reasonable care, and diligence. Furthermore, the broker must disclose potential conflicts of interest that might arise and diminish her performance as the vendor's agent.[34] Potential or actual conflicts of interest may be consented

---

[30] *See* Shinberg v. Bruk, 875 F.2d 973 (1st Cir. 1989) (under New Hampshire or Massachusetts law, attorney not entitled to finder's fee since not licensed as a broker).

[31] *See* Wolfram, Modern Legal Ethics (1986).

[32] Ronald B. Brown, Joseph M. Grohman, and Manuel R. Valcarcel, *Real Estate Brokerage: Recent Changes in Relationships and a Proposed Cure*, 29 Creighton L. Rev. 25, 62 (1995).

[33] *See, e.g.,*New Jersey State Bar Assn. v. Northern N.J. Mortgage Assocs., 32 N.J. 430, 161 A. 2d 257 (1960).

[34] Drake v. Hosley, 713 P.2d 1203 (Sup. Ct. Ala. 1986).

to by the vendor only after full disclosure by the broker. Similarly, a single broker may represent both Vendor and Vendee in the same transaction if she fully and completely discloses the potential for conflict of interest and obtains the consent of both parties to the dual representation.[35]

In *Haymes v. Rogers*, the issue was whether a broker's disclosure of a vendor's willingness to sell the property below the list price violated his fiduciary duty to the vendor.[36] The vendor listed a piece of property with the broker for $9,500, agreeing to pay the broker a 5% commission for the sale. The broker's salesman described the property to prospective vendees, stating that he thought the vendor would accept between $8,250 and $9,500 for the property, and that the vendees could probably buy it for $8,500. Later, the vendees visited the vendor's property without the salesman and negotiated a contract to purchase the property for $8,500. The broker sued the vendor for the 5% commission. The court, in finding for the vendor, held the broker breached his fiduciary duty to act in the best interest of the vendor, thereby forfeiting any right to a commission.

The fiduciary relationship which exists between the vendor and the broker places the broker in a position of knowledge as to the vendor's selling needs. While this knowledge is necessary to allow the broker to perform his responsibilities in terms of procuring a sale, if the knowledge is conveyed to third parties, the vendor is placed in a disadvantageous bargaining position. Consequently, such breaches of the fiduciary duty of loyalty are discouraged by the forfeiture of commissions.

[1]   Conflicts Created by Multiple Listing Services

The increasing use of the MLS has created many problems with respect to the fiduciary relationships and duties of brokers that have yet to be definitively resolved by the courts. When a seller executes a listing agreement with a broker, an agency relationship with all of its attendant duties is explicitly established between the listing broker and the vendor. However, usually a selling broker who is not the listing broker is also involved in transactions through the MLS, and is traditionally regarded as a subagent[37] of the vendor,[38] since his commission and his contractual obligation to sell the real property arise from the listing agreement executed by the vendor and the listing broker. This subagency relationship also places substantial potential liability on both the listing broker and the vendor for the actions of the selling broker, even though the listing broker

---

[35] Wilson v. Lewis, 106 Cal. App. 3d 802, 165 Cal. Rptr. 396 (1980).

[36] Haymes v. Rogers, 70 Ariz. 527, 219 P.2d 339 (1950).

[37] *See* Restatement (Second) of Agency 5(1) (1957) (defining "subagent" as "a person appointed by an agent empowered to do so, to perform functions undertaken by the agent for the principal, but for whose conduct the agent agrees with the principal to be primarily responsible").

[38] Ronald B. Brown, Joseph M. Grohman, and Manuel R. Valcarcel, *Real Estate Brokerage: Recent Changes in Relationships and a Proposed Cure*, 29 Creighton L. Rev. 25, 34 (1995).

and the vendor typically have little knowledge of, or control over, the actions of the selling broker in dealing with the buyer. Although the vendee may contact and deal exclusively with a selling broker in his attempt to purchase the property from the vendor, operating under the misconception that the selling broker is advocating his interests, the traditional approach views the vendee as unrepresented in the transaction unless he explicitly contracts with a broker for representation. However, a realistic analysis of the roles and relationships between the parties suggests that the selling broker should be regarded as the agent of the vendee and not of the vendor.[39]

Brokers and their trade associations are addressing this issue in listing agreements and by promoting legislation that may resolve this problem. Many state legislatures have recently enacted disclosure statutes requiring brokers to provide potential buyers with a written explanation of the broker-client relationship in order to help dispel the common misconceptions concerning a selling broker's fiduciary duties. For example, under some statutes a selling broker must make a written disclosure to the prospective buyer of both the type of relationship that the broker has with the seller, and the type of relationship offered to the buyer.

Furthermore, the MLS rules no longer require listing brokers to make an offer of subagency to non-listing brokers as a prerequisite for submitting a listing to the service, but allow listing brokers to offer "cooperation and compensation" to brokers who help make a sale, thus moving from agency law to contract law.[40] However, an offer of subagency is still mandatory for in-house sales, where the listing and selling brokers are employed by the same firm. Despite this move away from agency law to contract law which has been promoted by the National Association of Realtors (NAR), brokers still typically use the subagent approach.[41]

This change in the MLS rules, allowing that the selling broker is not necessarily a subagent of the listing broker, enables selling brokers to act exclusively as agents of the buyer (*Buyer's Brokers*) in states that recognize this new concept.[42] Additionally, some states allow brokers to maintain a non-representative, independent contractor status in which they act as facilitators of the deal, putting buyers and sellers in contact with one another without being bound by fiduciary duties. However, this approach has been criticized as undermining the expectations of both the buyer and the seller, who presume that the broker will act with

---

[39] *See* Comment, *A Reexamination of the Real Estate Broker-Buyer-Seller Relationship*, 18 Wayne L. Rev. 1343 (1972).

[40] Ronald B. Brown, Joseph M. Grohman, and Manuel R. Valcarcel, *Real Estate Brokerage: Recent Changes in Relationships and a Proposed Cure*, 29 Creighton L. Rev. 25, 38 (1995).

[41] *Id.*

[42] *Id.* at 43.

loyalty in exchange for compensation and is not endorsed by the National Association of Realtors.[43]

[2]   Conflicts Created by the Broker's Duty to Disclose

In many states, the broker has a duty to disclose to the vendee material defects of the property known to the broker or reasonably discoverable by the broker upon inspection.[44] This duty to disclose defects is based on the broker's expertise in the sale of real property and the "trust and confidence" that arises between vendee and broker that leads the vendee to expect "the broker to protect his interest."[45] Consequently, although the broker is the agent of the selling vendor, she has a duty of disclosure that benefits the vendee.

For example, assume that Vendor executes an exclusive listing agreement with First Broker Co. Broker, employed by First Broker Co., visually inspects the listed property and discovers no material defects. If there is a material defect in the premises—for example, an old furnace that has been temporarily patched up but needs to be permanently replaced within the next year—unbeknownst to Broker, but known to Vendor, should or must Vendor disclose that information to Broker?

The answer appears to be no, unless the defect is a known dangerous condition that is not discoverable upon inspection. Vendor profits by withholding this type of relevant information from her agent, Broker, because Broker must disclose such information to the vendee. As a result, a conflict of interest is created between Vendor and Broker because of Broker's duty to make a full and complete disclosure to the vendee.

One method to address the conflicts generated by the fiduciary relationships and conflicting duties that arise between the vendor-broker-vendee in the typical transaction is to ignore the formalistic method of analysis employed by the common law that results in the broker being viewed exclusively as the agent of the vendor. Instead one can employ a functional approach that attempts to realistically apportion duties in accordance with the responsibilities and expectations of the parties. Hence, for certain purposes the broker should be viewed as the agent of the vendor—for example, when it involves a discussion of price or terms of the sale. But for other purposes, i.e., when it involves the condition of the premises being sold, the broker should be regarded as the agent of the vendee. This "shifting" agency relationship may be more difficult and costly to police and monitor. Nonetheless, given the complexity of the relationships between the parties and the recognition that the perfect solution—the vendor's representation by her exclusive broker and the vendee's representation by a broker

---

[43] *Id.* at 45.

[44] Easton v. Strassburger, 152 Cal. App. 3d 90, 199 Cal. Rptr. 383 (1984).

[45] *Id.* at 93. *See* Note, *Real Estate Brokers' Duties to Prospective Purchasers,* Brigham Young L. Rev. 513 (1976).

devoted exclusively to his interests—is too costly and, therefore, inefficient in the typical transaction, the additional cost is justified.

In *Easton v. Strassburger*, the issue was whether a real estate broker has a duty to disclose all defects he knows or should know exist to prospective vendees.[46] The vendee purchased the property for $170,000 through a broker who did not disclose any defects in the property. Shortly thereafter, several earth movements on the property caused massive destruction, decreasing the property's value to approximately $20,000. The vendees sued the selling broker on the basis of his failure to disclose the erosion problem that the vendees alleged the broker knew or should have known to exist.

The court held that a real estate broker has a duty to disclose defects in real property which he knows or should know exist at the time of sale. Furthermore, the court found that this duty includes the affirmative responsibility to conduct a reasonably competent and diligent inspection of the residential property. In this case, the broker was liable to the vendee because there were "red flags" discoverable upon inspection indicating that the property had soil problems of which the vendee should have been warned.

As described in *Easton*, the imposition of such a duty on brokers creates ample incentive for them to disclose information to prospective vendees. Aside from the conflict of interest it creates for the broker in his dealing with the vendor, the burden appears reasonable because it is easily fulfilled by the broker and meets the vendee's expectation that the broker will relay accurate information. In fact, this duty to disclose is imposed on many brokers by their own code of ethics.

[C]   Self-Dealing

The one rule governing real estate transactions that has remained constant is that the broker cannot personally profit from her access to information provided by the vendor with respect to the real property listed. In other words, the broker cannot engage in self-dealing and profit at the expense of her principal by purchasing, either directly or through nominees, real property that she believes is undervalued in order to resell it at a higher price.[47] Nor can the broker purchase the property from the vendor and then resell it at a profit to a prospective vendee whose identity the broker became aware of during the listing agreement.[48]

[1]   Net Listing Agreements Create Conflicts of Interest

Net listing agreements,[49] create conflicts of interest because of the potential for self-dealing that can arise when these unique listing agreements are used.

---

[46] Easton v. Strassburger, 152 Cal. App. 3d 90, 199 Cal. Rptr. 383, 46 A.L.R. 4th 521 (1984).

[47] Ornamental and Structural Steel, Inc. v. BBG, Inc., 20 Ariz. App. 16, 509 P.2d 1053 (1973).

[48] Zichlin v. Dill, 157 Fla. 96, 25 So.2d 4 (Sup. Ct. 1946).

[49] For a definition of net listing agreements, see *supra* § 2.02[B].

As a result, the National Association of Realtors frowns upon the use of net listing agreements, suggesting "that a Realtor who enters a net listing arrangement with a customer violates a professional obligation to serve clients as a fiduciary rather than an antagonist and is subject to disciplinary action."

§ 2.06   The Quality of the Subject Property

In addition to the broker's duty to disclose defects of the property of which he is aware or should reasonably be aware, modern sellers of real property sometimes have a duty to disclose defects to prospective sellers. Courts have considered various factors in determining whether a seller has a duty to disclose, such as: 1) whether the vendor has concealed an inherent defect which could not be reasonably discovered and which will affect the market value of the property; 2) whether the vendor affirmatively acted in order to preclude discovery of the property's defect; and 3) any difference in intelligence or sophistication between the contracting parties.[50] However, limitations are placed on the seller's duty to disclose to the buyer so as not to impede the transferability of property, an instrumental end of property law.

[A]   The Common Law Doctrine of Caveat Emptor

The common law doctrine of caveat emptor, or "let the buyer beware," is still applied to purchasers of used property with respect to *patent* defective conditions, which are either obvious or discoverable upon reasonable examination of the property by the purchaser. In the absence of an express agreement or misrepresentation concerning the quality of the land by the seller, the buyer must inspect the property herself to determine its condition. Similarly, the vendor generally is not liable for patent defects existing at the time of transfer that result in harm to others.[51] Furthermore, caveat emptor can only be applied where the buyer has an unobstructed opportunity to inspect the premises prior to purchase, and will not preclude recovery for fraud or misrepresentation.[52] Since nearly every building has defects of some kind, application of the doctrine of caveat emptor protects against potentially endless litigation surrounding transfers of property.

[B]   Exceptions to the Application of Caveat Emptor

[1]   Latent Defects

With respect to material, hidden defects in the property that are not reasonably discoverable by the purchaser (*latent defects*), the vendor is under a duty to disclose such defects of which she is aware or should be aware that may present an unreasonable risk of harm to persons on the premises.[53] Furthermore, if a

---

[50] Pitre v. Twelve Oak Trust, 818 F. Supp. 949 (Miss. 1993).

[51] W. Prosser and K.P. Keeton, The Law of Torts § 64, at 447 (5th ed. 1984).

[52] Layman v. Binns, 519 N.E.2d 642, 644 (Ohio. 1988).

[53] *See* Loewer v. Harris, 57 F.368 (2nd Cir. 1893) (holding that if the vendor chooses to make some representations concerning the quality of the property to the buyer, the vendor must then make a complete disclosure of all relevant facts).

vendor attempts to conceal latent defects of which she knows, the doctrine of caveat emptor does not preclude recovery for fraud.[54] To determine whether a defect is latent, courts rely on the nature of the defect and the parties' ability to determine its existence through a reasonable inspection of the premises. A material defect is any information that a reasonable buyer would want to know before agreeing to purchase the property.[55]

For example, termites present a common illustration of a latent defect, as they are quite obvious when in season, but hardly noticeable when not in season. Generally, sellers are required to disclose any knowledge of a termite infestation,[56] and may not necessarily represent the property as "termite-free" just because they have not seen any termites themselves. Sellers are advised to take preventive measures to avoid termite problems, and in order to protect themselves from liability for nondisclosure of a latent defect, should supply prospective buyers with a pest inspection report.[57] With respect to defects in property that are not physical or legal impairments of the property, some courts have treated such *psychological defects* similarly to a latent defect in the property since such a defect's intangible nature would not cause it to be discoverable through reasonable inspection of the property.[58]

[2] Misrepresentations by the Vendor

The doctrine of caveat emptor does not protect the seller of a pre-owned home from tort liability for affirmative misrepresentation or concealment of defects in the property. Though some "puffing" and sales talk is permissible, sellers must act reasonably in order to avoid a future misrepresentation claim. Sellers must disclose any known information that might affect the buyer's decision to purchase, and they are held just as liable for concealing the truth as they are for telling outright lies.[59]

Purchasers should expressly inquire about the condition of the property and the surrounding neighborhood, and should request that the seller include such representations in the contract. Furthermore, purchasers should obtain copies of all past inspections and reports related to the quality of the property.[60] In response to an inquiry by a prospective vendee, a seller's active misrepresentation,

---

[54] Klott v. Assoc. Real Estate, 322 N.E.2d 690, 692 (Ohio. 2d 1974). *But see* Cornelius v. Austin, 542 So.2d 1220 (Ala. 1989) (holding that concealment does not necessarily amount to fraud).

[55] George Lefcoe, Real Estate Transactions 113 (3rd ed. 1992) (citing Bart Pachino, Senior Vice President and General Counsel, Kaufman and Broad Home Corporation).

[56] *See* E.T. Tsai, Annotation, *Duty of Vendor of Real Estate to Give Purchaser Information as to Termite Infestation*, 22 A.L.R.3d 972 (1968).

[57] Lefcoe, *supra* note 55, at 112.

[58] Van Camp v. Bradford, 63 Ohio Misc.2d 245, 623 N.E.2d 731 (1993).

[59] Lefcoe, *supra* note 55, at 109.

[60] *Id.* at 109.

concealment, or nondisclosure of a material fact, even if it concerns a psychological defect in the property, is considered evidence of the seller's breach of her duty to disclose.

For example, *Van Camp v. Bradford*[61] was a case in which serious, violent crimes had occurred on and near the property at issue, but were not disclosed by the seller even when the buyer explicitly inquired about the security bars on the home's basement windows. The court held the seller liable for nondisclosure of the property's psychological stigma to the buyer.[62] However, in order to protect against limitless recovery for "insubstantial harms and irrational fears," the misrepresentation at issue must concern a material fact, induce justifiable reliance on the part of the vendee, and result in damages to the vendee.[63] A misleading seller may be exonerated from a misrepresentation claim if she can prove that the buyer had actual knowledge of the defect before contracting, thus negating the requisite element of reliance.

[3] "As is" Clauses in the Contract for Sale

An "as is" clause included in the sales contract indicates that the property is to be sold in its presently existing condition on the date of the contract's execution, shifting the risk of defects in the property onto the vendee. However, in almost all states the vendor still has a duty to disclose all known defects to the buyer,[64] and the use of an "as is" or other disclaimer clause will not bar suit against the vendor for affirmative misrepresentation or concealment of defects in the property.[65] A reduction in the sales price of the property is often taken by courts as evidence of the buyer's assumption of the risk involved in buying the property.[66] Furthermore, the "as is" clause only protects the seller, and not the seller's broker, from suits by the buyer.[67] The appearance of the clause tends to caution the buyer about the potential existence of hidden defects in the property, encouraging a thorough inspection.

[4] Professional Homebuilders and Subdividers

[a] Disclosure Requirements

As compared to the average pre-owned home transaction where both the buyer and the seller are amateurs, professional builders and subdividers have greater knowledge of the hazards and limitations inherent in the property that they are offering for sale and are in a better position to prevent and correct defects. As

---

[61] 63 Ohio Misc.2d 245, 623 N.E.2d 731 (1993).

[62] *Id.* at 733.

[63] *Id.*

[64] Loughrin v. Superior Ct., 19 Cal.Rptr.2d 161 (Cal. Ct. App. 1993).

[65] Kaye v. Buehrle, 457 N.E.2d 373 (Ohio App. 3d. 1983).

[66] Pitre, *supra* note 50, at 950.

[67] Carroll v. Dungey, 223 Cal.App.2d 247 (1963).

a result, such professionals are held to higher standards than the amateur seller, and often must comply with statutory warranties or court-imposed duties of disclosure to prospective buyers.[68]

[b] Implied Warranty of Habitability

Recently, an implied warranty of habitability has been applied to sellers of new homes, so that residential homes constructed are guaranteed to be of reasonable workmanship and fit for habitation.[69] This movement away from caveat emptor has developed in response to the typical disparity in expertise between the vendee and the builder-vendor. The average buyer lacks the necessary knowledge to make a competent inspection of the premises, and expert advice can be prohibitively expensive. Furthermore, the builder-vendor is in better position to prevent problems from occurring in the first place. As standard form contracts for purchase have become the norm when dealing with subdivision developers, it is no longer practical or affordable for buyers to attempt to extract an express warranty from the builder-vendor, and insurance policies obtained from builders or third parties often exclude certain types of repairs or limit coverage to defects rendering the property uninhabitable.

[5] Statutory Duty to Disclose

Though professional builders and subdividers have been subject to disclosure requirements for a considerable time, recently even some amateur vendors have been required to observe exacting disclosure laws enacted by state legislatures. These state statutes require sellers to disclose all known defects in quality to the buyer, whether obvious or latent, and also provide buyers with an opportunity to rescind after receiving disclosure reports. Over half of the states have executed mandatory disclosure laws that either codify or modify the vendor's current duties under common law, and many other states are contemplating enacting similar legislation. Real estate brokers actively support mandatory disclosure for sellers, since it takes some of the pressure off brokers, who are typically blamed if problems arise with the property.[70]

In the majority of states, the seller's statutory duty to disclose does not include conditions outside of the boundary of the property for sale; however, some states additionally require sellers to disclose offsite defects, such as earthquake fault lines or hazardous waste dump-sites in the area. It is always safest for the vendor to disclose everything that could potentially influence the buyer's decision to purchase, though most states limit disclosure obligations to physical defects and do not require sellers to disclose psychological ones.[71]

---

[68] Lefcoe, *supra* note 55, at 105.

[69] McDonald v. Mianecki, 398 A.2d 1283 (N.J. Sup. Ct. 1979).

[70] Lefcoe, *supra* note 55, at 113.

[71] *Id.*

As of 1993, twenty states and the District of Columbia have responded to judicial decisions imposing a duty to disclose psychological defects on sellers of real property by enacting *nondisclosure statutes*. These statutes are aimed at protecting sellers from liability for failing to inform buyers of stigmatizing events, such as the fact that a house is allegedly haunted or is the scene of a recent murder. However, even under such statutes, a seller must completely and truthfully answer when questioned by a buyer.[72] Nondisclosure statutes merely protect sellers from the burden of voluntary disclosure of potential stigmas associated with the property.

[a] Rationale and Critique

A state's imposition of a statutory duty to disclose assists buyers of property in pinpointing potential problem areas and accurately assessing the worth of the property before purchase. Additionally, such a duty may encourage sellers to make necessary repairs of the property prior to putting it on the market in order to avoid having to disclose defects.[73]

However, the existence of disclosure laws provides an advantage to sellers who do not comply over those who do, and thus enforcement must be taken seriously by sellers for the statutes to work. Additionally, there is a risk that buyers will be overburdened by thick disclosure documents and will not take the time to read them. Also, upon disclosure, sellers who have already discounted their property to reflect the existence of serious defects may reach deadlocks over price with buyers seeking a reduction upon learning of the defects for the first time.[75]

An additional problem with the imposition of a mandatory duty to disclose is determining where to draw the line with respect to where the duty ends. For example, is a neighbor's habit of having noisy, drunken arguments in the middle of the night a material fact to be disclosed? An unattractive neighbor's fondness for sunbathing in offensively skimpy attire on an adjacent deck? Furthermore, buyers may have a difficult time proving that the seller knew about the defect before the sale, since the seller can always insist that the defect did not exist when the seller owned the house. Rather than relying on the seller to admit to a defect's existence after the fact, unhappy buyers must look to other sources, such as past service workers, for proof that the defect is recurrent and not new.[76]

---

[72] McDonald v. Mianecki, 398 A.2d 1283, 1285 (N.J. Sup. Ct. 1979).

[73] Lefcoe, *supra* note 55, at 114.

[75] *Id.*

[76] *Id.*

CHAPTER

3

THE REAL ESTATE PURCHASE AND SALE CONTRACT

SYNOPSIS

§ 3.01 Introduction

When most people think about the agreements that are involved in purchasing real property, they think about the listing agreement with the broker and the deed that is executed at closing, transferring the real property. Rarely do they give much thought to the most important agreement involved in the transaction, the standard real estate purchase and sale contract. However, the purchase and sale contract defines the parties' rights and responsibilities with respect to the sale of the real property, and thus determines whether the purchase and sale will take place, or whether it will be aborted because one of many contingencies cannot be met pursuant to the terms and conditions of the contract. Furthermore, the purchase and sale contract defines what type of title and deed must be delivered at the closing and thus whether the vendee will be forced to accept the title and deed tendered at the closing. Thus, although it is true that the typical purchase and sale contract is temporally short-lived, it plays an integral part in the disposition of real property because of its definitional role, and is perhaps the most frequently litigated aspect of the typical residential real estate transaction.

§ 3.02   The Standard Real Estate Purchase and Sale Contract

As a caveat, note that a short-term real estate purchase and sale contract should not be confused with an *Installment Land Sale Contract.* The real estate purchase and sale contract establishes the parties' rights and responsibilities during the interval, frequently referred to as the *"executory interval,"* between the signing of the agreement and the date of closing, and defines the real property being transferred at the time of closing. On the other hand, an installment land sale contract is a mortgage substitute or alternative financing device that remains in effect often for as long as twenty or thirty years.[1] One way to distinguish the two types of contracts is to think of the standard real estate purchase and sale contract as a short-term marketing contract that allows the parties to prepare for the closing, which will usually occur within some period stated in days, typically 30, 60, or 90 days. In contrast, the installment land sale contract should be viewed as a long-term contract pursuant to which the putative vendee goes into possession immediately upon execution of the agreement (there is no closing), and begins to make periodic (usually monthly) payments to the vendor.

[A]   Statute of Frauds

The vast majority of states require an agreement for the conveyance of real property to meet the specifications of the Statute of Frauds—in other words, to be in writing. Usually, this condition is met by the execution of a written purchase and sale contract signed by both of the parties. Other states require the writing to be signed only by the party to be charged, the vendee, since it is he who has the obligation to pay pursuant to the contract.

Although the Statute of Frauds is normally satisfied by the parties' execution of a standard purchase and sale contract, it is not required that the parties execute a formal purchase and sale contract in order to comply with the Statute of Frauds. The Statute of Frauds only requires a memorandum in writing that describes with sufficient detail the subject matter and terms of the agreement.

In *Schwinn v. Griffith,*[2] the issue was whether the statute of frauds is violated when a purchase agreement is executed by an auctioneer but not signed by a purchaser following an auction in which the respondent purchaser is the high bidder.[3] In *Schwinn,* the vendor's property was auctioned, and the vendee was the highest bidder. After the auction, a purchase and sale agreement was prepared and signed by the vendor and auctioneer. The vendee subsequently refused to sign the agreement or accept delivery of the property. The vendor sued for specific performance. The trial court held that a written agreement signed by only the vendor, and not accepted by the vendee, is void under the Statute of

---

[1] *See infra* § 3.04.

[2] 303 N.W.2d 258 (Sup. Ct. Minn. 1981).

[3] *Id.*

Frauds. However, in this case, the Supreme Court of Minnesota found that the auctioneer was acting as the vendee's agent when the auctioneer signed the purchase and sale agreement. Therefore, the contract was valid and the vendor was entitled to specific performance.

By determining that the auctioneer was the seller's agent, the court in *Schwinn* created a limited exception to the strict requirements of the statute of frauds. The protective function advanced by the statute is satisfied when an impartial auctioneer memorializes the transaction immediately after the auction.

[1] Part Performance

In most jurisdictions, "part performance" of the real estate purchase and sale contract is defined as either the (i) vendee's taking possession of the property (the most liberal standard) or, (ii) vendee's possession of the property plus partial or total payment of the purchase price to the vendor (the intermediate standard) or, (iii) vendee's possession plus the construction of valuable improvements on the property or some other action that would cause the vendee irreparable harm if the contract is not enforced (the strictest standard).

Generally speaking, part performance is enough to take an oral real estate purchase and sale contract out of the Statute of Frauds, thereby creating an enforceable contract. However, compare *Baliles v. Cities Service Co.*,[4] holding that part performance alone will not take the contract out of the Statute of Frauds. Nonetheless, "the harshness of this rule has been mitigated by the application of the doctrine of equitable estoppel in exceptional cases where to enforce the Statute of Frauds would make it an instrument of hardship and oppression, verging on actual fraud."[5]

[B] The Basics: Parties, Description of Property, and Consideration

In order to have an enforceable agreement conveying real property, certain basic information such as the parties to the contract, a description of the property to be transferred, and the consideration to be paid must be contained in the agreement or writing in order to comply with the Statute of Frauds.

[1] Parties

The parties to the contract must be identified in order to have an enforceable agreement to convey realty.

[2] Description of the Property

This requirement is more complicated than it might first appear. Although more liberal courts are willing to accept only a street address along with parol evidence to establish the location of the property to be sold to the exclusion of any other

---

[4] 578 S.W.2d 621 (Sup. Ct. Tenn. 1979).

[5] *Id.* at 624.

property in the world,[6] the better view is to require a description which standing alone, that is, without parol evidence, sufficiently identifies the property being conveyed by the agreement to the exclusion of any other property.

For example, Vendor agrees to sell property to vendee located and identified in the contract as 123 Main Street, Anytown, California. Although this description is not a legal description, courts will normally uphold the description if the street address is referenced to a city and a state and it is the only such address located in that city and state.[7]

However, compare the minority view expressed in *Martin v. Seigle*,[8] in which the Washington Supreme Court refused to order specific performance of a contract that identified the property by its street address, including city, county and state, but failed to provide the parcel's lot and block numbers, although such information was available in parol.[9]

[a] Legal Description

In all jurisdictions, a reference to the parcel's lot and block numbers (if the property is located in a subdivision) or a metes and bound or other legal description of the property suffices to satisfy the requirement of describing the property. Hence, the legal description of the property should be taken from the deed pursuant to which the vendor acquired his interest in the property and used to satisfy this requirement.

[3] Consideration

A contract must be supported by consideration in order to be enforceable, and the amount to be paid must be stated in a valid contract for purchase and sale. The issue of a lack of consideration rarely arises in the typical residential real estate transaction since the property is normally sold for a substantial amount. A donative transaction or gift is not supported by consideration and, therefore, does not give rise to an enforceable contract. However, when the donor has the requisite intent to make a gift, delivers a deed to the donee, and the donee accepts the gift, the donative transaction will be valid and treated as a completed gift.

[C] Conditions in the Contract

A typical real estate purchase and sale contract contains many conditions that must be completed or waived before the contract can be fully performed at closing. Conditions allow the parties to provide each other with relevant information that cannot be conveyed at the time of closing, but which information

---

[6] Stachnik v. Winkel, 50 Mich. App. 316, 213 N.W.2d 434 (1973), *rev'd on other grounds*, 394 Mich. 375, 230 N.W.2d 529 (1975).

[7] *See* Ray v. Robben, 225 Ark. 824, 285 S.W. 2d 907 (1956).

[8] 35 Wash. 2d 223, 212 P.2d 107 (1949).

[9] *Id.* For a thorough discussion of the specific description requirement as affecting the enforceability of the contract to convey real property, see 73 ALR 4th 135 (1989).

must be conveyed either before or at the time of closing. A condition should be viewed as a prerequisite to the party's performance of the promise to buy or sell. Thus, conditions make the parties' promises to perform contingent upon the happening or non-happening of some occurrence, anticipating some potential risks and contingencies. Though typically a breach of one of the major contract conditions relating to title, financing, or land use will result in the termination of the contract, not all contingencies stipulate that the contract will be terminated if a condition is not completed. Rather, contract contingency clauses may specify different consequences for the non-occurrence of a condition.[10] Other commonly-used conditions include the provision that the closing is: 1) subject to the sale of the vendee's existing residence; 2) subject to the ability to obtain a new zoning classification for the property; 3) subject to existing mortgages; and 4) subject to an attorney's approval of the contract's terms and conditions.

For example, Vendee promises to purchase Blackacre from the vendor for $100,000 contingent upon the condition that the property is appraised by a reputable and qualified appraiser at $100,000 some number of days prior to the date of sale. In a well-drafted contract, the duty to hire and pay for the appraiser will be allocated to one or both parties. The good faith duty to obtain an appraisal is not a covenant or promise in the contract but a condition which must be satisfied before the vendee is contractually bound to perform his obligation or promise to purchase Blackacre for $100,000. If the condition is not met, Vendee cannot be sued for specific performance or breach of contract nor can his deposit be retained by Vendor.

[1] Bilateral Contract

The real estate purchase and sale contract is a typical bilateral contract, requiring both parties to carry out conditions contained in the contract as part of the complete and full performance of the contract. If the contract requires either the vendor or vendee to discharge a condition as a prerequisite to the performance of the contract, the party charged with the performance of the condition must perform or be in breach of the contract, unless the contract specifically provides to the contrary or the performance of the condition is waived by the party who is benefitted by enforcing the condition.

A typical contract may require the vendee to place an additional deposit with the vendor or his agent within a specified time period following execution of the real estate purchase and sale contract. Thus, if the contract requires the vendee to deposit $5,000 within 48 hours of the execution of the contract, failure to do so will constitute anticipatory breach of contract, excusing the vendor's performance of her conditions in the contract and allowing her to pursue any and all remedies against the defaulting vendee for breach of contract.[11] Of course, the

---

[10] For a discussion of breach of the purchase and sale contract and associated remedies for the parties involved, see *infra* Chapter 5.

[11] For a discussion of the vendor's remedies, see *infra* § 5.04.

(Matthew Bender & Co., Inc.)

vendor may unilaterally waive the provision requiring the additional deposit, seeking to enforce the contract despite the vendee's failure to timely perform the condition provided in the contract.

The purpose of this type of condition is to provide the vendor with some degree of certainty that the putative vendee is really interested in purchasing the property by forcing the vendee to make a large deposit which ties him financially to the purchase of the real property. What follows is an examination of the most frequently used and litigated "conditions" typically contained in the real estate purchase and sale contract.

[2] Financing

Absent contractual language to the contrary, the financing default rule assumes that the vendee will be purchasing the property in cash, placing the financing risk on the buyer-vendee. Under the default rule, the vendee is obligated to purchase the property or be in breach, even if she is unable to obtain necessary financing. Thus, every well-drafted contract should contain a comprehensive "subject to financing" clause (unless the purchase is an exchange or all cash transaction) that provides that the vendee will not be required to purchase the property unless she can obtain suitable financing as specified in the real estate purchase and sale contract. A financing condition allows the vendee to avoid a contractual obligation to purchase the property if she is unable to secure necessary financing, but may also benefit the vendor if it provides earlier notice of a buyer's ability to finance the purchase by requiring proof of a firm loan commitment. Without such a clause, the seller may not know of a buyer's inability to fund the transaction until the date set for closing, when the obligation to pay for the property matures. At a minimum, a "subject to financing" clause typically defines: 1) the amount of the mortgage loan to be procured, 2) the minimum allowable loan term (for example, 20 or 30 years), and 3) the maximum allowable interest rate to be paid on the loan. If applicable, the clause should also state the number of points to be paid by the vendee to the lender to obtain the loan at the applicable interest rate.[12]

For example, assume that Vendees' offer to purchase Blackacre for $100,000, paying $20,000 as an earnest money deposit, or downpayment, against the purchase price. The contract contains a condition that the Vendees will not be committed to the purchase of the property unless they can obtain a commitment for a conventional loan from a bank or savings and loan association in the amount of $80,000, secured by a mortgage and amortized over a minimum of twenty years at a rate of interest not higher than 10%. The Vendees have a good faith obligation to obtain financing by applying for the loan at a "reasonable" number

---

[12] A point represents one percent of the loan principle. For example, one point on a $100,000 loan is $1,000, and the existence of such a point effects the loan's true yield or interest rate. For further discussion of points and the terminology applicable to all mortgages, see *infra* § 6.09.

of qualifying institutions. However, if they are unable to obtain the loan on the terms provided in the condition, they can terminate the contract and obtain the return of the deposit.

[a] Applying for Financing

The contract's condition may require either or both the vendor and vendee to apply for financing, though typically only the vendee is required to apply for the financing. As a result, the vendee has a good faith duty to apply for financing upon the terms and conditions set forth in the purchase and sale contract. The "subject to financing" condition imposes on the vendee a duty to apply to a reasonable number of financial institutions for financing.[13] However, the vendee does not have to apply to multiple lenders if such action would be futile. For example, if all the institutional lenders belong to a central appraisal bureau, and thereby have access to the information that caused the initial institution to reject the vendee's application for a loan, the vendee need not perform the futile exercise of applying to additional institutional lenders.[14]

In *Liuzza v. Panzer*,[15] the issue was whether the vendee fulfilled the financing requirement of a purchase and sale agreement.[16] The vendor and vendee entered into an agreement for the sale of real property at a price of $37,500. The contract contained a financing clause which stated the sale was conditional upon the ability of the vendee to borrow $30,000 of the purchase price at an interest rate not to exceed 9%. If the vendee was unable to obtain financing, the agreement was null and void and all deposits would be returned. The vendee applied to one institution and was told the appraised value of the property was $32,151.20 and that they would not lend in excess of 80% of that amount ($25,000). The vendee attempted to rescind the contract. The court held that the financing clause implicitly imposed a duty on the vendee to make a good faith effort to acquire the loan. The court found that the vendee had not made a sufficient effort by applying only to one institution.

Implying a duty of good faith in the conditional clause of the contract effectively prevents the parties from employing such clauses to rescind the contract at will. Here, the vendee attempted to use the financing contingency opportunistically as an "out" when he discovered he had agreed to pay too much for the property according to the appraisal done on the property.

[b] Vendor Financing

Unless the contract provides to the contrary, the vendor may offer to finance the sale upon the terms and conditions set forth in the contract in order to meet

---

[13] *See* Liuzza v. Panzer, 333 So.2d 689 (La. App. 4th Cir. 1976).

[14] *See* Katz v. Chatelain, 312 So.2d 802 (La. App. 4th Cir. 1975).

[15] 333 So.2d 690 (1976).

[16] *Id.*

the financing contingency. In the absence of exculpatory language in the contract, the vendee must accept the financing or breach the contract.

Since financing and the ability to make a monthly payment of a certain amount play paramount roles in the sale of real property, the use of a financing contingency clause allows the putative vendee to set parameters on the risk he may be undertaking in the purchase of the property. In other words, the vendee does not want to lose his downpayment or deposit because he is unable to obtain a loan which he can afford to pay off. Hence, the financing clause gives the vendee an "out" by allowing for the return of the deposit if the property cannot be financed as anticipated.

Occasionally, some vendees may use the financing clause as a substitute for obtaining an appraisal on the property. Institutional lenders will not make secured loans on real property unless the property is worth a certain value when compared to the amount requested to be borrowed—often expressed as the "loan-to-value ratio."[17] Generally, most lenders will not take a first mortgage on the property unless the property is appraised at or above the sales price. Hence, an inability to obtain financing may signal that the piece of real property is overpriced, while simultaneously relieving the vendee from an obligation to purchase the property.

[3] Title

Given the magnitude and importance of real estate transactions, the vendor must unequivocally establish that she is the true owner of the property being sold.[18] Since non-possessory rights in real property can be created easily and are frequently beneficial to the value of the property, the vendor may also convey the real property subject to acceptable covenants, conditions and restrictions that affect the use of the real property. In addition, the vendor must provide a warranty or guarantee that no unacceptable interests exist which detrimentally affect the use of the real property and would thereby prevent the putative vendee from using the property as she intended. An example would be if the vendor promises to convey good and marketable title to the vendee on the date set for closing pursuant to a full or general warranty deed, with the exception of easements of record granted to or held by public utility companies to service the property and adjacent land.

This title covenant provides the vendee with information on the state of the title to be conveyed at the time of closing. Thus, notwithstanding the prospective vendee's lack of knowledge about the state of title, she can rest assured that the title received on the date of closing will be that set forth in the condition in the real estate purchase and sale contract. If not, the vendee can cancel the purchase and sale contract and refuse to go forward with the purchase.

---

[17] *See infra* § 6.02[C].

[18] *See infra* Chapter 10.

As with most conditions in contracts, conditions in real estate contracts must be read very carefully to insure that they are performed properly. The title condition discussed here requires the vendor to deliver the quality of title described in the purchase and sale contract on the date of closing. The fact that the vendor does not possess the requisite title on the date of the execution of the real estate purchase and sale contract is irrelevant, as long as the vendor performs the condition at the time required: the date of closing.

For example, suppose that the vendor promises to convey marketable title to the vendee on September 1st, the date set for closing, free and clear of all encumbrances with no exceptions. At the time of contracting, not only is there a mortgage on the property in the amount of $50,000, but the vendor does not even own the property at issue. However, the vendor's promise to convey good and marketable title is not breached when the contract is executed; it is breached, if at all, on September 1st when the vendor is called upon to do what he promised in the contract. Presumably in the executory interval between the signing of the contract and the delivery of the deed on September 1st, the date set for closing, the vendor will acquire title to the property and remove the encumbrance (the mortgage) from the property. The vendor's failure to perform either task by the date set for closing will give rise to a breach of the express condition in the contract to deliver marketable title.

[a] Marketable Title

There is an implied covenant in every contract for the sale of real property that the title that is conveyed be marketable. Marketable title is defined most frequently, and with some degree of circularity, as title:

[T]hat may be freely made the subject of resale. It is title which can be readily sold or mortgaged to a person of reasonable prudence, the test of the marketability of a title being whether there is an objection thereto such as would interfere with a sale or with the market value of the property. The law assures to a [vendee] a title free from reasonable doubt, but not from every doubt and the mere possibility or suspicion of a defect. . .does not demonstrate an unmarketable title.[19]

This implied covenant can be negated by language in the contract, expressly affirmed, or expanded by the use of appropriate language requiring either record title or insurable title (both of which—"record" and "insurable" title—are terms of art and are discussed *infra* below). Matters that detrimentally affect title and may cause title to be unmarketable are listed and discussed separately below.

[i] Encumbrances

Any encumbrance reducing the value of the land (for example, leases, mortgages, easements, mineral reservations, and liens) is an encumbrance that

---

[19] Regan v. Lanze, 40 N.Y.2d 475, 481-82, 387 N.Y.S.2d 79, 83, 354 N.E.2d 818, 822 (1976).

affects the marketability or value of the land and can cause title to be unmarketable if not properly excepted.

[ii] Visible Easements

Although easements affecting the use of land are encumbrances, visible easements that the vendee is or should be aware of and should have taken into account in her decision to purchase the property are *not* regarded as encumbrances affecting title.

[iii] Lack of Access

Lack of access to a public road can render a title unmarketable.

[iv] Violations of Private Covenants

Even if the vendor has agreed to take title subject to existing covenants, conditions and restrictions of record, a violation of any of those covenants, conditions, or restrictions may cause title to be unmarketable. Such a violation exposes the owner of the land to a potential lawsuit that can have a detrimental impact on the value of the property.

For example, assume that Barb Buyer has agreed to purchase Blackacre from Vern Vendor pursuant to a contract that contains the following language: Buyer agrees to take Blackacre subject to all existing easements and encumbrances of record. Buyer subsequently discovers that there is a telephone easement on the property that allows the local utility to run a telephone line across the boundary line of Blackacre. In addition, Buyer discovers that when the property was subdivided, the original owner/grantor placed a restriction that required that each structure be at least 20 feet from any boundary (a set-back restriction designed to insure the orderly and attractive development of the subdivision or neighborhood). The mere existence of the utility easement and the covenant—the promise by the owner not to build within 20 feet—do not violate the clause in the contract and make title unmarketable. However, if Buyer has a physical survey completed and discovers that the attached garage is built within 10 feet of the east boundary line of the property that constitutes a violation of the covenant that makes title unmarketable. More importantly, Buyer does not have to show that a lawsuit is pending or forthcoming. It is the violation which creates the mere possibility of a lawsuit to which Buyer did not agree that constitutes a violation of marketable title. At some point, the owner may be forced to move the garage back 10 feet or more in order to comply with the covenant at considerable cost.[20]

---

[20] Note that Vendor may claim that the garage has been present for a period longer than that required by the statute of limitations for adverse possession and argue therefore that no one has the right to enforce the setback covenant against him or a subsequent buyer. If that is factually the case, the issue of whether Vendor has breached his duty to deliver marketable title turns on whether Vendor must deliver "record" marketable title or whether Vendor can prove marketable title by facts outside the record or what's recorded in the County Recorder's Office. For a discussion of this issue, see *infra* text § 3.02[C][3][e].

[v] Zoning and Local Ordinances

The existence or *violation* of zoning or other ordinances affecting the land does *not* impede or affect the marketability of title since both parties have equal access to information about the rules and ordinances that affect the use of property.[21] Conditions that do affect marketability can best be characterized as those conditions that are within the knowledge of, or are easily determinable by, the vendor. Such conditions should be disclosed by the vendor (or "excepted") in the contract at the time of contracting. The requirement of marketable title serves as a device to allocate the duty to disclose information. It requires the party with the best access to the information, the vendor, to discover and either disclose the information (by explicit exceptions to the quality of title conveyed in the contract) or accept the potential risk of loss that may occur as a result of defects in the state of title that the reasonable vendee may find unacceptable. Since information concerning public bodies, such as zoning boards, their rules and regulations, and any violation thereof, is equally available to both parties, such information does not affect the marketability of the property. The same rationale supports the exception for visible easements.

However, if the vendee contemplates a specific, unique use of the premises that is not disclosed to the vendor or made a condition of the contract, then the risk that the real property cannot fulfill that use is placed on the vendee, who is in the best position to insure ex ante that the use contemplated can be accomplished following his purchase.

[b] Excepting Encumbrances that Affect Title

The best way to convey information to the vendee about the condition and state of title to be transferred at the time of closing is to either "except" all of the encumbrances that may affect title by listing them in the contract, or to state that the vendee takes "subject to all encumbrances of record." The preferred method is to list all the encumbrances individually because some may not be publicly recorded. In addition, a well-advised vendee may reasonably object to such a general statement excepting encumbrances when the vendee is unaware of the specific nature of the encumbrances which could detrimentally impact the value of the property.

[c] Insurable Title

Insurable title is a term of art and represents an alternative to marketable title. Insurable title is title that a reputable title insurance company will insure without exception, unless the exception(s) is stated in the contract. Insurable title can be used in conjunction with marketable title or can be used to supplant the implied

---

[21] *Compare* Dover Pool and Racquet Club, Inc. v. Brooking, 366 Mass. 629, 322 N.E. 2d 168 (1975), in which the court granted rescission of the real estate contract based on mutual mistake of fact when both parties erroneously believed that the zoning laws in effect permitted the vendee's anticipated use of the premises.

requirement that marketable title be delivered on the date of closing. However, the sufficiency of insurable title must be explicitly expressed in the contract before it can be used by the vendor to satisfy his duty to deliver title on the date of closing.

Suppose that the vendor promises to deliver title that is either marketable or insurable on the date of closing. Since marketable and insurable are stated in the disjunctive, the vendor can satisfy this condition by delivering either. Compare this to the situation where the vendor promises to deliver marketable *and* insurable title. In this situation, since the requirement is stated in the conjunctive, the vendor must deliver title that is both marketable and insured by a reputable title insurance company in order to perform.[22]

In *Laba v. Carey*,[23] the issue was whether a vendee is entitled to rescind a purchase and sale contract when the vendor is contractually required to deliver "title such as any reputable title company would approve and insure," subject to covenants, restrictions and easement[s] of record, and there are easements, restrictions and covenants of record that the title company refuses to insure.[24] In *Laba*, the vendor and vendee entered into a contract for the sale of real property, agreeing that the vendor would convey title that any reputable title company would approve and insure. A title company issued title insurance on the property, excepting a telephone easement and a "Waiver of Legal Grades" relating to the grade of the sidewalk. At closing, the vendee refused to accept this title, claiming it was not good, marketable and insurable title because it was not unconditionally insured by the insurance company. The vendee then sued the vendor for the return of his deposit.

The court held that the "insurance" clause must be read in conjunction with the "subject to" clause in the purchase and sale contract, which only required the vendor to tender an insurable title subject to encumbrances of record, as long as those encumbrances (easements and covenants) were not violated.

Contractual provisions defining the quality of title to be delivered by the vendor must be read carefully to determine the quality of title that the vendor must deliver. Blanket statements requiring the vendor to deliver marketable title may be qualified by later "subject to" clauses, excepting matters that affect title. In addition, clauses excepting encumbrances to title do not include violations of either public (zoning) restrictions on the property that are the subject of pending litigation or enforcement actions on the part of a governmental body (violations that are not being prosecuted do not make title unmarketable) or private (easements/covenants) restrictions on the property.

---

[22] *See* Conklin v. Davi, 76 N.J. 468, 388 A.2d 598 (1978).

[23] 277 N.E.2d 641 (1971).

[24] *Id.*

"Subject to" clauses are interpreted broadly to allow the vendor to convey relevant information to the vendee regarding the restrictions (not violated) that affect title to the property. "Subject to" clauses are necessary because very few, if any, parcels of real property are totally free of any valid restrictions on use. For example, without a "subject to" clause a telephone easement that improves the property's value that if not otherwise excepted would cause title to be unmarketable.

[d] Insurable Title Compared to Marketable Title

Since title insurance companies are in the insurance business and may agree to certain risks at a given cost, a title insurance company may issue a title insurance policy without exception on real property that may not be marketable (for example, a reasonable vendee may defend an action for specific performance brought by the vendor against her by proving defects in title) in exchange for an acceptable premium based on the company's belief that the odds are worth taking that they will not have to pay on the policy.[25]

As an example, presume that Vendor transfers insurable title to the vendee. The title insurer insures title unequivocally even though a search of the records reveals an ancient, but apparently still valid easement. The easement is not visible upon inspection of the property, but cuts through the middle of the lot being conveyed. The beneficiary of the easement is presumed dead. It is important to note that even though the title insurer may issue the vendee a policy protecting the vendee's interest in the property, that does not mean that the vendee will be able to transfer the property to a subsequent purchaser for value or that the subsequent purchaser for value will be able to obtain a similar policy protecting any interest in the property he may purchase. Quite the contrary, if the risk increases (perhaps the heirs have discovered their interest in the property and are threatening to enforce their easement rights unless they are paid off) while the vendee owns the property, the insurer may refuse to issue a new policy to any subsequent vendee and, as discussed below, the current vendee's policy will not be transferable to a subsequent vendee. Hence, the vendee will have insurable title that is not marketable.

[e] Record Title

If the vendor promises to deliver record title, the vendor is promising to convey title that can be proved by looking to the record alone and without resort to any extraneous matters.[26] The use of record title precludes the vendor from proving title via adverse possession that has not resulted in title being adjudicated in the vendor in a successful action to quiet title. The vendor must prove title only by reference to documents filed of record in the court recorder's office.

---

[25] Title insurance and title insurers are discussed *infra* § 9.03.

[26] The "record" is discussed *infra* in Chapter 10.

[f]   Record Title Compared to Marketable Title

Perfect record title does not necessarily mean good title. For instance, one of the deeds in the chain of title establishing the record title may be a forgery or signed by an incompetent or someone not capable of making the transfer.

[4]   Time of Closing

The real estate purchase and sale contract should always contain an agreed upon date for closing, the time at which title is to be transferred from the vendor to the vendee. At law, time is always of the essence and failure to perform on the date indicated in the contract may cause the late party to be liable in damages for the delay.[27] However, in this situation, the aggrieved party's legal damages may be very small since the party eventually receives what was promised—the real property—pursuant to the contract.[28]

In equity, the vendor or vendee's failure to perform, or close, on the date stated in the contract is not a breach of contract unless the contract expressly states that "time is of the essence," or the circumstances, known to the other party, make the time of performance essential. Thus, in *Century 21 All Western Real Estate v. Webb,*[29] the issue was whether the vendor had breached the purchase and sale agreement by refusing to perform.[30] The vendor and vendees had entered into a purchase and sale agreement for the purchase of a home for $28,000. During the executory interval, the vendees discovered that the vendor had a personal debt in the amount of $5,000 which was secured by an assignment of her interest in the property at issue. The vendees refused to proceed with the purchase until the lien on the property was retired (paid off). The vendor, in turn, refused to proceed until the vendees paid the purchase price lien. At a later date, the vendees, without changing their position as to the lien, arranged a closing. When the vendor failed to attend, the vendees sued the vendor for breach of the contract.

The court held that the vendees had not placed the vendor in breach because the contract contained no declaration that time was of the essence. Given the unresolved dispute, the court found that the vendees had not unconditionally tendered their performance of the contract.

Where the executory contract does not contain a clause declaring that time is of the essence, both parties' obligations to perform can continue for a reasonable period of time beyond the date set for closing. The contract is not capable of being breached until the party seeking to establish a breach unconditionally tenders performance as required by the contract. As a practical matter,

---

[27] *See* Richardson v. Van Dolah, 429 F.2d 912 (9th Cir. 1970).

[28] *See also* Corbin, Contracts § 713 (1951).

[29] 645 P.2d 52 (Sup. Ct. Utah 1982).

[30] *Id.*

this case demonstrates the hazards confronted by a vendee when: (1) the contract fails to clearly state that time is of the essence, and (2) the parties fail to address adequately the timing of payments of liens or encumbrances on the property.

[a] Treatment by Equity Courts

However, in equity, if time is not of the essence, the party who is late maintains her right to enforce the contract by seeking specific performance if she is ready to perform within a reasonable time, as judged by the circumstances.[31] Since "reasonable" is such a vague term, one cannot be certain what a judge will determine in hindsight to be a reasonable tender, given the circumstances. One way to avoid this issue is to state in the contract that as a condition of closing, time is of the essence.

For example, suppose that Vendor and Vendee agree to close on September 1st. On September 1st, the vendor notifies the vendee that she is unable to close because she cannot deliver marketable title, as was promised pursuant to the contract, until October 1st. If the clause stating the closing date includes the intent of the parties that time is of the essence, the vendee can refuse to accept the vendor's proffered late tender, terminate the contract, and either seek to rescind the contract with a return of her deposit, or alternatively, seek a return of her deposit and damages proximately caused by the vendor's failure to timely perform. However, if the contract or the circumstances do not make time of the essence, the vendor's late tender of performance may very easily be deemed reasonable by an equity court, and the vendee may have to accept the later closing date or be in breach of contract.

[5] Good Faith and the Duty to Perform

As with most contracts containing multiple conditions and covenants, the question often arises as to whether the purchase and sale contract is too indefinite to be enforced when certain terms are vague or ambiguous. Alternatively, arguments may be made that the contract is illusory and should not be enforced when the conditions are phrased in general terms and the fulfillment of the conditions (for example, obtaining financing) is left to the exclusive control of one party (in this case, the vendee). The courts use the doctrine of "good faith" to police and monitor the behavior of the parties and to insure that parties do not renege on terms of performance.

Frequently, a party to an agreement will point to a technical violation of the contract in an attempt to rescind the agreement when the real problem (for example, tenants in possession of the premises pursuant to a valid lease), is not covered by the contract or does not give the aggrieved party a right to terminate. In these situations, courts should, and are likely to, look at the real reason for the party's reluctance to perform the contract, basing the outcome of the case

---

[31] For a discussion of the equitable remedy of specific performance, see *infra* § 5.03 and § 5.04[A].

on whether the parties addressed the real issue in the contract. In other words, the courts will not allow an aggrieved party to be released from a bad deal by pointing to a harmless technical violation of the contract when the problem actually causing the harm could have been addressed by the aggrieved party ex ante at the time of contracting. To do otherwise would reward subterfuge instead of good drafting.

[a] Unreasonably Detailed Clauses

The doctrine of good faith is also used to insure that excessively detailed clauses are not used by one party as a subterfuge to evade obligations pursuant to an onerous contract. Good faith in performance is required when the contract is drafted with excessive detail.[32]

[D] Equitable Conversion

Because equity courts regard what ought to and will be done as already done, the roles and risks assigned during the executory interval reflect the fact that, upon the date set for closing or shortly thereafter, the putative vendee will become the owner of the real property, and the current vendor will be the recipient of money or other property. As a result, during the executory interval, a *fictional* transmutation in the characterization of the property is effectuated by courts of equity. This fictional transmutation has far reaching ramifications during the executory interval.

[1] Characterization of the Parties' Interests

Let's assume that Vendor and Vendee sign a real estate purchase and sale contract on June 1st, with closing set for September 1st, time being of the essence. During the executory interval between June 1st and September 1st, equity regards as done what will be done on September 1st—namely the fact that the vendee will be the owner of *real property* on September 1st, and the vendor will be the owner of *personal property* (money paid for the sale of the real property) on September 1st. Hence, during the executory interval, the vendee's personal right to receive the property on September 1st (if he performs all conditions of the contract) is fictionally transformed into an equitable interest in the real property. Conversely, the vendor's interest in the real property is fictionally transformed into the personal right to receive the proceeds generated by the sale if he performs all of his conditions in the contract. Thus, during the executory interval, the vendee is said to possess an interest in the real property, and the vendor is said to possess an interest in personal property. Though the "legal" title to the property will remain with the vendor until it passes to the vendee at closing, the doctrine of equitable conversion maintains that the vendee has "equitable" title upon the execution of a *valid and enforceable* real estate purchase and sale agreement.

---

[32] *See* Note, *Contingency Financing Clauses in Real Estate Sales Contract in Georgia*, 8 Ga. L. Rev. 186 (1973).

Equitable conversion operates to change the nature and character of the property held in the hands of the vendor and the vendee during the executory interval.

[2] Risk of Loss

At common law, equitable conversion operates to place the risk of loss for any fortuitous destruction of the premises on the *vendee* during the executory interval. This is true even if the vendor remains in possession, because courts of equity regard the vendee as the owner of the realty during the executory interval as soon as there is a completed, enforceable contract. Note that the doctrine of equitable conversion and the risk of loss rule arise only when the contract is capable of specific performance—in other words, all the contract conditions must be satisfied before this equitable action becomes available.

Continuing the above hypothetical, if the house located on the property at issue is destroyed by a fire not intentionally caused by the vendor on August 1st during the executory interval, the vendee remains bound to purchase the property, notwithstanding her legitimate claim that the doctrine of frustration of purpose, i.e., the house has been destroyed and cannot be used as a residence per the parties' intent, should be applied to allow her to rescind the contract. Because the vendee has an equitable interest in the premises at the instant of the execution of the purchase and sale contract, the vendee has an insurable interest in the real property that she can, and should, protect by obtaining insurance.

[a] Minority or Modern View

Though the doctrine of equitable conversion has been adopted by a majority of American courts, the common law view of equitable conversion as it applies to the risk of loss in the event of the fortuitous destruction of the premises can be criticized for several reasons. First, equitable conversion is not in accord with the expectations of the parties since the vendee may not know that she will bear the risk of loss once the contract is signed and is capable of specific enforcement and usually believes she is not responsible for the property until the legal title is transferred to her at closing. Second, equitable conversion is inefficient because it places the risk of loss on the party least able to bear or control the risk—the party out of possession. Third, it often leads to the issuance of two insurance policies simultaneously covering the same parcel of property,[33] since the vendee is encouraged to obtain her own policy regardless of whether the property is still covered under the vendor's existing policy.

As a result, the minority view posits that the default or "off-the-rack" rule governing the typical transaction in the absence of customized language in the contract (which, if present, should always be referred to and given effect since it reflects the parties' allocation of rights) should place the risk of loss on the *vendor* until the date set for closing. Such an allocation would then allow the

---

[33] *See* Sanford v. Breidenbach, 111 Ohio App. 474, 173 N.E. 2d 702 (1960).

vendee to rescind the purchase and sale contract during the executory interval on the basis of the contract doctrines of impossibility or frustration of purpose, or possibly to allow specific performance with a price abatement reflecting the diminution in value caused by the act of destruction.

In *Sanford v. Breidenbach*, the issue was whether the vendee or the vendor bears and/or may insure against the risk of loss during the executory interval.[34] In this case, the vendee agreed to purchase the vendor's property and the home thereon for $26,000. During the executory interval, the house was entirely destroyed by fire. Both the vendor and the vendee had insured their interest in the property against a loss by fire with different insurance companies. Each insurance company and the vendor and vendee disputed who would be held responsible for the loss.

The court found that the risk of loss during the executory interval is on the vendor, unless the vendor has the right to enforce the sales contract through specific performance and the parties specify in the contract that they intend to shift the risk of loss to the vendee. In this case, only the vendor had an insurable interest in the property; therefore, he and his insurance company were liable for the loss, and the vendee did not have to perform the contract.

In this case the court followed the minority view, holding that the risk of loss is on the vendor until the vendor has performed all of the conditions in the contract *and* the parties intend title to transfer. Not only is this rule in line with the parties' expectations, but given that the vendor normally retains possession of the premises until the date set for closing (and can therefore simply keep his insurance policy in force), placing the risk of loss on the vendor is more efficient.

As a result of the dissatisfaction with the majority or common law view towards the doctrine of equitable conversion, many alternatives have been put forth for the allocation of the risk of loss during the executory interval. Those views are summarized in *Skelly Oil Co. v. Ashmore*:[35] (i) the risk of loss is on the vendor until the date of closing even if the vendee is in possession, (ii) the risk of loss is on the vendor until the date of closing, and thereafter on the vendee, unless the vendor has not performed the conditions of the contract (for example, is in breach, in which case the risk of loss remains on the vendor), (iii) the risk of loss is on the party in possession, and (iv) the risk of loss is on the vendor unless the court can discern a different intent from the contract.[36]

[b]   Rationale for the Majority View of Equitable Conversion

The doctrine of equitable conversion may initially appear to treat the vendee inequitably by requiring her to bear the risk of loss on the property during the

---

[34] *Id.*

[35] 365 S.W.2d 582, 587 (Sup. Ct. Mo. 1963).

[36] *Id.*

executory interval. However, ignoring the doctrine of equitable conversion's fictional transformation of an interest in personal property into one in real property and vice versa, one way to support the doctrine is to recognize that after signing the contract to purchase real property, the vendee has an interest in the property that is enforceable by the remedy of specific performance.[37] Pursuant to that remedy, the vendee can force the vendor to complete the sale of the property (assuming the parties have a valid contract and the vendee has performed all of his obligations pursuant thereunder) irrespective of any favorable events that occur during the executory interval that have an impact on the value of the property. For example, if oil is discovered beneath the real property during the executory interval and the property increases in value ten-fold, the vendee obtains the windfall represented by the higher value of the property. Since the vendee receives the benefit of any increase in the value of the property during the executory interval, she must also be the one to suffer any loss to the value of the property during that time. Hence, those who support the common law view argue that equitable conversion should be considered an extension of this doctrine.

[c] The Uniform Vendor and Purchaser Risk Act (UVPRA)

Due to dissatisfaction with the common law rule on risk of loss, thirteen states, California, Hawaii, Illinois, Iowa, Michigan, Nevada, New York, North Carolina, Oklahoma, Oregon, South Dakota, Texas, and Wisconsin, have adopted the UVPRA in full or in part. The Act reads as follows:

"Any contract hereafter made in this State for the purchase and sale of real property shall be interpreted as including an agreement that the parties shall have the following rights and duties, unless the contract expressly provides otherwise:

(a) If, when neither the legal title nor the possession of the subject matter of the contract has been transferred, all or a material part thereof is destroyed without fault of the purchaser or is taken by eminent domain, the vendor cannot enforce the contract, and the purchaser is entitled to recover any portion of the price that he has paid;

(b) If, when either the legal title or the possession of the subject matter of the contract has been transferred, all or any part hereof is destroyed without fault of the vendor or is taken by eminent domain, the purchaser is not thereby relieved from a duty to pay the price."[38]

[3] Insurance

Practically speaking, the party bearing the risk of loss during the executory interval should obtain an insurance policy to protect her interest in the property at issue. Thus, in jurisdictions following the majority view that the vendee has

---

[37] For a discussion of the doctrine of specific performance, see *infra* § 5.03 and § 5.04[A].

[38] 14 U.L.A. 469 (1990 & Supp. 2000).

the risk of loss, the vendee is best advised to obtain her own policy. However, as insurance coverage is typically required by a lender-mortgagee, the vendor will usually carry a policy at the time that the contract is executed. Thus, if the vendor chooses to keep an existing policy in effect during the executory period, the vendor can either name the vendee as an insured party under her policy, or can endorse the policy, allowing the vendee to share in any proceeds.

However, if none of these methods are used to provide explicit coverage for the party bearing the risk of loss, the equitable principles of conversion, constructive trusts, and subrogation will be used to determine the outcome, though the results are not always easy to predict. Though an insurance policy is considered to be a personal contract between the insurer and the insured, some courts in states following the majority rule have held that the insured vendor holds the proceeds in a trust for the uninsured vendee. In other words, once the named insured party receives the proceeds of the policy, equity courts may require the proceeds to be placed in a constructive trust to benefit the uninsured party who suffers the risk of loss. However, it is not clear that the constructive trust theory operates in reverse—when the vendee is insured, but the vendor is held to have the risk of loss. Furthermore, in jurisdictions following the majority rule but where the vendor holds the policy, after a loss occurs and the vendee benefits from the proceeds of the policy, courts typically require the vendee to reimburse the vendor for insurance premiums paid.

In *Gilles v. Sprout*,[39] the issue was whether the vendee or the vendor bears the risk of loss to the property during the executory interval after the contract is signed and before the date set for closing.[40] The vendor and vendee had executed a purchase and sale contract for the sale of a lot and the building thereon for a stated price, though the contract was silent as to the insurance obligations of the respective parties. While the vendee was in possession of the premises during the executory interval, a fire destroyed the building and the vendor received insurance proceeds from an existing policy. At closing, the vendor and vendee disputed whether or not there should be an abatement in the purchase price equivalent to the amount of the insurance proceeds recovered by the vendor to reflect the loss of the building.

The court held that the risk of loss during the executory interval is on the vendor and granted specific performance of the purchase and sale contract with the insurance proceeds credited to the vendee against the purchase price of the property. Adopting the minority view, the court reasoned that by placing the risk of loss during the executory interval on the vendor, both parties were able to receive the benefit of their bargain. The vendor received the contract price for the property, while the vendee was only required to pay for the value of the

[39] 293 Minn. 53, 196 N.W.2d 612 (1972).

[40] *Id.*

property he actually received. Though this result prevents the vendor from having a windfall (selling the property for the full original amount and collecting insurance proceeds in addition), it can be criticized as allowing the vendee to receive a windfall. For example, the vendee may have planned to tear down the structure which was destroyed by fire, and therefore received land worth more than was bargained for at a reduced price. In situations like this, it can be argued that the court instead should have given the vendee the option to rescind or perform pursuant to the terms of the contract.

§ 3.03   Option Agreements

Although related to real estate purchase and sale contracts, option agreements represent a separate agreement pursuant to which one party, normally the putative vendee, is given the option to purchase the real property at a price set forth in the option agreement. An option is a promise by the putative vendor to sell the property to the optionee at a certain price. It is an offer, and not a binding contract, to sell the real property, and it is held open to the optionee for a fixed period of time. An option agreement differs from a real estate purchase and sale contract in that it gives the optionee, the putative vendee, the ability to determine unilaterally whether she will exercise the option by purchasing the property from the optionor/vendor during the period of time specified in the option agreement.

[A]   Mechanics of Option Agreements

Like any other contractual agreement, an option agreement must be supported by consideration in order to be enforceable. Hence, the option itself is viewed as a separate agreement supported by consideration. If the option is exercised, it will eventually be memorialized as a real estate purchase and sale contract. As a result, the option agreement should be drafted as though it will become the real estate purchase and sale contract, and should include all the terms and conditions normally contained in the real estate purchase and sale contract. Failure to include key terms may render the option agreement indefinite, and thereby unenforceable.

[1]   Specific Performance

The option agreement is specifically enforceable by the optionee if she validly exercises the option during the period the option is in effect.

[2]   Equitable Conversion

The doctrine of equitable conversion does *not* apply to option agreements.[41]

[3]   Time is of the Essence

Although it should be stated expressly in the agreement to avoid confusion, the fact that time is of the essence will be implied in an option agreement.

---

[41] *See supra* § 3.02[D].

[a]   Late Payment of Consideration

Although time is of the essence with respect to the *exercise* of the option within the time period defined in the option agreement, late payment of the consideration for the option does not destroy the optionee's right to exercise the option in a timely fashion, as long as no harm is caused by the late payment.[42]

[B]   Rule Against Perpetuities

The Rule Against Perpetuities invalidates interests in real property that may fail to vest within twenty-one years of the creation of the interest. An option is a contingent interest in real property that may fail to vest within twenty-one years of its creation and is, therefore, subject to the application of the rule. The Rule Against Perpetuities, requires that the option must be exercised, if at all, within the period fixed by the Rule.[43]

As an example, let's say that Vendor grants Vendee an option of 120 days to purchase certain lands at an agreed upon cash price, with the option period beginning when the city in which the land is located rezones the property for commercial purposes. This option agreement violates the technical requirements of the Rule Against Perpetuities because the city may rezone the property for commercial purposes beyond the applicable perpetuities period (say, 150 years from now).[44]

§ 3.04   The Installment Land Sale Contract or Contract for Deed

The Installment Land Sale Contract (ILSC), or Contract for Deed, is discussed in depth as a device to finance the purchase of real property in Chapter 6. As previously mentioned,[45] ILSCs should not be confused with real estate purchase and sale contracts because ILSCs are financing devices used by the vendee to purchase an interest in real property. As such, the issues and questions raised by the use of ILSCs are very different from the issues and topics addressed in this chapter. Those issues and topics are addressed *infra* at Chapter 6. However, courts often do not clearly distinguish between real estate purchase and sale contracts and ILSCs and frequently apply rules designed to deal with one type of contract inappropriately to the other.

ILSCs are easily distinguishable from real estate purchase and sale contracts due to their length (usually in excess of ten years) and the fact that the vendee

---

[42] *See* Holiday Inns of America, Inc. v. Knight, 70 Cal 2. 327, 74 Cal. Rptr. 722, 450 P.2d 42 (1969).

[43] United Virginia Bank/Citizens & Marine v. Union Oil Co. of California, 214 Va. 48, 197 S.E.2d 174 (1973).

[44] *Id. Compare* Isen v. Giant Food, Inc., 295 F.2d 136 (D.C. Cir. 1961) (an agreement to lease land upon obtaining favorable zoning was upheld on the theory that the option agreement impliedly required that the rezoning must take place within "a reasonable time" which was less than twenty-one years).

[45] *See supra* § 3.04.

is entitled to possession of the real property while the ILSC is in effect. If both of these elements are present, the parties have more than likely created an ILSC and should be treated like mortgagor/mortgagee instead of vendee/vendor, as is the case pursuant to a real estate purchase and sale contract.

However, it is important to remember that having determined that ILSCs are distinguishable from other contracts does not mean that the issues raised regarding their use and operation are unique. For example, the risk of loss issue raised by the doctrine of equitable conversion applies equally to ILSCs and real estate purchase and sale contracts. What happens if the property is destroyed while an ILSC is in effect and the vendee is in possession? Here, it may make sense to apply the common law rule and place the loss on the vendee who also happens to be in possession. When one is dealing with an ILSC, the key determination to resolving any issue is to ask why the issue is raised. Should it make any difference that the parties are involved in a long-term financing arrangement represented by an ILSC? If the answer is yes, the law or answer generated by the use of real estate purchase and sale contracts should not mechanically be applied. If the answer is no and there is no distinction between the interests of the parties using an ILSC and those using a real estate purchase and sale contract, then the same rule should be applied to both. Thus, ignore the label of the transaction and look at the interests being affected before determining whether analogous rules should be applied.

CHAPTER

4

THE CLOSING

SYNOPSIS

§ 4.01 Introduction

The closing may be handled by an escrow agent,[1] by attorneys representing both parties, by one attorney representing both parties (although this may cause some ethical problems),[2] or by the parties themselves. Irrespective of who is involved, the objective of the closing remains the same: to accomplish a transfer of the vendor's interest in the real property as set forth in the real estate purchase and sale contract to the vendee, with the concomitant payment of money or performance of conditions by the vendee to the vendor.

§ 4.02 The Escrow Agreement

In most parts of the country, an escrow agreement is used to define the rights and responsibilities of the parties at closing. The escrow agreement will provide the necessary timing and other instructions necessary to effectuate the transfer of title and, hence, property, from the vendor to the vendee. Pursuant to the escrow agreement, the parties have to fulfill certain conditions prior to the date set for closing, such as the vendor's delivery of proof of title to the escrow agent, and the escrow agent must perform certain duties, i.e., verifying the status of the vendor's title, prior to, or on, the date set for closing. Ultimately, the vendee delivers funds to the escrow agent and the escrow agent is responsible for removing liens, etc., from the property and remitting the remaining funds to the vendor. As a result, escrow instructions, detailing what each of the parties—the vendor, the vendee, and the escrow agent—must be drafted and agreed to by the vendor and vendee contemporaneous with the execution of the purchase and sale contract if an escrow is used to transfer title. Hence, the escrow instructions can be viewed as supplemental to the real estate purchase and sale contract.[3]

[A] Escrow Agents

In most states, escrow agents are licensed and regulated. Hence, in many respects they are treated like real estate brokers.

[B] Disputed Funds

In disputes involving escrowed funds, the escrow agent must maintain a neutral position with respect to the dispute since the agent or holder is the agent of both the vendor and the vendee. Thus, if a dispute over the disposition of funds does arise, the agent must act neutrally and hold the funds until the dispute is resolved by the court or by the parties. However, if there is no dispute and conditions are verifiably met, the escrow agent cannot assert a subjective belief or view

---

[1] For a discussion of escrow agents and the escrow agreement, see *infra* § 4.02.

[2] *See In re* Lanza, 65 N.J. 347, 322 A. 2d 445 (1974).

[3] *See* Harris v. Skyline Corp., 342 Mass. 444. 173 N.E. 2d 644 (1961).

that certain conditions have not been met or performed unless the escrow agent is given that express authority to act subjectively. In other words, the escrow agent performs the duty properly by strictly following the instructions set forth in the escrow agreement.

For example, in *Harris v. Skyline Corp.*,[4] the issue was whether the escrow agent had fulfilled his duties per the terms of the escrow agreement. The issue arose because during the closing the vendor and vendee had established the escrow account to receive and pay funds for the cost of completing grading and landscaping for the property being sold. The agreement required the escrow agent to remit funds to the vendor upon the vendor's presentation of a Veteran's Administration certificate indicating that the work was completed. That certificate was presented by the vendor to the escrow agent some four months after the sale was completed. However, the vendees contended that the work remained incomplete. The escrow agent petitioned the court to take possession of the check and to require the parties to litigate the issue between themselves. The court held that the escrow agreement imposed a duty on the agent to examine the certificate presented to him by the vendor and to express any doubts regarding the validity of the certificate directly to the vendor. If, however, the certificate was authentic and complied with the instructions, the escrow agent had no discretion and must remit the funds to the vendor per the terms of agreement. *Harris* demonstrates that the escrow agent cannot attempt to vary the terms of the performance of the parties after the instructions have been drafted and finalized.

§ 4.03 Formalities of Transfer

On the date set for closing in the purchase and sale contract, the vendor and the vendee, or their duly appointed representatives, meet to conclude the prescribed aspects of the sale of the real property. In particular, the following items are taken care of according to either the relevant terms of the purchase and sale contract or any applicable escrow agreement in effect to govern the closing.

For example, assume that there is no escrow agreement governing the details of closing, the real estate purchase and sale contract requires vendor to deliver marketable title to vendee by warranty deed on the date of closing. In order to satisfy this contractual obligation, on the date of closing, the vendor has to both prepare a warranty deed naming the vendee as grantee and prove to the satisfaction of a "reasonable" vendee that he has marketable title. On the other hand, if the parties are using an escrow agreement in addition to the purchase and sale contract to manage the closing, the escrow agreement should require the vendor to deposit (with the escrowholder if one is used) both an executed warranty deed with vendee as grantee and proof of marketable title with the escrowholder within 24 hours of the date set for closing. The vendee would then

---

[4] *Id.*

(Matthew Bender & Co., Inc.)   (Pub.3127)

be required to object to the condition of title within 24 hours of his receipt of the vendor's proof of marketable title or be deemed to have accepted the title.

[A] Title

Immediately prior to closing or as close thereto as possible, the vendor must prove, as required by the purchase and sale contract, both her ownership interest in the property and the fact that no intervening detrimental interests have been created during the executory interval following execution of the purchase and sale contract.

[B] Delivery of Deed

The deed delivering title to the property in the quality[5] required by the purchase and sale contract must be prepared and executed by the vendor to transfer his interest in the real property to the vendee.

[C] Financing

All of the paperwork for any financing needed to purchase the real property must be completed and accompanied by the deposit or delivery of any cash required to be paid by the vendee on the date of closing. The purchase price may then be conveyed to the vendor upon the vendor's delivery of the deed to the vendee.

[D] Title Insurance

In order to protect the vendee's interest in the purchased real property, title insurance or other methods of title assurance must be ready to take effect upon execution and delivery of the deed to the vendee.

[E] Accounting and Prorations

Prorations must be made on the date of closing for such items as property taxes, homeowners' association dues and fees, and homeowner's insurance.

[F] Recording

In order to protect the vendee's interest in the real property from third parties, arrangements must be made to have the deed to the vendee recorded as soon as practicable following execution and delivery.[6]

§ 4.04 Delivery of the Deed

The delivery of the deed from vendor to vendee signals a completed sale and, thus, the end of the vendor's interest in the real property and the beginning of the vendee's interest. More importantly, it signals the end of the parties' contractual relationship pursuant to the real estate purchase and sale agreement,

---

[5] *See infra* § 4.04.

[6] For a discussion of what can happen when the vendee fails to timely record her interest, see *infra* Chapter 10.

and in most cases, mandates resort to the deed to determine what, if any, promises or warranties were made to the vendee by the vendor. Consequently, the deed is very important not only because it transfers the vendor's interest in the property to the vendee, but also because it contains the vendor's warranty and continuing promise regarding the quality of title that the vendor has delivered to the vendee. Typically the warranties or promises made in the deed, or lack thereof, supersede any promises or warranties made in the purchase and sale contract pursuant to the doctrine of merger.

[A]   The Doctrine of Merger

As a result of the doctrine of merger, the purchase and sale contract and any warranties or promises made therein regarding the quality of title to be conveyed by the vendor to the vendee is superseded once the deed to the real property is delivered. Thus, any inconsistent or contradictory terms in the purchase and sale contract are rendered null and void even if the deed conflicts with the language in the contract of purchase. As a result, the deed is the sole repository of any warranties of title that survive the execution and delivery of the deed. In effect, the merger doctrine provides the vendee with post-closing rights based only on the promises contained in the deed. Any pre-closing rights based on promises or the warranties set forth in the purchase and sale contract are merged into the deed and, therefore, negated.

For example, let's assume that the vendor promises to deliver marketable title via a general or full warranty deed on the date of closing. On the date of closing, the vendor tenders a quitclaim deed which is accepted by the vendee. The vendee is subsequently evicted from the property by the true owner. Pursuant to the doctrine of merger, the vendor's promise to deliver marketable title via a general warranty deed was merged into and became nullified by the vendee's acceptance of the quitclaim deed. Hence, the vendee must look to the deed to determine which, if any, warranties may provide a cause of action against the vendor in this situation. Since a quitclaim deed was used, the vendee would have no recourse against the vendor in the absence of fraud.[7]

[1]   Limitations on the Merger Doctrine

The doctrine of merger is a rule of construction as opposed to a rule of law, and therefore gives the courts some leeway with respect to its application. As a result, when the rights of third parties are not affected, the courts may not strictly construe the doctrine of merger and may accept parol evidence concerning whether or not the doctrine was "intended" to be applied by the parties.

[B]   Contract Liabilities that Survive the Delivery of the Deed

As a rule of construction, the merger doctrine can be expressly negated by the parties' insertion of the appropriate language in the purchase and sale contract.

---

[7] For a discussion of quitclaim deeds, see *infra* § 4.04[C][3] .

The parties must explicitly express their intention that the warranties and other obligations in the purchase and sale contract survive the expiration of the contract and the delivery of the deed.

The merger doctrine makes sense when the rights of third parties are considered. Any subsequent purchaser from the initial vendee will look to the record state of title to determine what promises any remote vendor-grantor made regarding the state of the title being conveyed. In other words, since the deed is normally recorded and the contract of sale is not, the only evidence available to remote vendee-grantee is that which appears in the deed. The remote vendee-grantee, who was not privy or party to the original purchase and sale contract, cannot be heard to complain that she relied on promises made in that contract because she had no knowledge of the promises made in that contract. Thus, as to third parties not privy to the contract, the merger doctrine is both efficient and practical, limiting the inquiry to matters of record. However, as between the contracting parties, the doctrine may work a hardship on unsophisticated vendees and can be criticized on the basis that a vendor should not be allowed to evade his express promises in the contract merely because a remote grantee will not rely on them.

[C] Types of Deeds

By statute or custom, certain standard deeds have evolved as vehicles to convey title from the vendor to the vendee. The type of deed used in conveying title, unless it is a customized deed drafted specifically for a unique transaction, designates the warranties made by the vendor with respect to the quality or state of title being conveyed to the vendee. Although the effect of the covenants contained in the standard deeds are described in detail in § 9.02, a brief outline of the three standard deeds is provided below.

[1] Full or General Warranty Deed

This deed contains six covenants of title: (1) covenant of seisin; (2) covenant of right to convey; (3) covenant against encumbrances (this first triad of covenants are referred to as the *present covenants*); (4) covenant of quite enjoyment; (5) covenant of general assurances; and (6) covenant of warranty (this second triad of covenants are referred to as the *future covenants*) and is referred to as a deed containing full or English covenants of title. The full or general warranty deed provides the maximum protection to the vendee when a standardized deed is used. In some states, the use of one or a few symbolic words (for example, "this is a General Warranty Deed") in the deed will, by statute, automatically cause the deed to be characterized as a full or general warranty deed.

For example, the vendor transfers property to the vendee using a deed which is captioned "General Warranty Deed" or which, in the habendum clause (the to have and to hold clause of the deed), states that the vendor "warrants" or "warrants generally" the state of title. As a result of the use of these magic words and nothing more, in certain states the vendor has used a full or general warranty deed that contains the six covenants discussed above.

[2]   Special or Limited Warranty Deed

The use of a Special or Limited Warranty Deed means that the vendor has conveyed something less than a full or general warranty deed and something more than a quitclaim deed. However, each state and each case must be looked to individually in order to determine exactly what is meant by the term. Nonetheless, two major variations appear to be applicable to the use of the term.

[a]   California

In California, a special or limited warranty deed contains the six covenants discussed above. However, it differs from a general warranty deed because the vendor's warranties and representations made with respect to the covenants relate only to *her* actions that affect title and not to any predecessor(s) in interest. Thus, the vendor-grantor is only warranting that *she personally* has done nothing to detrimentally affect the title to the real property.

[b]   Other States

In other states, a special or limited warranty deed may also include or refer to a deed that contains less than the six covenants described above. For example, if the vendor-grantor transfers title to the vendee-grantee via a deed containing the first triad of covenants (the present covenants), the vendor is using a special or limited warranty deed.

[3]   Quitclaim Deed

A Quitclaim Deed is a deed that contains no covenants of title, delivering the quality of title (if any) that the vendor owns at the date of the transfer to the vendee. For example, let's assume that the vendor delivers to the vendee a quitclaim deed to Blackacre even though he is an adverse possessor who has not possessed the property for the required period of time in order to have his possession ripen into ownership. If the vendee is evicted by the true owner before the statutory period to bring an eviction claim has expired, the vendee has no cause of action against the vendor. On the other hand, the vendee may tack his period of possession to that of his vendor in order to prove that the true owner's action is barred by the statute of limitations.

[4]   Customized Deeds

Although warranty, limited, and quitclaim deeds make up the vast majority of deeds used to convey property, customized deeds may be used by the parties to reflect the state of title to be conveyed by the vendor. In this respect, the parties are only limited by their needs and imaginations is drafting a deed that is best suited for their transaction.

§ 4.05 Federal Legislative Intervention

Calls for national uniformity in the real estate market areas of closing costs, financing, title assurance, etc., have lead to increasing pressure on the federal government to intervene and preempt local or state real estate laws. The first area in which this increasing federal legislative intervention manifests itself is the closing.

[A] The Real Estate Settlement and Procedures Act (RESPA)

The Real Estate Settlement and Procedures Act (RESPA),[8] enacted in 1974, reflects Congressional concern that residential real estate consumers are not provided with sufficient information regarding settlement costs. Pursuant to RESPA, vendees must be given an itemized estimate of projected closing costs prior to closing and a Housing and Urban Development (HUD) booklet explaining the closing and various closing costs. Additionally, RESPA makes certain practices illegal (for example, giving real estate brokers kickbacks for generating loans).

---

[8] 12 U.S.C.A. §§ 2601 et seq.

5

BREACH OF THE PURCHASE AND SALE CONTRACT

SYNOPSIS

---

§ 5.01   Introduction

When executed, the real estate purchase and sale contract creates certain contractual rights and responsibilities by and between the parties. Consequently, the parties have the right to demand timely performance of the contract pursuant to its terms and conditions. One party's failure to perform may constitute a breach of the contract, giving rise to a panoply of remedies. The key question and the primary focus raised by breach of contract is how, if at all, the remedies provided are affected because the contract is for the sale of real property, as opposed to personal property. A related question is how the parties may use the various remedies provided to exploit a strategic advantage in the hopes of obtaining a favorable resolution of the dispute.

§ 5.02   What Constitutes Breach

As with most complicated bilateral contracts, there are many ways in which the purchase and sale contract may be breached, ranging from a party's clear outright refusal to perform to a party's good faith tender which is rejected by the receiving party as non-conforming. The latter rejection leads to a lawsuit over which party was responsible for the breach. Although the details of each fact situation are different, the cases fall into two distinct categories depending on the timing of the breach.

[A]   Anticipatory Breach

During the executory period between execution of the purchase and sale contract and the date set for closing, either party may undertake some action or inaction that has the effect of materially breaching the purchase and sale contract, indicating to the other party their intention not to perform pursuant to the contract.[1]

[B] Breach at Closing

Perhaps more typically is a party's failure to perform pursuant to the terms and conditions of the purchase and sale contract on the date set for closing, giving rise to the other party's claim for breach of contract.[2]

[1] Merger

Complete performance of the conditions set forth in the purchase and sale contract on the date set for closing is normally required by the parties because of the effect that the doctrine of merger has on the parties' post-closing rights and remedies.[3]

§ 5.03 Remedies for Breach

There is no over-arching theory of damages that leads to an easy resolution of the issues that arise when there has been a breach of a real estate purchase and sale contract. Rather, the type of remedy chosen by the injured party will play an inordinately large role in determining the remedy ultimately provided by the court. Hence, the injured party, because of her power to select the remedy, may gain an unfair advantage by choosing a remedy that will convey a benefit exceeding the harm caused by the breach. Simply put, the injured party may be able to manipulate the remedial system to extract excessive, or even punitive, damages from the breaching party.

What follows is the common law treatment of remedies when either the vendee or the vendor breaches the real estate purchase and sale contract. However, these remedies have mostly been supplanted by language in the purchase and sale contract that delineates the remedies available in the case of breach. Thus, the first inquiry in these types of cases is whether the available remedies are expressly defined and limited by the contracting parties in the purchase and sale agreement.

The issue of whether or not a breach of the purchase and sale contract has occurred is a question of fact governed largely by the law of contracts, and therefore is beyond the scope of this text. However, the remedies that are available to a party injured by the breach of a purchase and sale contract are uniquely shaped by the fact that real property, as opposed to personal property, is the

---

[1] *See* Freedman v. Rector, Wardens & Vestrymen of St. Mathias Parish, 37 Cal. 2d 16, 230 P.2d 629 (1951) (vendees wrote letters prior to closing indicating that they would not perform because of groundless objections to the vendor's state of title, thereby causing a repudiation of the contract).

[2] *See* Tristram's Landing, Inc. v. Wait, 367 Mass. 622, 327 N.E.2d 727 (1975) (on the date set for closing, the vendee did not appear and refused to pay the remainder of the purchase price as required by the contract).

[3] For a discussion of the doctrine of merger, see *supra* § 4.04[A].

subject of the contract in this case. The so-called uniqueness of land, its lack of fungibility, its immobility, and its permanence, have caused a confusing and sometimes contradictory body of law to be applied when the courts are confronted with the breach of a real estate purchase and sale contract. From the perspective of contract law, if the goal of the remedy is to make the injured party whole, many of the remedies discussed below will appear either overinclusive or underinclusive Unfortunately, the current state of the law is such that these apparent anomalies and inconsistencies cannot be avoided.

§ 5.04 Vendee's Remedies—An Overview

Although cases in which the vendor breaches a purchase and sale contract are relatively rare, the typical situation involves the vendor's failure to perform a condition required by the contract. In the situations detailed below, the vendee may pursue her remedy of a vendee's lien in order to obtain the return of her deposit. However, a vendee's lien may be unsatisfactory if the vendor does not own a sufficient interest in the land to which the lien can attach. Similarly, when the vendor's failure to perform is traceable to a defect in title, the vendee's remedy of specific performance is worthless, since the last thing the vendee wants is to be forced to accept the vendor's defective title. Hence, in most cases, damages and rescission will be the vendee's preferred remedies. However, in the rare case in which the real property has significantly increased in value and the vendor breaches the purchase and sale contract by refusing to perform due to the fact that she has a competing and a better offer for the said property, specific performance may represent the vendee's optimal remedy.

[A] Specific Performance

When atypical circumstances prevent the remedies that are available in the courts of law from making the injured party whole, an equitable remedy may be pursued in the court of equity. Hence, specific performance will be allowed only when the injured party's remedies are inadequate at law. The definition of "inadequate at law" is the subject of many complex theories of remedies and the current topic of many law review articles. It is sufficient to note that most courts allow specific performance if the subject matter of the contract is *unique*.[4] Since land is unique, it is alleged that money damages are inadequate to compensate the injured party for her loss when a purchase and sale contract is breached. As a result, the remedy of specific performance is made available in such situations.

As an example, let's assume that Vendee and Vendor enter into a contract pursuant to which Vendee agrees to buy Blackacre for $100,000, simultaneously placing a $10,000 down payment on Blackacre. On the date set for closing,

---

[4] For a discussion of the remedy of specific performance, see Ulen, *The Efficiency for Specific Performance: Toward a Unified Theory of Contract Remedies*, 83 Mich. L.Rev. 341 (1984).

Vendee tenders the balance of the purchase price, $90,000, but Vendor refuses to deliver the title to Blackacre. Vendor states that she has received on offer of $125,000 from a second vendee, Vendee #2, which must be matched by Vendee #1 before she will deliver a deed to Blackacre. Since Blackacre is the only piece of realty in the world occupying the space where it is located, it is unique, and therefore Vendee #1 may seek specific performance of the purchase and sale contract.

[1]   *Lis Pendens*

When a vendee files a lawsuit seeking specific performance against a defaulting vendor, the case may not be resolved until months or even years after the date originally set for closing. In order to insure that the subject property is procurable by the vendee once it is adjudicated that she is entitled to specific performance of the purchase and sale contract, the vendee will file a *lis pendens* in the County Recorder's Office of the county in which the property is located. The vendee will file the *lis pendens* at the same time or shortly after she files her lawsuit seeking specific performance. The *lis pendens*, which is a notice stating that there is a lawsuit or dispute over the ownership of the property defined in the notice, is filed against the vendor's name or tract (depending upon whether a grantor-grantee or tract index is used) so that notice of the *lis pendens* is in the vendor's chain of title.[5] Thus, the *lis pendens* gives notice to any subsequent purchaser for value that the property is subject to an existing claim or lawsuit, and that any purchaser or transferee from the defaulting vendor takes subject to the resolution of that claim. As a result, once the *lis pendens* is filed, the marketability of the subject property is seriously impeded, and the property is usually not transferred until the dispute is resolved. Moreover, in the rare case that the property is transferred prior to the settlement of the claim, the purchaser must discount the value of the property by the probability that the vendee's lawsuit will ultimately be successful.

The vendee gains a tremendous strategic advantage over the vendor in any settlement negotiations by pursuing her remedy of specific performance in combination with filing a *lis pendens*. The *lis pendens* has the effect of tying up the property through the duration of the litigation and essentially forces the vendor to maintain the property at his cost during the lawsuit. Furthermore, the vendee may be able to obtain a favorable settlement in a situation in which the vendor independently values the transferability of the property that is the subject of the suit. If the vendor is selling Blackacre and using her equity in the premises to purchase other property, the vendor's plans may be impacted detrimentally by her failure to sell Blackacre.

For example, in *Askari v. R & R Land Co.*,[6] the issue was whether a vendor is entitled to recover consequential damages for a vendee's breach of a purchase

---

[5] For a discussion of chain of title and the recording acts, see *infra* Chapter 10.

[6] 179 Cal. App. 3d 1101, 225 Cal. Rptr. 285 (1986).

and sale contract. In *Askari*, the vendor and vendee entered into a purchase and sale agreement for the sale of property for the price of $1,250,000. However, the vendor and vendee could not agree on the meaning of the agreement's financing clause, and the escrow failed for lack of common instructions. The parties then sued one another for breach of contract, and the vendee filed a notice of *lis pendens* simultaneously with filing suit. The vendor then claimed consequential damages based on his inability to resell the property due to the presence of the *lis pendens* on the title.

The court in *Askari* held that a vendor is entitled to recover consequential damages only if she diligently attempts to resell the property after the vendee has breached the contract. If the vendor is found to have diligently attempted to resell the property, but was unable to do so because of the filing of the *lis pendens*, the vendor can recover operating expenses, lost interest, and diminished property value (measured by the difference in value between the contract price and the value of the property on the date the *lis pendens* is removed, freeing the property for resale), offset by any amount of the real property's appreciation over the contract price.

By filing a *lis pendens*, the vendee essentially blocks the vendor's efforts to sell the subject property and therefore is responsible for the vendor's loss in value during the period the *lis pendens* is in place should the filing of the *lis pendens* be subsequently adjudicated as wrongful.

[a] Slander of Title

One should note that state law must be consulted to determine whether the vendee has the right to place a *lis pendens* (called a "slap" in the vernacular of the trade) on the property. Due to the severe impact of a *lis pendens* on the alienability of the property, thus negatively affecting the property's value, the penalties for wrongful use of a *lis pendens* in order to extract negotiating leverage are substantial. Technically speaking, slander of title occurs when title to real property is disparaged wrongfully causing damage. Slander of title actions in some states result in the offending party paying punitive damages for the wrongful filing of a *lis pendens*.

[2] Practical Operation of Specific Performance

Continuing our example from above, if the vendee seeks to compel specific performance of the purchase and sale contract, she must allege: 1) that she is ready and able to perform pursuant to the contract (that she herself is not in breach of the contract); 2) that the subject of the contract is unique (which is easily done with real property); 3) that any remedy at law is inadequate; and 4) that in equity, the court should compel the vendor to do that which she is bound to do pursuant to the contract—namely to transfer title to Blackacre to the vendee upon receipt of the purchase price of $90,000.

[a] Abatement

When there is a defect in the quality of the title to be conveyed pursuant to the purchase and sale contract that is *not* excepted in the contract, the vendee occasionally may seek the remedy of specific performance with an abatement in the purchase price to reflect the diminished value of the premises caused by the defect. Exercising its equitable power, the court may order specific performance of the purchase and sale contract with an abatement in the purchase price as long as the defect is nominal and the amount of the abatement is small relative to the purchase price stated in the contract.[7] Courts are loathe to substantially revise the purchase and sale contract, including changing the price significantly. By so doing, the court would be ordering a new contract, rather than enforcing a previously existing agreement between the parties.

[b] Uniqueness and Condominiums

As will be discussed in Part 2, the recent growth in the use of condominiums has caused the courts and commentators to call into question some previously established legal doctrines, including the applicability of the equitable remedy of specific performance to situations involving the sale of condominiums and other less unique types of real property. For instance, in *Centex Homes Corp. v. Boag*,[8] the New Jersey court refused to allow specific performance when the object of the suit was one of 3,600 condominium apartments. The court in *Centex* viewed the subject condominium as non-unique and fungible, thus its loss was adequately compensated by money damages.

[B] Vendee's Lien

The vendee's lien is a statutory lien on the subject property given to the vendee so that she can recover her deposit or downpayment made on the vendor's property. It arises by operation of law in most states when the vendor refuses to perform according to the contract or refuses to return sums received pursuant to the contract. Though available, the vendee's lien is rarely used for two reasons. First, the remedy it provides—the return of the vendee's deposit—is not the vendee's preferred remedy in most situations since it has the same effect as rescission. Second, and more importantly, it is a remedy that is easily avoided by the vendor if she alienates the property to a subsequent purchaser for value. At best, the vendee's lien aids the vendee if she seeks to exercise her right to rescind the purchase and sale contract and to obtain a return of her deposit.

Continuing our hypothetical, assuming that Vendee does not want to obtain specific performance of the contract when Vendor breaches, it is a virtual

---

[7] *See* Merritz v. Circelli, 361 Pa. 239, 64 A.2d 796 (1949) (court refused to order specific performance with an abatement when, among other reasons, it would have reduced the purchase price from $12,500 to $3,200).

[8] 128 N.J. Super 385, 320 A.2d 194 (Ch. Div. 1974).

certainty that Vendee will want her deposit or down payment of $10,000 returned. If Vendor refuses to return the deposit, Vendee may seek to enforce a vendee's lien against the property for the return of the deposit, as discussed below.

[1]   Practical Operation of the Vendee's Lien

The vendee exercises her lien in the property by foreclosing it (for example, by having Blackacre sold to the highest bidder either judicially or at a private sale). The funds generated by the foreclosure sale are then applied to refund the money owed to the vendee. Upon reimbursing the vendee for the amount of her deposit, the lien is satisfied and canceled. Any funds generated in excess of the vendee's lien will be remitted to junior lien holders or returned to the vendor.[9]

Since most purchase and sale contracts are not recorded, the vendee's lien which arises by operation of law is not recorded. As a result, a subsequent purchaser from the vendor will take without notice of the vendee's interest in the real property either pursuant to the vendee's purchase and sale contract or the vendee's lien. Consequently, the subsequent purchaser from the vendor will take free of the vendee's lien and the vendee will have to pursue the vendor *personally*, as opposed to proceeding against the land. Hence, as a practical matter, the vendor can easily avoid the vendee's lien by later alienating the property to a subsequent purchaser for value.

[C]   Rescission

In a clear cut case, following non-performance of the purchase and sale contract, the parties to the breached contract may enter into a separate agreement to rescind the original agreement by each party agreeing to return to the other anything received of value. This exchange would return the parties to the status quo which existed prior to the execution of the purchase and sale contract, and may be done either in writing or orally. The Statute of Frauds is said not to apply because though it prevents the parties from going forward and making a new contract orally, it does not prevent them from going back (for example, returning to the status quo ex ante). This "agreement to rescind" is often referred to as mutual rescission and is sometimes argued to be the only valid form of rescission.[10]

[1]   Election to Rescind

It is occasionally alleged that a party's actions following breach provide evidence of that party's intention to rescind the contract. This "election" to rescind, as indicated by the party's actions, can be used by the breaching party to bar any further, or any inconsistent, action by the injured party (for example, a separate suit for damages). Although this claim is infrequently successful, it

---

[9] For a discussion of foreclosure, junior lien holders, and priority problems generated by multiple liens, see *infra* Chapter 8.

[10] *See* Corbin, 5 Contracts § 1236 (1963).

demonstrates the quagmire that the injured party finds herself in once the contract is breached.

To avoid any claim by the breaching party that the injured party has "elected" to rescind by her actions, the injured party should explicitly preface her subsequent actions by notifying the breaching party that such actions do not represent her election to rescind, and that she continues to hold the breaching party liable for any and all damages or other remedial benefits available as a result of the breach of contract.

[D] Damages

Though an award of damages may be a very common remedy available to the vendee when the vendor breaches, it unfortunately is not the least complicated of the potential remedies. Rather, in order to determine the measure of her damages, the vendee must first determine whether the English or the American rule applies in the jurisdiction in which the property is located.

[1] English Rule

The English rule is based on the view that uncertainties in the quality or status of title are caused by complex rules that the vendor cannot be held accountable for or does not understand. Thus, if the vendor's inability to perform the contract is caused by a title defect beyond her control, the English rule limits the vendee's damages to a return of her deposit with interest, and recovery of her expenses incurred as a result of the failed purchase. In other words, if the vendor's inability to deliver good title is not her doing, the vendee is limited to the rescission measure of damage and may not obtain the benefit of her bargain.

There are legions of cases concerning whether the vendor's defect in title is of the type caused by the vendor for which she should be held accountable and which would thus allow the vendee to bypass the English rule in order to obtain the benefit of her bargain. It is clear that if the vendor willfully refuses to convey or is guilty of fraud or deceit, she has breached the purchase and sale contract and the vendee is entitled to the benefit of her bargain. However, tough cases arise when a defect is known to the vendor at the time of contracting, which she believes she can cure prior to closing but actually cannot.[11] A review of the cases reveals that courts following the English rule have no principled basis for deciding these difficult cases. As assessing fault is typically a question of fact, the resolution of such cases is usually left to the trier of fact. Thus, the cases are all over the map in terms of defining criteria relevant to making this determination. Some factors frequently discussed include whether the defect was latent or patent, whether the defaulting vendor acted in good or bad faith (which

---

[11] *See* Raisor v. Jackson, 311 Ky, 803, 225 S.W.2d 657 (Ct. App. 1950) (vendor unable to perform because spouse who owned a one half interest in the property refused to convey her interest in the property).

is a circular argument in the extremis), whether the defaulting vendor knew or should have known that she could not cure the defect. However, these and all other tests really boil down to whether the court believes the vendor is a "good" or a "bad guy", and damages are granted accordingly.

The leading case on this matter, *Raisor v. Jackson*,[12] demonstrates the exception to the English rule which may potentially become the majority rule. In *Raisor*, the issue was whether a vendor is liable for breach of contract when a known title defect prevents her performance at the time of contracting.[13] The vendee purchased property at a public auction for $22,252 and paid a $4,500 deposit. When the vendee contacted the vendor a few days later, the vendor refused to convey the property since his wife, who owned a one-half interest in the property, would not join in the deed. Shortly thereafter, the vendor and his wife sold the property to another party. The court held that a vendee is entitled to substantial damages without regard to a vendor's good faith where that vendor agrees to convey real property knowing he has no title or having knowledge "of an outstanding interest therein owned by a third party." By looking to the vendor's subjective knowledge or lack thereof with respect to the state of the title, vendees may be able to prove that a vendor acted in bad faith.

[2] American Rule

Many courts, perhaps a slim majority, have rejected the English rule in favor of the American rule, which allows the injured vendee to obtain the benefit of her bargain regardless of whether the defect is caused by the vendor or not.[14] That benefit will be measured as the difference between the contract price and the fair market value of the premises at the time of breach.[15]

The American rule is preferable to the English rule for numerous reasons. First and foremost, the vendor's uncertainty of the quality of title, the rationale behind the English rule, has been largely vitiated by "advances" in assuring title, which are discussed *infra* in Chapter 10. In other words, it is no longer true that it is difficult for the granting vendor to ascertain the true state of her title prior to the transaction. In fact, today it is quite easy to determine the state of one's title by obtaining a title report from an attorney or title insurer. Hence, a breaching vendor cannot state that she failed to detect the defect in her title that caused the breach of contract in good faith.

Furthermore, the American rule, a clear "black-letter rule," is easier to administer and thus, more efficient than the English rule. The vendor is in the

---

[12] 225 S.W.2d 657 (1950).

[13] *Id.*

[14] *See* Donovan v. Bachstadt, 91 N.J. 434, 453 A.2d 160 (1982) (court rejected the complicated and confusing English rule in favor of the American rule awarding the injured party the benefit of his bargain).

[15] For a further discussion of the vendee's benefit of her bargain, see *infra* § 5.04[D][3].

best position to determine the state of the title being conveyed and to assure that it is as warranted in the purchase and sale contract. As a result, vendor is the cheapest cost-avoider, and she should bear the burden to ensure that the state of the title to be conveyed is as represented in the contract.

In *Donovan v. Bachstadt*,[16] the issue was the amount of damages a vendee is entitled to receive upon a vendor's breach of a contract for the sale of real property.[17] In *Donovan,* the vendor and vendees entered into an agreement for the sale of property pursuant to which $14,900 of the purchase price was to be paid in cash and the remaining balance was to be paid by a purchase money mortgage from the vendor with a $10\frac{1}{2}\%$ interest rate. The vendor breached the contract when he was unable to deliver marketable title. Thereafter, the vendees purchased another house, obtained a mortgage loan bearing a rate of $13\frac{1}{8}\%$ per annum from a commercial lender, and sued the vendor for the difference between a $10\frac{1}{2}\%$ and a $13\frac{1}{8}\%$ mortgage rate as compensatory damages. The court adopted the American rule which entitles the vendees to the benefit of their bargain. However, the court held that the vendees could not recover the difference in mortgage rates because the vendor had provided the low mortgage rate as an inducement to purchase this particular piece of property. Therefore, the $10\frac{1}{2}\%$ rate was not a lost market opportunity for the vendees. Thus, at the time the vendees contracted with the vendor, the market rate was $13\frac{1}{8}\%$ and not $10\frac{1}{2}\%$.

[3]   Measuring Damages

As noted above, the English rule only allows for the return of the vendee's deposit and the reasonable and unavoidable expenses incurred by the vendee in her attempts to perform the contract. In contrast, the American rule allows the injured vendee to recover the benefit of her bargain. Although the "benefit of the bargain" is a simple principle to apply in contracts dealing with fungible goods, difficulties appear when it is applied to contracts for the purchase of real property.

The benefit derived from a bargain may consist of certain gains such as return of deposits, interest, costs, expenses incurred in connection with the sale, and generally, the difference between the market price at the time of breach and the contract price. Whether or not it includes other elements, depends upon whether those aspects are unique to the transaction or represent a market opportunity lost by the vendee. For instance, in *Donovan,*[18] if the vendee's loan commitment had come from an outside mortgagee and could not be recaptured in the later transaction, the vendee perhaps may recover the difference in mortgage interest rates.

---

[16] 91 N.J. 434, 453 A.2d 160 (1982).

[17] *Id.*

[18] *Id.*

[a] Fair Market Value

If the vendor breaches and the vendee is entitled to the benefit of her bargain, that benefit will be measured as the difference between the contract price and the fair market value of the premises at the time of breach. Thus, in our continuing hypothetical, if Blackacre was worth $100,000 or less, the vendee has no claim for damages since, if you recall, the contract price was $100,000. However, if the fair market value of the premises is in excess of the sales price, vendee is entitled to damages as a result of the breach which should equal the difference between $100,000 and the fair market value of the premises. If the fair market value of the property is $125,000, our vendee would thus be entitled to damages of $25,000.

There are two problems with this approach when it is applied to real property. First, since the property is unique, ascertaining its objective fair market value is fraught with difficulty. *Fair* market value is a very subjective term when applied to real estate.[19] Second, assuming fair market value can be accurately and objectively determined, the damages are measured from the date of the breach, theoretically ignoring fluctuations in value that occur after that date, but before trial or judgment. Hence, the vendee may recover damages if she can prove that the property's value on the date of the breach exceeded the contract price, notwithstanding the fact that the value later plunged after the contract was breached.

In passing, note that valuation problems are further complicated by the calculation of the timing of the breach. If anticipatory breach is proven, is the value of the property ascertained on that date or the date set for closing? What if there is a reasonable question on the vendee's part about whether the vendor will be able to perform? Should the vendee wait until the date of closing or declare the contract breached at the first hint that vendor may not be able to perform?

In measuring damages, it is very easy to conclude that the burden should be placed on the breaching party to prove that the fair market value of the property on the date of the breach is not as alleged by the injured party. However, in an area as subjective as the valuation of real property, frequently, the only objective verifiable evidence before the court concerning the value of the property is the price in the purchase and sale contract, which presumably was set by the market and reached by arms-length bargaining between the parties. Thus, courts will frequently ignore expert testimony and find that the only damages arising from the breach are incidental damages because the value of the property equals the contract price.

---

[19] *See* Askari v. R. & R Land Co., 179 Cal. App.3d 1101, 225 Cal Rptr. 285 (1986) (upon a claim for breach of contract by vendor against vendee, the appraisers for the two parties were $400,000 apart in their valuation of property that had a contract price of $1,200,000).

[b]   Incidental Damages

Apart from the out of pocket expenses that the vendee is entitled to as a result of the vendor's breach, complicated questions are raised concerning the extent of incidental damages that the vendee is entitled to due to the nature of the typical real estate transaction. For example, in *Donovan*,[20] the vendee claimed that he was entitled to the difference between a 10½% and a 13⅛% interest rate on a mortgage as compensatory or incidental damages since interest rates on mortgages had risen following the vendor's breach of the purchase and sale contract. The court refused the vendee's request, holding that the vendor was not in the business of lending or guaranteeing the rates on loans to purchase realty.

§ 5.05   Vendor's Remedies—An Overview

The vendor's remedies parallel the remedies available to the vendee. Thus, the full panoply of remedies available to the vendor includes specific performance, rescission, vendor's lien, and damages. However, all of the vendor's remedies are affected by the fact that the vendor normally has in her possession a substantial deposit (sometimes referred to in the contract as "earnest money") that may be as much as 10% of the contract price. Thus, in the case of the vendee's breach, the vendor may be content to retain the deposit and resell the premises to a subsequent vendee. If the property is sold to a subsequent vendee for a price in excess of that agreed to in the original breached contract, however, whether the vendor will be able to retain the deposit depends on the contract and the remedial strategy undertaken by the vendor following the vendee's breach.

As an example, suppose that Vendor and Vendee enter into a real estate purchase and sale contract pursuant to which Vendee agrees to pay $100,000 for Blackacre. Upon tendering the accepted offer to purchase Blackacre, Vendee deposits $10,000 with Vendor's broker, characterized in the purchase and sale contract as earnest money. On the date set for closing, Vendee refuses to perform, breaching the contract.

[A]   Specific Performance

Specific performance is one of the few remedies unaffected by the use of deposits. However, a theoretical problem arises when specific performance is requested by the vendor. When the vendee is seeking specific performance, it is granted, if at all, on the basis that the real property at issue is unique. On the contrary, when the vendor petitions for specific performance, the vendor is merely attempting to enforce the contract by obtaining the balance of the money owed to her pursuant to the contract, $90,000 in our example. The most frequently cited theory to explain this anomalous situation references the doctrine of mutuality. Essentially the doctrine of mutuality posits that since the remedial right

---

[20] 91 N.J. 434, 453 A.2d 160 (1982).

of specific performance is recognized in the vendee, the vendor has a corresponding right to obtain specific performance. In equity, specific performance cannot be obtained by either party unless there is mutuality of remedy.

Today, the better view is that "mutuality of remedy is satisfied if the decree of specific performance operates effectively against both parties and gives to each the benefit of the mutual obligation or performance. It is not necessary to serve the ends of equal justice that the parties shall have identical remedies."[21] Nevertheless, specific performance is routinely granted in favor of the vendor simply because it is available to the vendee. This result makes little sense given the stated rationale for specific performance as a viable remedy in unique situations where damages are inadequate.

In *Centex Homes Corp. v. Boag,*[22] the issue was whether the remedy of specific performance is available to a vendor of a condominium when the vendee breaches the purchase and sale contract.[23] In *Centex*, Vendor and Vendee entered into a purchase and sale contract for a condominium. A few weeks later, the vendee advised the vendor that he would be unable to perform the contract. The vendor then sued for specific performance of the contract. The court held that condominiums are akin to personal property because they have no unique qualities and therefore, the remedies available at law are adequate, and hence, specific performance is unavailable. In addition, the court held that the mutuality requirement was not an appropriate basis for automatically granting vendors of real estate the concomitant right to specific performance.

In *Centex*, the court based its categorization of condominiums as personal property on the identical physical properties of the units, the generic manner in which condominiums are sold, and the uniformity in the pricing of the units. The court effectively analogized these attributes to the general attributes of personal property and the market in which personal property is sold. The court in this case found that the extraordinary remedy of specific performance was not supported by the qualities of the property at issue.

In the case of vendee breach, innocent vendors rarely petition for specific performance, and should never seek this remedy in a rising real estate market. In order to obtain specific performance, the vendor must hold himself ready to perform and be able to perform when so ordered by the court. This is an uncertain process which could literally take years. During this time, the vendor must effectively remove the property from the market and hold it until the disposition of the claim for specific performance is completed. Rather, due to potential fluctuation in the market and the potentially long period during which the property must be held and maintained by the vendor, it is typically in the vendor's best

---

[21] Restatement of Contracts § 372 (1).

[22] 128 N.J. Super. 385, 320 A.2d 194 (1974).

[23] *Id.*

interest to resell the property to a subsequent purchaser for value, and pursuing other remedies against the breaching vendee.

In the leading case, *Tombari v. Griepp*,[24] the issue was whether a vendor could obtain specific performance of a purchase and sale contract when the co-owner of the real property (spouse) has not signed the contract. In *Tombari*, a husband and wife jointly owned a parcel of real property. The husband-vendor and the vendee signed a purchase and sale agreement for the sale of the property, but the vendee thereafter refused to perform the contract, claiming it was void due to the absence of the vendor-wife's signature. The vendors sued for specific performance. The court held that the lack of the vendor-wife's signature rendered the contract voidable but not void, and that once the vendor-wife had affirmed the contract by joining in the present action, the contract became binding on all the parties. Vendors were then entitled to enforce the contract via specific performance.

Tombari demonstrates two disparate principles. First, the outcome in this case illustrates that the mutuality requirement needed for specific performance at common law (before either party is able to obtain specific performance, both must be able to obtain specific performance) is relaxed in modern cases and is *not* required at the time the parties enter the contract. Second, by holding that the wife's failure to initially join in the purchase and sale contract made the contract voidable as opposed to void, the court created an option contract that could be enforced by the vendors, at their election, but not by vendee. This case can be criticized because of this second aspect.

[B]　Vendor's Lien

In order to prevent unjust enrichment, the vendor's lien arises by operation of law to secure the vendor's claim for the balance owed her pursuant to the purchase and sale contract against the land that the vendor conveyed to the vendee. A vendor's lien is rarely used because it can only be utilized effectively if the vendor's lawyer has done a horrendous job by allowing his client to transfer title to Blackacre without obtaining either the balance owed pursuant to the purchase and sale contract, or a mortgage or other lien evidencing the balance due to be paid on the purchase and sale contract.

Moreover, like the vendee's lien, the vendor's lien is ineffective in protecting the injured party's interest if the property is conveyed to a bona fide purchaser for value without notice of the existence of the vendor's lien. Because the vendor's lien arises by operation of law, the vendor must take steps to have it memorialized in some recordable fashion before it will be transferred to subsequent purchasers with the requisite notice.[25]

---

[24] 55 Wash.2d 771, 350 P.2d 452 (1960).

[25] *See* Uniform Land Transactions Act § 2-508 (providing for recordation of a vendor's lien).

[C]   Rescission

The vendor's rescission remedy parallels that of the vendee. By mutual agreement the parties may rescind the purchase and sale contract and agree to the disposition of any deposit made by the vendee. Similarly, the vendor can attempt to prove unilateral rescission either by seeking judicial termination of the contract if the vendee fails to perform on the date set for closing, or by simply declaring that the vendee's actions constitute grounds for rescission.

Rescission will rarely be used by the vendor because its purpose is to annul the agreement and return the parties to their ex ante position prior to the execution of the purchase and sale contract. Unless a separate agreement is reached, the vendor must consequently return any deposit to the vendee.

[1]   Efficacious Use of Rescission

If the vendee records the contract of sale, it may detrimentally affect the marketability of the property. One way to remove the cloud on the vendor's title is by claiming rescission.

[D]   Damages

Unlike the other remedies discussed above, the vendor's remedies in damages do not parallel those available to the vendee for two distinct reasons. First, there is no English or American rule complicating the measure of damages. The vendor is entitled to the benefit of her bargain, defined as the difference between the sales price stated in the contract and the fair market value *at the time of breach*. Resales, which occur subsequent to the date of breach, constitute evidence of value on the date of breach but do not automatically determine the amount of damages in a declining market.[26] The second factor, which causes the vendor's damage remedy to differ from that of the vendee, is the vendor's potential retention of the vendee's deposit. The vendor may wish to retain the vendee's deposit as her sole remedy in the event of breach or as an offset against actual damages suffered as a result of the breach. Interesting questions arise if the vendor wishes to retain the deposit, but is unable to prove damages by traditional methods. The best way to analyze the vendor's damage remedies in light of a deposit is to distinguish between the vendor's remedies in a rising market and those available in a falling market, examining the strategies each party would respectively pursue.

In *Royer v. Carter,* the issue was the timing of the calculation of damages for the breach of contract to purchase real property.[27] The vendee agreed to buy the vendor's house and lot for $24,000, paying a $1,000 deposit. The vendee was then unable to acquire additional financing and breached the agreement. The vendor placed the property back on the market, and after three months in a

---

[26] *See* Royer v. Carter, 37 Cal.2d 544, 233 P.2d 539 (1951).

[27] *Id.*

declining market, resold the property for $18,500. The vendor then sued the vendee for damages.

The court held that damages must be computed at the time of the breach by first determining the amount which would have been due to the vendor under the contract, and then subtracting the value of the property at the time of breach from that amount. Thus, in this case, the resale price of the property could not be utilized to determine the value of the property to the vendor because it did not reflect the property's value at the time of breach.

Although the resale price cannot be used to help establish the vendor's damages, it can be used as a piece of evidence with respect to the vendor's damages if the resale takes place within a reasonable time after the breach. However, the best evidence of the value of the property at the time of breach is the contract price agreed upon between the parties. Hence, the vendor's damages are frequently determined to consist solely of extra costs incurred in re-selling the property.

[E]   Strategy in a Rising Market

Returning to our hypothetical, if Vendor ultimately is able to sell Blackacre for a price in excess of $100,000, the original contract price, Vendor has a number of options. First, she can seek to formally rescind the contract, return the $10,000 deposit, and seek recovery for any incidental damages caused by the breach. However, if the subsequent sale occurs shortly or immediately after the breach, Vendor will have a difficult time proving such damages. Moreover, the traditional damage remedy may be unavailable if the fair market value of the property was in excess of the contract price at the time of breach.

A more difficult question arises if Vendor seeks to retain Vendee's deposit after Vendee's breach. To determine Vendor's rights in this situation, one must first look to the purchase and sale contract to determine what, if any, language addresses this issue.

[1]   Contract Allows Vendor to Retain Deposit

Even if the vendor cannot prove damages, most courts will uphold the enforceability of a contract clause allowing the vendor to retain the vendee's deposit as liquidated damages, as long as the amount forfeited is not considered excessive or punitive. To determine whether a contract provision is enforceable as liquidated damages, the amount of actual damages must be difficult to compute ex ante or ex post, the parties' intentions cannot be penal in nature or an attempt to extort performance, and the amount to be retained by the vendor must be reasonable in light of the facts. Another emerging view is that as long as there was no unfairness in the bargaining process ex ante (for example, as long as the contract is not one of adhesion and no unconscionable means were used to obtain it), the parties should be allowed to "bond" the performance of their promise by paying a premium in the form of liquidated damages (even if the amount of liquidated damages bears no relation to actual damages suffered) in order to ensure performance.

As a note, one should be careful with the language used to draft a liquidated damages clause so as not to run afoul of the traditional bar of punitive liquidated damage provisions. Also, the use of mandatory language, like "shall," when referring to the vendor's option to retain the deposit as liquidated damages instead of precatory language, like "may," can result in a court holding the remedy of liquidated damages to be the vendor's sole remedy, precluding specific performance and any other damage remedy.[28] Rather, the contract drafter should be careful to frame the right to retain liquidated damages as an election or option to be exercised by the vendor.

[2] Contract Omits Reference to Disposition of Deposit

The custom that the vendee should forfeit her deposit upon breach is so well accepted that courts have upheld the vendor's retention of the deposit even in the absence of such a clause. Thus, the expectations of the parties may be used to support an argument that the vendor should be entitled to retain the deposit.

[F] Strategies in a Declining Market

Going back to our hypothetical, if Vendor re-sells the property for $80,000, $20,000 less than the original contract price, Vendor will retain the $10,000 deposit and seek to obtain other compensating damages from the defaulting Vendee. Her success may depend on the language in the contract.

[1] Contract Allows Vendor to Retain Deposit

As discussed above, if the contract states that the deposit "shall" be forfeited as liquidated damages, some courts have held that the vendor is limited to the amount of the deposit as her damages and may not pursue any other legal remedies. On the other hand, contracts which state that the vendor "may" retain the deposit as liquidated damages provide the vendor with an election to retain the deposit as liquidated damages or to pursue any other available remedy, including her remedy of damages.[29]

[2] Contract Omits Reference to the Disposition of Deposit

Contracts that are silent as to the disposition of the deposit in the case of breach are treated like contracts that allow the vendor an option either to treat the vendee's deposit as liquidated damages and her sole remedy, or to pursue the vendee for any other available remedies. In other words, if she so chooses, the

---

[28] *See* Hatcher v. Panama City Nursing Center, Inc., 461 So.2d 288 (Fla. App. 1985).

[29] *See* Mahoney v. Tingley, 85 Wash.2d 95, 529 P.2d 1068 (1975) (vendor was limited to retention of deposit as her damage remedy when the contract stated that the deposit *shall be forfeited as liquidated damages* unless the vendor elects to proceed with an action for specific performance).

vendor may retain the deposit as an offset against her actual damages but not as liquidated damages. Thus, the vendor will be given the opportunity to show her damages are in excess of the amount of the deposit, and if she is successful, she will first apply the deposit to partially satisfy those damages, seeking recovery of any outstanding amount from the breaching vendee.

(Pub.3127)

CHAPTER

6

FINANCING THE TRANSACTION

SYNOPSIS

----

§ 6.01 Introduction

In both the residential and the commercial real estate markets, financing has
become the most important and complex element of many transactions. Today,
rarely is real property purchased without the use of some type of financing.
Indeed, mortgaging and other financing of real estate purchase contracts drives
a multi-billion dollar industry in the U.S., allowing the majority of residential
homeowners to purchase property when they possess only a fraction of the
purchase price at the time of purchase. A national real estate market has evolved
with significant regulation at the federal level due to the historical development
of the amortizable, level payment mortgage. That "traditional" mortgage developed as a result of changes wrought by the Depression of the 1930s, and requires
a nominal downpayment of as little as 5% of the purchase price. Because of
the development of the secondary mortgage market on a national level, what was

once examined on a state-by-state basis is now scrutinized on a national basis, resulting in the increasing homogenization of the residential real estate market.

§ 6.02   The Traditional Mortgage

[A]   Documentation

Due to the increasing influence of the federal government on the real estate market and the fact that mortgages are packaged and sold as investment devices on the secondary money market through institutions like the Government National Mortgage Association ("Ginnie Mae"), the forms that have developed to document the typical real estate transaction have become nationally uniform. In fact, the Federal National Mortgage Association ("Fannie Mae"), originally a governmental entity but now a private body charged with maintaining a secondary market for the purchase and sale of residential mortgages, requires mortgagees and mortgagors to use forms that it has approved. Thus, banks interested in selling their mortgages on the secondary market[1] must use standardized forms, a practice which has further contributed to the homogenization of the real estate market.[2]

[1]   Promissory Note

The promissory note is the instrument signed by the mortgagor identifying the borrower (mortgagor), the lender (mortgagee), the indebtedness, and the terms of payment. The note also indicates the mortgagor's promise to pay the debt to the mortgagee. If drafted properly, the note is considered a negotiable instrument pursuant to all the rules and regulations of the Uniform Commercial Code (UCC) and subject to all of the UCC rules and regulations regarding transferability.[3]

[2]   Mortgage

Although the note and the mortgage together are often referred to by consumers as "the mortgage," mortgage is a term of art connoting an instrument signed by the mortgagor and the mortgagee that secures a debt evidenced by a promissory note between the same parties. The mortgage itself creates and grants the mortgagee a security interest in the borrower-mortgagor's real property.

The mortgage, when compared to the note, is a lengthy and complex document that defines the parties' rights and responsibilities with respect to the real property. The mortgage essentially curtails the use and alienability of the property

---

[1] The secondary mortgage market refers to that network of buyers and sellers of pre-packaged mortgages. In order to raise money, banks and other financial entities will package mortgages they own and sell them to investors for a lump sum. The investors who are interested in the rate of return (interest), purchase these relatively safe investment vehicles because the loans are secured with mortgages in real property, thereby reducing risk. Hence, an investor in California may purchase a package of mortgages that originated in New York City by a New York bank.

[2] For further discussion of the nationalization of the real estate market, see *infra* § 7.02[A].

[3] For a discussion of the issues presented concerning the transferability of a note secured by a mortgage and its interpretation pursuant to UCC rules, see *infra* § 7.04[B].

by the mortgagor/owner to acts intended to protect or insure the value of the property as a security interest for the mortgagee. For example, the mortgage may provide that the mortgagor cannot, without the permission of the mortgagee, commit waste or transfer the property without triggering acceleration of the remaining amount of the debt.[4] In addition, the mortgage creates, in the mortgagee, certain valuable rights to reach and dispose of the secured property should the mortgagor default on his obligations pursuant to the note.

Never lose sight of the important fact that "a mortgage" consists of two separate and distinct instruments: the note and the mortgage. The note or the debt can exist without the mortgage, and promissory notes evidencing debts are often used in typical business transactions when loans are made that are either unsecured or secured with assets (such as pledges, inventory, and accounts receivables) other than real property. However, the mortgage, which is nothing more than a security interest, technically cannot exist when there is no debt to secure. Hence, a mortgage without a note is well-nigh impossible. Furthermore, though these two instruments are often used together, they must be distinguished because the rights and remedies provided by each are different and at times even contradictory.

As discussed below, a body of commercial law has developed in the last fifty years with the primary goal of facilitating the transferability of instruments (notes) evidencing debts in an attempt to aid the free flow of commerce. Unquestionably, the UCC is the preeminent national authority on the creation and transferability of debts represented by notes. However, it is argued that real property law has not and cannot be adapted to the developments of the last half century with respect to the creation of debt, given the immobile nature of the asset involved. The variance between the two systems, the UCC and real property law, has created incredible conflicts which have yet to be resolved.

[3] The Level Pay Fully Amortized Mortgage

The financing device commonly referred to as the traditional mortgage is a level monthly payment, fully amortized mortgage pursuant to which the mortgagor (the vendee purchasing the house and making the monthly payments) pays the same amount each month to the mortgagee (the bank lending the funds). A portion of that amount pays the interest that has accrued on the outstanding debt since the previous payment, while the rest of the monthly payment pays down the principal amount of the loan or indebtedness. Typically after 20 or 30 years, the mortgagor will pay off the indebtedness by making her last payment, and will own the property free and clear of the mortgage. Since the vendee-mortgagor owes the maximum amount when she makes her first payment, a significant portion of that payment is attributable to the payment of interest. Only a small amount of the early payments is applied to pay down the principal amount of the loan.

---

[4] For a discussion of acceleration, see *infra* § 6.09[E].

For example, assume that Mortgagor purchases Blackacre for $110,000 by making a $10,000 downpayment/deposit to the vendor and arranging for a loan (actually a first mortgage) from First Bank for the remaining amount of $100,000. Mortgagor signs a promissory note and mortgage securing the debt to repay the $100,000 over 30 years, with interest calculated at a rate of 12% per annum. If Mortgagor closes and takes possession of the premises on September 1, by the time her first payment is due on October 1, she would have had the use of the borrowed money for 1/12 of the year, or roughly 30 days. If she decides to pay off the remainder of the mortgage on October 1, she would then owe $101,000 instead of $100,000—the extra $1,000 represents the payment of interest for the use of the $100,000 during the month of September. Hence, if her monthly payment is $1,028, $1,000 of that amount is used to pay for the interest that accrued during the month of September, and the remaining $28 is used to pay down the principal. During the month of October, $997.20 in interest will accrue on the outstanding amount of the debt (1% of $99,972, which is the principal balance owed on the loan after the October 1 payment). Thus, when the same $1,028 is paid on November 1, $997.20 will be applied to interest, and the remaining $30.80 will be applied to reduce the principal. The balance owed after the November 1 payment will be $99,941.20. This process will continue until the end of the mortgage term (in this case, 30 years), when the last monthly payment of $1,028 represents the remainder of the principal due pursuant to the mortgage and by then only a nominal amount of interest.

It may seem odd that after two payments totaling $2,056, the debtor-mortgagor has only "paid off" $58.80 of the principal amount of the loan. However, the mortgagor must pay for the privilege of using the mortgagee's money, and the fact that the bulk of the early payments is attributable to interest reflects this fact. Thus, excluding insurance, taxes, and homeowner association dues, the mortgagor will pay a total of $368,080 for her purchase of Blackacre, assuming that she has not made any prepayments (see below for a discussion of prepayments). That is, the mortgagor will pay $268,080 in interest to the mortgagee-bank over the 30-year term for the use of $100,000 to cover the original purchase price.

[B]   The Effect of Interest on the Market

One easy example will demonstrate the impact that the interest rate has on the real estate market. Returning to the facts of our previous hypothetical, if you assume that the interest rate on mortgages is 6% instead of 12%, our mortgagor's payments would be cut in half to $514 a month, saving her $184,040 over the 30 years of the mortgage. More importantly, if we assume that the mortgagor will want to purchase the most expensive home that her financing will allow, as is usually the case, if the rates fall from 12% to 6%, our mortgagor may opt to pay the $1,028 a month anyway, but she can now purchase a more expensive house. Assuming our mortgagor can come up with the appropriate down payment, she can obtain a mortgage for $200,000 at the lower 6% interest rate (rather than for $100,000 at the 12% rate), thus doubling the price of the home that she can afford to purchase.

[1] Deductibility of Interest

Underlying the mortgagor's desire to maximize the monthly mortgage payment for which she is qualified in the eyes of institutional lenders (normally somewhere between 25% to 30% of the mortgagor's monthly income), is the deductibility of the interest for federal income tax paid on mortgages and other financing devices used to purchase both a primary residence and one secondary home with a value not in excess of $100,000 (there is no limit on the value of the primary residence on which the interest on any loans used to finance the purchase may be deducted). The interest on loans used to purchase the principal residence and the vacation home (subject to the limit noted above) is fully deductible against the mortgagor's gross income, and as such reduces her federal tax liability to a significant degree. In a very real sense, the federal government is partially subsidizing the mortgagor's purchase of her home through a transfer of income known as a deduction.

For example, suppose that Mortgagor grosses $4,000 a month as a new associate at Big Firm, Inc. Assuming she has sufficient cash to make the requisite down payment, Mortgagor will qualify for a loan which results in a monthly payment of roughly $1,000 when amortized. Thus, if the interest rate is 6%, she can qualify for a $200,000 mortgage; if the rate is 12%, she qualifies for a $100,000 mortgage. Once the hurdle of amassing the down payment is removed, the total amount of the loan may be irrelevant to a vendee-buyer, who will be primarily concerned with the amount of her monthly payment. It is the amount of the monthly payment, as a percentage of the mortgagor's income, which will determine the amount of the loan, and therefore the price of the house that the mortgagor will be able to purchase.

As demonstrated *supra*, if the mortgagor borrows $100,000 at 12%, a little less than $12,000 (which we will round to $12,000 for ease of computation) will be paid as interest during the first year of the mortgage. If $12,000 is deductible as interest paid, it reduces Mortgagor's taxable income from a gross of $48,000 ($4,000 × 12 mos) to $36,000. At the current maximum tax rate of 28% (and assuming erroneously that every dollar, even the first, is taxed at 28% instead of the lower rate of 15%), $36,000 yields a tax of $10,800 ($36,000 × 28%), assuming no other deductions. However, if Mortgagor was renting the same house and had no deductions, her tax would be 28% × $48,000, or $13,440; $2,640 more than her tax with the mortgage. Thus, in excess of 20% or 2½ monthly payments of the mortgagor's payments are being "paid" for by the federal government through a tax break. With higher income taxpayers and larger mortgages, the tax savings gained from owning a home become even more pronounced.

(Matthew Bender & Co., Inc.)

[C]   Loan-to-Value Ratio

In addition to proving that her gross income will support the monthly payments, the successful mortgage applicant must show that the property securing the mortgage is worth at least the amount of money borrowed. In the event of default, the property may be sold to satisfy the debt. More particularly, banks and other commercial lenders recognize that the property should be worth some amount in excess of the amount borrowed in order to protect their investment in the property. Hence, the "loan-to-value ratio" is used to determine whether the property securing the mortgage (the security) is worth enough to support the loan requested by the potential mortgagor.

Changing the hypothetical slightly for ease of mathematical computations, let's assume that the mortgagor has placed a $10,000 deposit/downpayment on Blackacre, which she has agreed to purchase for $100,000. Mortgagor applies to First Bank for a first mortgage in the amount of $90,000. The appraiser hired by First Bank (although probably paid for separately or as part of the mortgagor's closing costs) appraises the property at $100,000. Assuming all other aspects of this transaction are in order, First Bank will approve the loan if its policy is to grant loans when the loan-to-value ratio is 90% or lower (most banks and other financing institutions will not lend money for any reason when the loan-to-value ratio exceeds 95% for the reasons noted below).

The ratio is easily computed by comparing the amount of the loan to the value of the land and expressing that ratio as a percentage. Hence, in this transaction, the loan is 90/100 of the value of the land, or 90%. Conversely, immediately after the closing, the mortgagor's equity in the property is the flip side of her debt—10/100 or 10%. As another example, if the mortgagor borrows $40,000 as a first mortgage against a house appraised at $50,000, the loan to value ratio is 80%—for those of you who care about the math—$40,000/$50,000 = .80 × 100 = 80%. Hence, if the numbers are 38,000/50,000 the first thing you would do is get rid of the zeros (although you don't have to) to make it easier to compute. Divide 38 by 50 and the product is .76. Multiply that by 100 and you get 76 or 76% which is the correct loan-to-value ratio. Loan-to-value is important also because any loan-to-value ratio at 90% or higher requires the mortgagor to obtain, at a very high cost, private mortgage insurance (PMI) in order to obtain a mortgage from a commercial lender (Bank).[5]

[1]   Effect of Loan-to-Value Ratio on Foreclosure

Studies have shown that the loan-to-value ratio has an incredibly disproportionate impact on the risk of foreclosure; the higher the loan-to-value ratio, the higher the risk of foreclosure. This, coupled with the lender's desire to be fully protected (secured) should there be even a slight decline in the value of property not attributable to waste or activities of the mortgagor leads most lenders to require

---

[5] PMI is discussed *infra* at § 6.09[C].

that the loan-to-value ratio not exceeding 90%. Of course, risk is a function of the marketplace, and a buyer with a higher loan-to-value ratio may be able to obtain a loan by paying a higher interest rate, and paying for PMI, thus purchasing the right to create a riskier investment for the mortgagee. However, until recently the standard loan-to-value ratio on a first mortgage was stable at 80% for savings and loans and 90% for other commercial, institutional lenders.

[2] Moral Hazard

The explanation for the strong corollary relationship between the loan-to-value ratio and the rate of foreclosure may be found by examining the moral hazard inherent in a high loan-to-value ratio. Simply put, the higher the mortgagor's equity in the premises, the greater the incentive she has to protect her investment by properly maintaining the residence, paying the taxes, etc. For every incremental decrease in the value of Blackacre, the mortgagor herself will lose a fraction of her equity in the premises. Thus, if the loan-to-value ratio is 60% and the equity-to value ratio is 40%, for each dollar of the property's decrease in value, the mortgagor theoretically loses 40 cents if she were to sell the house immediately. More importantly, due to the manner in which foreclosure is structured, the mortgagor loses her money "off the top" rather than in proportion to the total loss. The mortgagee gets its money first from the proceeds of the foreclosure and only if there is any money left after the mortgage is paid off does the mortgagor regain all or part of her equity in the premises.[6] Hence, it stands to reason that the higher the mortgagor's equity, and thus the lower the loan-to-value ratio, the safer the loan.

Conversely, if the mortgagor has no equity in the property and the value of the property declines to the point that the property is worth less than the mortgage, the mortgagor has a strong incentive to default on the mortgage. In this scenario, all of the risk and the resulting loss falls on the mortgagee. This is especially true if the state prohibits deficiency judgments[7] or if the mortgagor places no monetary value on the harm done to her credit as a result of her default. From an economic perspective, it would be in the mortgagor's best interest to walk away from a loan anytime the loan-to-value ratio exceeds 100%.

[D] Theories of Title: Effect on Possession

Historically, a mortgage was treated either as a "dead pledge" (*mortgage*) in which the lender took possession of the land and used the profits for her own gain, or as a "live pledge" (*vif gage*) in which the lender took possession, but used the profits to reduce the indebtedness. As a result of the history of the mortgage's development, in some jurisdictions today lenders are entitled to possession and any rents or profits generated by the land until the debt is paid

---

[6] For a discussion of foreclosure, see *infra* Chapter 8.

[7] For a discussion of deficiency judgments, see *infra* § 8.07.

off. Three different rules have developed to address the issue of who is entitled to possession of the property during the term of the mortgage.

[1] Lien Theory

The vast majority of states follow the lien theory of title. Under this theory, a lien is created against the secured property upon execution of the mortgage, and in the absence of a contrary provision, only the *mortgagor* is entitled to possession and rents until a foreclosure sale is held and the mortgagor's equity of redemption and statutory redemption are foreclosed.[8]

[2] Intermediate Theory

In four states, Illinois, New Jersey, North Carolina, and Ohio, the default rule provided by both statute and common law grants the mortgagor the right to possession until first default,[9] at which point the mortgagee has the right to take possession.[10]

[3] Title Theory

In the four title theory states, Alabama, Connecticut, Maryland and Tennessee, upon execution of the mortgage, the *mortgagee* has the right to take possession of the property. In fact, upon execution of the mortgage, the mortgagor's title to the property is transferred to the mortgagee, subject to defeasance. Title will remain in the mortgagee unless and until the mortgagor pays off the debt secured by the mortgage. The payment of the debt is the divesting condition that causes title to shift back from the mortgagee to the mortgagor.

[4] Effect on Rents and Profits

The real issue raised by which theory is employed is who is entitled to rents and profits generated by the land in a commercial setting following the mortgagor's default. In other words, can the mortgagee use or benefit from the use of the property prior to foreclosure? The best way to handle the issue in a commercial context is by express agreement, which will trump the default rule employed by the particular state.

However, in *Taylor v. Brennen,*[11] the Texas Supreme Court held that a rents and profits clause in a receivership agreement (similar to bankruptcy) is ineffective "until the mortgagee obtains possession of the property, or impounds the rents, or secures the appointment of a receiver, or takes some other action." However, what constitutes "taking possession" is not entirely clear. Some courts

---

[8] For a discussion of equity of redemption and statutory redemption, see § 8.03 and § 8.06 respectively.

[9] For a discussion of default, see *infra* § 8.02.

[10] *See* Kratovil, *Mortgages—Problems in Possession, Rents, and Mortgagee Liability,* 11 De Paul L.Rev. 1, 4-6 (1961).

[11] 621 S.W.2d 592 (Tex. 1981).

have held that a refused demand for possession of property is sufficient, while others have found a greater requirement of affirmative action is required on the part of the mortgagee. Finally, some courts have held that the appointment of a receiver is enough to satisfy the taking possession requirement and thereby entitles the mortgagee to any rents that accrue following the appointment of the receiver.

[a] Minimizing the Impact of Title Theory

The impact of the historical rules regulating mortgages in title theory states can be ameliorated by either express contractual agreement or by statute to allow the mortgagor to remain in possession and collect rents on the property unless otherwise agreed. In those title theory states in which statutes are used to delay the mortgagee's right to possession pursuant to her title until mortgagor's first default, these states have in effect been transformed into intermediate theory states.[12] In those title theory states which have no relevant statutes, the particular mortgage must be scrutinized to determine the rights of the mortgagee with respect to possession. The right to take possession without foreclosure is a valuable right, especially if the mortgagor is in default and the property secured is either threatened or will generate significant rental income that can be used to satisfy the debt.

[E] Federal Intervention and Sound Financial Practices

In this era of deregulation and amidst the controversy over the failure of the savings and loan industry, which precipitated a federal bailout, it is hard to believe that there is federal intervention in the financial marketplace. Nevertheless, in obtaining a mortgage or other loan secured by real property, the first question one should ask is what type of lender is financing the loan. If the lender is a federally insured savings and loan, the rules governing that loan (ranging from the type of form used for the loan application to the maximum loan-to-value ratio permitted) will be determined by federal regulations issued by the Federal Home Loan Bank Board and will be applied uniformly to all other such banks in that region. However, state chartered banks and other institutions may not be subject to the federal government's regulatory intervention.[13]

[F] Usury

Until recently, loans made at usurious rates were a matter of significant concern to every real estate lawyer. Usury is defined as a loan in which the debtor is required to pay interest at a rate in excess of a benchmark or absolute maximum interest rate set by statute and occurs when the lender enters into the transaction

---

[12] *See supra* § 6.02[D][2].

[13] In certain situations mandated by the legislature and constitutionally supported by the Commerce Clause, such institutions are subject to federal intervention. However, these situations are relatively rare.

knowing that the rate is usurious (for example, the interest rate was not mistakenly calculated so as to violate the interest limitation). Two factors have coalesced to cause usury rules to be primarily of historical significance. First, usury statutes themselves have become incredibly complex, unworkable, and riddled with exceptions such that proving usury has become increasingly difficult. Second, and more importantly for residential purchasers of realty, federal law governing federally insured savings and loans and banks[14] preempts state regulations, exempting those financial institutions (essentially all relevant institutions) from state usury limitations. However, with respect to commercial developers who borrow from institutions or individuals exempt from federal control and regulation, most states have corporate borrower exemptions that limit the applicability of usury limitations.

§ 6.03   Deed of Trust

For various reasons having to do with obtaining a deficiency judgment and being permitted to bid at the foreclosure sale, a deed of trust is used instead of a traditional mortgage to finance the purchase of real property in many states. Similar to the structure of a traditional mortgage, two instruments are executed to create a deed of trust. First, the parties use a note to memorialize the existence of the debt. A bond may also be used to establish a debtor/creditor relationship, though this is rare because of its deleterious impact on transferability. Second, similar to the mortgage instrument, the deed of trust sets forth the rights and responsibilities of the three parties (the trustor, the beneficiary, and the trustee) with respect to the property.

[A]   Trustor

The trustor is the mortgagor. Whenever you are dealing with a deed of trust and the trustor, you are, in fact, dealing with the mortgagor, since the obligations and identity of the trustor and the mortgagor are identical, for all intents and purposes. In the arcane language of trusts, the mortgagor is referred to as the trustor or settlor because it is she who has the obligation—in this case, to make the monthly payment to the trustee pursuant to the trust for the benefit of the beneficiary. More importantly, as part of the transaction, the trustor agrees to transfer title to the real property to the trustee (the beneficiary's nominee or agent) as security for the trustor's obligation to pay off the debt evidenced by the note.

[B]   Beneficiary

The beneficiary is the mortgagee. Whenever you are dealing with the beneficiary of the deed of trust, you are dealing with the mortgagee, since the obligations and identity of the beneficiary and the mortgagee are identical, for all intents and purposes. In the arcane language of trusts, the mortgagee is referred to as the beneficiary because she gets the benefit of the trust—in this case, the

---

[14] See discussion of transferability of mortgages below.

receipt of the monthly payments made by the trustor-mortgagor. Upon default by the trustor, the instrument will state whether the beneficiary must request that the trustee begin foreclosure proceedings, or whether such proceedings will begin automatically. The beneficiary, per the rights granted in the deed of trust, may have other rights that she can exercise or request that the trustee exercise given the occurrence of certain events during the term of the deed of trust (for example, acceleration of the amount of the debt upon transfer of the premises by the trustor).

[C]   Trustee

The trustee is the only new party introduced by the deed of trust and does not have an analogous counterpart in the typical mortgagee-mortgagor transaction. The trustee is supposed to be an independent third party bound by the provisions of the trust to act in a fiduciary capacity to both the trustor and the beneficiary of the trust. However, since her role in the typical real estate transaction is to: 1) collect and forward payments from the trustor to the beneficiary; and 2) upon default, to conduct the foreclosure sale to maximize the interest of the beneficiary, her real interests lie with the mortgagee-beneficiary. The trustee should always be thought of as an agent of the mortgagee-beneficiary because the trustee is selected, retained, and controlled by the mortgagee as beneficiary of the trust. In practice, the trustee's primary responsibility is to arrange for the sale of the real property securing the debt in the event of default.

[D]   Critique

The deed of trust is largely of historical significance. It was used by banks as a vehicle to avoid certain restrictions imposed on mortgagees and to accomplish objectives forbidden to mortgagees at law. Thus, by using a deed of trust, the bank or lender could obtain a foreclosure of property through private sale when such was not permitted of mortgagees, or bid at the foreclosure sale when bidding was prohibited of mortgagees. Furthermore, although various arcane restrictions prevented the "mortgagee" from obtaining a deficiency judgment, in certain states a "beneficiary" could obtain the equivalent of a deficiency judgment in the absence of prohibiting language in the deed of trust.

This triumph of form over substance has been refuted in all states either by statute or by decisions unifying the treatment of residential mortgages and deeds of trust. In some instances, what was previously forbidden to mortgagees—like bidding at the foreclosure sale—has been granted by statute to mortgagees, thus negating the primary use of trustees. In other instances, what was previously permitted of beneficiaries of deeds of trust was subsequently forbidden when the laws applicable to mortgages and deeds of trust were unified (for example, in states prohibiting deficiency judgments, the prohibition was extended to real property loans secured by deeds of trust as well as those secured by mortgages).

Currently, the laws regulating mortgages and deeds of trust are treated uniformly by the courts for all intents and purposes. While local practice and custom may determine which arrangement is used to finance the purchase of realty or for the securitization of real property (for example, lenders in the Commonwealth of Virginia use deeds of trust), the various arrangements are interchangeable with respect to their legal treatment and interpretation (and shall be treated as such throughout the remainder of this text). In this text, the simpler terminology of mortgagor/mortgagee will be used to describe the typical transaction.

§ 6.04　Mortgage Substitutes

The deed of trust was perhaps the most frequently used mortgage substitute until courts and legislatures thwarted lenders' attempts to evade its characterization as mortgagees. However, the desire to avoid characterizing an arrangement as a mortgage is still alive due to both real and perceived benefits that may accrue to one not considered a mortgagee. From simple attempts to evade anti-deficiency statutes to complicated schemes to provide the lender with the option of being secured (if such security is deemed advantageous at the time of default),[15] lenders continue to attempt to avoid being characterized as a "mortgagee" in large part due to consumer oriented laws designed to protect mortgagors from harsh treatment. Mortgagee status invokes an entire panoply of rights and regulations that the lender often prefers to avoid. What follows is an examination of the three most important mortgage substitutes in descending order of use and importance.

[A]　Installment Land Sale Contract or Contract for Deed

At first glance, the Installment Land Sales Contract (ILSC), or Contract for Deed as it is known in certain locales in the Midwest, resembles a real estate purchase and sale contract.[16] The ILSC is a contract between the vendor and the vendee pursuant to which the vendee agrees to pay a certain total amount of money over a period of time to purchase Blackacre, and the vendor agrees to deliver a specified quality of title, as defined in the contract, to the vendee upon receipt of payment of said sums. Like the real estate purchase and sale contract, the ILSC is an agreement governing the parties' rights and responsibilities during the executory interval between signing the contract and delivering the deed.

Suppose that Vendee and Vendor execute an ILSC for the sale of Blackacre for $50,000. Pursuant to the ILSC, Vendee agrees to pay $500 down and monthly payments of principal and interest of $475 a month, an amount reflecting an interest rate of approximately 10%, amortized over the term of the contract, 20

---

[15] *See infra* § 6.04[C].

[16] For a discussion of ILSC, see *supra* Chapter 3.

years. In accordance with the contract, the vendee immediately takes possession of the premises, pays the taxes and insurance on the premises during the period of the contract, and agrees to maintain the premises in good repair. If the vendee performs her contractual duties, at the end of the 20-year period, the vendor has a duty to deliver marketable title to the premises. Thus, under an ILSC, the vendee is in possession, although the vendor retains legal title.

[1] Differences Between the ILSC and the Real Estate Purchase and Sale Contract

The ILSC differs from the real estate purchase and sales contract in a number of very important ways. First, the ILSC is used as a financing device to allow the vendee to ultimately purchase title to Blackacre. On the other hand, the standard real estate purchase and sales contract merely establishes the parties rights and responsibilities during the executory interval between the date of the contract and the date of closing—the vendee must arrange her own financing independent of the purchase and sale contract. This is true even if the vendor agrees to assist the vendee in financing the purchase. For example, if the vendor agrees to execute a secondary mortgage on the property as part of the purchase price (thus acting as a purchase money mortgagee-vendor),[17] the vendor's rights as owner terminate on the date of closing when title is transferred from the vendor to vendee, and her rights as a mortgagee begin. However, the ILSC-vendor acts in the dual capacity of owner and financier until the last payment is received from the vendee, at which point the vendor is obligated to deliver the quality of title specified in the ILSC.

Second, as a result of the ILSC-vendor's dual role as owner and financier until the vendor's final payment, certain other differences become immediately apparent. Not only is the term of the ILSC much longer than the term of the typical purchase and sale contract, but the vendee is granted the right to possession during the term of the ILSC, which is not the case with the typical executory contract. The final and most important difference from the point of view of the vendor utilizing an ILSC is that since title is not transferred until receipt of the final payment, the vendor may use the forfeiture or liquidated damage provisions of the ILSC advantageously against unsuspecting or unsophisticated vendees. If the vendee defaults pursuant to the contract, the vendor may retain all previous payments made, thus destroying any equity that the vendee may have acquired in the property.

Continuing our hypothetical from above, assume that the Vendee remains in possession of Blackacre for 10 years, during which time she makes prompt monthly payments. In addition, as a result of the market and improvements that she has made to the premises, Blackacre has increased in value to $75,000. Unfortunately, on the anniversary of her 11th year on the premises, she is laid

---

[17] Discussed *supra* § 1.06[A].

off from her job, missing her monthly payment for the first time. The contract states that time is of the essence, so pursuant to the forfeiture clause, the Vendor declares the Vendee's interest in Blackacre to be forfeited and requests that the Vendee remove herself from the premises as quickly as possible since she is now a trespasser. Until recently, the Vendee would be forced to vacate the premises in this situation, regardless of the equity that she had built up in the property. In breach of the contract, the Vendee had no right to complain about the inequitable treatment she received at the hands of the "injured" Vendor. [18]

The ILSC is regarded by most as a pro-vendor financing device used to evade restrictions placed on mortgagees by state law. In our hypothetical, instead of being required to seek foreclosure of a mortgage, the Vendor can declare a forfeiture as provided by the ILSC, then can resell the property free and clear of any claim by the Vendee. In most jurisdictions, ILSCs are not recordable. However, even in those jurisdictions in which they are recordable, the vendor must first sign the ILSC in order for it to be accepted for recordation, a task which she will conveniently avoid until the contract has been totally paid in order to limit the possibility of a claim by a vendee in default.

[2] Treatment of the Forfeiture Remedy by State Courts

In *Russell v. Richards*, [19] the assignee-purchaser of property pursuant to an ILSC reduced the principal on a note by $10,782, leaving a principal amount owing of $26,504. The trial court refused to enforce a forfeiture of the vendee's equity in the property when the assignee-purchaser defaulted, stating that the forfeiture shocked its conscience. The trial court then awarded the vendee damages equal to the loss of her equity and the loss of her personal property. On appeal, the Supreme Court of New Mexico found that the trial court had abused its discretion by refusing to enforce the forfeiture. The supreme court held that whether a forfeiture shocks the conscience is to be determined by considering the amount of money already paid, the period of possession, the market value of the property at the time of default compared to the time of sale, and the potential rental value of the property. The Supreme Court of New Mexico's holding demonstrates the strict construction of ILSCs followed by courts exalting form over substance. Rather than treating the ILSC as a mortgage substitute, such courts focus on the language of the contract to determine the parties' rights and responsibilities.

Courts have taken three very different approaches in their treatment of ILSCs in situations where the vendee defaults after having made substantial payments or where the vendee alleges that she has significant equity in the premises. Some states, such as New Mexico, treat each forfeiture provision individually to determine if it should be upheld. If the forfeiture "shocks the conscience," then

---

[18] *See* Russell v. Richards, 702 P.2d 993 (Sup. Ct. N.M. 1985).

[19] 702 P.2d 993, 103 N.M. 48 (1985).

it may be set aside and specific performance of the original contract provided to the vendee, so long as she tenders the late payments plus the vendor's cost.[20]

Used in only a small number of cases, the second approach is to uphold the contract as written, denying the vendee any remedy under a contract providing for forfeiture unless the vendee can prove fraud or some other unfairness in the bargaining process (for example, unconscionability) which would serve to void the contract.

The emerging approach is to treat the vendor's interest in the property pursuant to an ILSC like a security interest by requiring the vendor to foreclose the vendee's interest in order to cancel the vendee's redemption rights.[21] In this respect, the ILSC is treated like a mortgage in certain cases since the vendee is given an opportunity to protect her equity in the premises by either exercising her redemption rights or bidding at the foreclosure sale, should one occur. In this limited fashion, ILSCs are being treated as a mortgage. Some would even allege, that the ILSC is being intentionally transformed into a mortgage, a position that may have some degree of merit.

In *Skendzel v. Marshall*,[22] the vendor of a piece of property pursuant to an ILSC sought a judicial declaration of forfeiture of the vendee's interest in the property though the vendee had already paid $21,000 of a $36,000 contract price. The Indiana Supreme Court applied the "equity abhors a forfeiture" principle, holding that the enforcement of the forfeiture clause would be "clearly excessive" and "unreasonable." Moreover, the court treated the ILSC as if it were a mortgage and held that "[t]o conceive of the relationship [between the vendor and the vendee] in different terms is to pay homage to form over substance."[23] Though the court did not rule out forfeiture in all cases, the court limited its application to cases of absconding or abandoning vendees and situations in which the vendee has paid a minimum amount and seeks to retain possession though the vendor is paying for taxes, insurance, and maintenance of the premises.

This case demonstrates the better, more realistic view of ILSCs taken by courts willing to look beyond the form of the transaction to its substance. The ILSC represents a mortgage substitute and implies that the parties' rights and

---

20 "To determine whether a forfeiture shocks the conscience of the court, this Court has applied the following equitable considerations: the amount of money already paid by the buyer to the seller; the period of possession of the real property by the buyer; the market value of the real property at the time of default compared to the original sales price; and the rental potential and value of the real property." *Russell, supra* 702 P.2d at 994.

21 *See* Petersen v. Hartell, 40 Cal.3d 102, 219 Cal.Rptr. 170, 707 P.2d 232 (1985). For a discussion of redemption rights and the foreclosure process, see *infra* § 8.03[A].

22 Skendzel v. Marshall, 301 N.E.2d 641, 261 Ind. 226 (1973), *cert. denied*, 415 U.S. 921, 94 S. Ct. 1421, 39 L.Ed.2d 476 (1974).

23 *Id.*

responsibilities should be governed by rules analogous to those governing the mortgagee-mortgagor relationship whenever possible.

Although well-intentioned courts have gone far in reducing some of the difficulties created by the use of the ILSC, many difficult and vexing problems remain. For example, in California, even if the vendee is given the right to redeem until her interest in the premises is foreclosed, that right means very little unless it is adequately communicated to the vendee. Thus, many vendees will unknowingly sacrifice their interest in the premises when told by a vendor that the forfeiture provision in the contract controls when the vendee misses or is late with a payment. With this hazard in mind, one might question whether ILSCs should be abolished entirely. However, one should remember that ILSCs are typically used by those unable to obtain conventional financing from institutional lenders, and thus may be willing to take on the increased risk of loss of equity in exchange for securing financing. Since the cost of a loan to those with poor credit is often greater than the cost to qualified mortgagors,[24] the ILSC often represents an attractive alternative to the traditional mortgage for those with poor credit. Thus, any attempt to eradicate or toughen the laws with respect to the use of ILSCs may hurt the very class of individuals that most legislative and judicial efforts to transform an ILSC into a mortgage attempt to protect.

[B]   Absolute Deed

In order to avoid the mortgagor's right to redeem from default,[25] mortgagees often attempt to use an "absolute deed" as a security transaction in order to camouflage a mortgage. For example, the putative mortgagee agrees to lend the putative mortgagor $100,000 at a 10% interest rate. However, instead of executing a mortgage, the parties structure the transaction as a sale with the putative mortgagor transferring title to the subject property to the putative mortgagee by deed upon receipt of the $100,000. The deed is then recorded, showing the putative mortgagee as the owner of record. However, either through an oral or written agreement (if written, it is never recorded because it would almost automatically transform the absolute deed of record into a mortgage), the parties agree that the new owner (the putative mortgagee) will reconvey the premises to the old owner (the putative mortgagor) if the putative mortgagee receives timely repayment of the amount lent plus interest from the putative mortgagor (if in writing, the agreement will state that time is of the essence). What is left after all this "hocus pocus" is a deed which, although absolute on its face, is defeasible upon the payment of the amount of the debt pursuant to the terms and conditions of the side agreement by the putative mortgagor.

---

[24] *See* Note, *Reforming the Vendor's Remedies for Breach of Installment Land Sale Contracts,* 47 So. Cal. L.Rev. 191, 193-198 (1973).

[25] For a discussion of this issue, see *infra* § 8.02.

[1] Burden of Proof

As expected, the burden of proof is on the party seeking to defeat the apparent meaning of written instruments to establish by clear and convincing evidence that the transaction is not what it appears to be and instead should be treated legally as a mortgage. If documents are produced to prove that the initial transaction is a debt rather than a sale, the court will treat the absolute deed as a mortgage. However, when such clear proof is unavailable, the courts will accept parol and other extrinsic evidence to show that an absolute deed is in fact a mortgage. Facts that lend credibility to an argument that an absolute deed is a mortgage are: 1) the putative-mortgagor's continued possession, maintenance, and operation of the premises; 2) the putative-mortgagor's acting as an owner would (for example, paying taxes and making improvements on the property); and 3) evidence of periodic payments from the putative-mortgagor to the putative mortgagee that can only be characterized as the payment of interest.[26]

[C] Negative Pledge or Covenant

A negative pledge or covenant arises when the owner of Blackacre promises a lender not to convey or encumber Blackacre in a subsequent transaction. Assuming it is not breached, this promise benefits the lender by assuring her that unencumbered assets can be reached and sold if the owner of Blackacre defaults on the underlying debt. However, if the borrower attempts to sell or encumber Blackacre, it is uncertain what rights, if any, the lender will have with respect to the land now negatively pledged as security for a new debt. If she can prove the existence of the negative pledge and breach by the borrower, the lender clearly has rights for breach of contract. However, that right to sue for breach of contract may be worthless if the borrower is judgment proof or her assets are exempt from judgment.[27] Thus, if the borrower's only significant asset is real property which would otherwise be beyond the reach of the lender, the lender may attempt to prove that she has an equitable mortgage on the land. This mortgage predates (was perfected before and has superiority over) intervening lienors with knowledge of her interest, including the borrower.[28] Here the lender is claiming that an instrument not technically in the form of a mortgage should in fact be treated as an equitable mortgage. In essence, this is the reverse of the situation involving the absolute deed where the lender attempts to camouflage a mortgage as a sale of real property.

Although it seems counterintuitive that the lender, typically the party with superior bargaining power, will not execute a standard mortgage when in a position to so do, instead preferring a negative pledge or covenant, one must

---

[26] *See* Cunningham & Tischler, *Disguised Real Estate Security Transactions as Mortgages in Substance*, 26 Rutgers L.Rev. 1 (1972).

[27] *See* Tahoe National Bank v. Phillips, 4 Cal.3d 11, 480 P.2d 320, 92 Cal.Rptr. 704 (1971).

[28] *See id.*

recall that it may be advantageous for the lender to be viewed as an unsecured creditor as opposed to a mortgagee in certain situations. For example, as an unsecured creditor, the lender may avoid a potentially time-consuming foreclosure process in the event of default if the property is unsecured or unencumbered in the hands of the borrower. In addition, the lender may also avoid restrictions on obtaining a deficiency judgment by avoiding mortgagee status. On the other hand, when the property has been transferred without the consent of the lender, or in other situations where the value of the security is threatened, it may be advantageous for the lender to treat the loan as an equitable mortgage giving the lender the status rights of a mortgagee. As Professor Hetland has cogently stated, the use of a negative covenant represents the lender's attempt "to have his cake and eat it too. . . ."[29]

[1]   Treatment by the Courts

Although initial efforts by lenders to cast the negative pledge as an equitable mortgage were fruitful,[30] more recent attempts have proven unsuccessful.[31] For example, in the leading case *Tahoe National Bank v. Phillips*,[32] a lender-mortgagee attempted to foreclose an "Assignment of Rents and Agreement Not to Sell or Encumber Real Property" as a mortgage. The California Supreme Court held that *Coast Bank v. Minderhout*[33] was no longer controlling and that the form used in *Tahoe* was generally not considered in the trade to be a security agreement. In construing the negative covenant, the court held that the language of the instrument was not "reasonably susceptible of interpretation" as a mortgage. In *Tahoe*, the court interpreted the ambiguous assignment in favor of the borrower who declared a homestead exemption on the property, concluding that since the bank was the party who selected the form of documentation, it was required to "bear the responsibility for the creation and use of the assignment it now claims as ambiguous. Legal alchemy cannot convert an assignment into an equitable mortgage . . . bestowing upon the bank the riches of a hypothetical title."

The California Supreme Court placed the burden on the drafting party, the lending bank, to specifically and expressly use a mortgage instrument if it desired to obtain and perfect a security interest in land. Anything less would *not* be construed as a mortgage. Thus, if the lender has the choice between executing a mortgage to secure its debt or using another device (such as an Assignment of Rents and Agreement Not to Convey), the lender will be held to its elected documentation.

---

[29] Hetland, Secured Real Estate Transactions 73 (1974).

[30] *See* Coast Bank v. Minderhout, 61 Cal.2d, 392 P.2d 265, 38 Cal.Rptr. 505 (1964).

[31] *See* Tahoe National Bank v. Phillips, 4 Cal.3d 11, 92 Cal.Rptr. 704, 480 P.2d 320 (1971). *See also* Equitable Trust Co. v. Imbesi, 287 Md. 249, 412 A.2d 96 (Ct. App. 1980).

[32] 4 Cal.3d 11, 92 Cal.Rptr. 704, 480 P.2d 320 (1971).

[33] 61 Cal.2d 311, 38 Cal.Rptr. 505, 392 P.2d 265 (1964).

The court's rejections of lenders' attempts to employ the negative pledge are buttressed on both theoretical and practical grounds. From a theoretical stand-point, courts and commentators alike have a difficult time understanding how a negative right can also constitute a positive interest such as a security interest in real property.[34] Practically speaking, the lender's claim to secured status is significantly undermined in light of the facts that the lender occupies the superior bargaining position and uses it to structure the form of the transaction. Hence, the courts have ruled that if the lender wishes to enter into a secured transaction, it is the lender's responsibility to select the appropriate form.

In *Equitable Trust Co. v. Imbesi*,[35] the debtor borrowed $60,000 from the Equitable Trust Company and executed a Covenant Not to Encumber or Convey Real Estate. The debtor subsequently placed an encumbrance on the property by executing a mortgage with another lender. Following default, the Equitable Trust Company sought to enforce the negative covenant, claiming that it had an equitable lien (for example, a mortgage) on the property. After an exhaustive examination of case law, the court held that an equitable lien or mortgage could not arise as a result of the execution of a negative pledge of the type used in this case. The court correctly distinguished between true equitable mortgages arising when parties use a homemade mortgage instrument and expressly intend to secure a debt with a mortgage, and negative pledges in which a lender attempts to create a negative right incapable of "morphing" into an affirmative lien against the property.

§ 6.05 Adjustable Rate Mortgages (Variable Rate Mortgages)

Unlike the traditional mortgage discussed in § 6.02, the adjustable rate mortgage (known early on as the variable rate mortgage, but referred to herein as an ARM) is a financing device in which the interest rate of the mortgage may fluctuate throughout the duration of the mortgage pursuant to the terms and conditions set forth in the mortgage. Thus, unlike the level payment feature of the traditional mortgage, requiring equal monthly payments to amortize the debt, the payments on the ARM may fluctuate wildly during the term of the mortgage within the bounds set forth in the mortgage instrument.

Suppose that Mortgagor enters into an ARM with First Bank for $100,000 at an initial interest rate of 8¾%, with a 2% cap annually and a 6% cap over the term of the loan. Interest is set annually on the anniversary date of the ARM by reference to an index measured for any change from one anniversary date to the next. The index used may be the Consumer Price Index, Federal Funds ("Fed Funds" such as U.S. Treasury security yields), the prime rate, or any other

---

[34] *See* Coogan, Kripke, and Weiss, *The Outer Fringes of Article 9: Subordination Agreements, Security Interests in Money Deposits, Negative Pledge Clauses and Participation Agreements*, 79 Harv. L.Rev. 229 (1965).

[35] 287 Md. 249, 412 A.2d 96 (1980).

acceptable, objectively verifiable index that measures the cost of inflation or (and they are actually the same) the change in the value of money.

Assuming the transaction as stated above, the mortgagor agrees to enter into a mortgage for $100,000, with an interest rate for the first year of only 8¾%. The initial interest rate is usually below the market rate and is called the "teaser rate" because it induces borrowers to take out ARMs instead of fixed rate mortgages. Also, it may be easier to qualify for an ARM than for a fixed rate mortgage since the initial payment, as a percentage of the mortgagor's income, is lower than what would be required for a fixed rate mortgage. However, on the first anniversary of the note, an economic snapshot is taken by reference to the index selected by the mortgagee—in this case, Fed Funds—and the interest is adjusted accordingly. If the index shows an increase of 2 or more points, the interest on the loan will be raised from 8¾% to 10¾%. However, the first cap (2% cap annually) guarantees that the interest will not be raised more than 2% a year, regardless of the rise in the index. In addition, the second cap (6% over the term of the loan) means that even with a series of 2% increases annually (assuming a wild, long-term inflationary spiral), the interest on this loan for any given year can never exceed 8¾% + 6% = 14¾%. Of course, over the term of the loan the interest may go up or down depending on the index and depending on what the note calls for in its terms and conditions. Thus, some ARMs provide that the interest rate may never fall below the initial rate (although these are believed to be a small minority), while others have no lower floor, but merely a higher cap.

The rationale behind such apparently complicated devices is quite simple and reasonable. The use of an ARM shifts the risk of possible higher interest rates during the term of the loan from the financial institution to the mortgagor. Similarly, it permits the mortgagor to benefit from declining interest rates. In addition, the use of ARMs represents one response to the question of the transferability of mortgages discussed in § 7.02. To understand how an ARM shifts the risk from the financial institution to the mortgagor, one must analyze the financial aspects of a typical mortgage.

Consider the following hypothetical:

At a time when market mortgage rates are 10% for fixed rate mortgages, the mortgagor and the mortgagee enter into a fixed rate, level payment, fully amortizable mortgage which extends over a thirty year term. What is not readily apparent is the cost to the bank or financial institution of the funds necessary to supply mortgages. Either by attracting depositors by offering a competitive interest rate or by paying interest on Fed Funds borrowed from the Federal Reserve, the financial institution incurs a cost in obtaining the funds which it gives out as loans. In order to make a profit on the loan, the bank-mortgagee must be able to obtain funds at a cheaper rate than the interest rate it charges to the mortgagor, with enough left over to cover its administrative costs.

Let us assume the bank-mortgagee is able to obtain funds at a rate of 8%, which it can then turn around and loan out at 10%. Problems develop when inflation strikes and interest rates rise. If competitors are paying 12% on deposits, the bank must raise its interest rates to remain competitive, or depositors will remove their funds. However, since it is locked into a fixed rate of return of 10%, the bank-mortgagee will lose money on the fixed-rate mortgage as depositor's investments mature and roll over into the higher 12% rate. The mortgagor's interest rate cannot rise to 12% to offset the inflation because she has a fixed rate mortgage below the market rate, which she is certain to hold to maturity as long as it remains below the market.[36]

One option (some would argue the only realistic option) open to the bank when interest rates rise is to sell the mortgage (really the right to receive its stream of income) on the secondary market, taking the proceeds, and reinvesting in a new mortgage that pays the market rate. However, the bank must discount the mortgage being sold to reflect its below market interest rate, and the bank will not earn the face value of the mortgage. Thus, ignoring for a moment the effect of points (see below for a definition of points) and transaction fees extracted from the mortgagor at closing, the bank is still losing money on the loan. The only way to cover this loss is to make it up on subsequent mortgages (spread the risk); thus, new mortgagees may pay a higher interest rate to the bank in order to subsidize its older, unprofitable mortgages.

The use of ARMs and other exotic financing devices discussed below, represents an attempt by financial institutions to shift the risk of later higher rates to the mortgagor. Mortgagors benefit from the use of ARMs by frequently obtaining lower interest rates ex ante since the mortgagee does not have to build the potential for future inflation or the error costs associated with prognosticating future rates over a thirty year period into its fixed rate mortgages. The end result of the development of the ARM is that it gives a mortgagor a choice, forcing her to pick the mortgage vehicle best suited to her needs. From a paternalistic standpoint, one might argue that the risk is better borne by the sophisticated bank when entering into these transactions. However, that view fails to take into account the risk-averse nature of banks and other financial institutions. If banks were forced to offer only fixed rate mortgages, their use of available risk spreading techniques would ultimately require a later class of mortgagors to subsidize previous, unprofitable mortgages. Moreover, one must also consider the risk-averse nature of mortgagors. The fact that both ARMs and fixed rate mortgages survive in a world that might theoretically be better with the use of either fixed rate mortgages or adjustable rate mortgages, but not a mixture of both, suggests that some borrowers are more risk-averse than others. Furthermore,

---

[36] Whether she can transfer the advantageous, below-market mortgage to a subsequent purchaser is a major issue addressed *infra* § 7.02 and § 7.03. This phenomenon is sometimes referred to as "portfolio lag."

banks do not have the market position or strength to force ARMs on all borrowers, nor are they able to perfect their risk spreading techniques so that mortgagors are efficiently subsidizing each others' losses through the use of only fixed rate mortgages.

§ 6.06   Exotic Financing Devices

As a result of the popularity of ARMs and the turmoil in the financial market created by consumer demands for mortgages that are customized to their individual situations, certain types of mortgages have developed in the last decade that are exotic in the sense that they differ from the typical mortgage transaction and the standard ARM mortgage. What follows is a list of the more popular exotic financing devices with a brief explanation of how each operates.

[A]   Graduated Payment Mortgages (GPMs)

GPMs look like ARMs in that the payments made on the mortgage vary according to a schedule set forth in the mortgage. However, unlike the ARM, the payments vary in a predetermined amount according to a schedule set at the time the mortgage begins. Typically, the payments gradually increase (hence, the term graduated) by a certain percentage each year for the early years of the mortgage, and then level off at the highest rate for the remainder of the term of the loan. GPMs are used when the mortgagor anticipates that her income will increase over the initial term of the mortgage so that she will be better able to support the larger payments in the later years of the mortgage. As a result, some GPMs feature negative amortization. With negative amortization, the mortgagor is not paying enough in the early years to cover all the interest that accrues on the mortgage, and the additional interest, which is not being paid, is added to the principal amount of the debt, which is paid off, as the payments increase during the term of the loan.

As an example, assume that a young associate enters into a GPM with First Bank that has an average interest rate over the term of 10½%. However in the first year of the loan, her payments reflect an interest of 8%. The second year her payments are increased to reflect an interest rate of 9%, the third year, 9½%, the fourth year, 10%, the fifth year, 10½%. The sixth year and every year thereafter to maturity, her payments would reflect an interest rate of 11%, covering the lower initial payments.

[B]   Shared Appreciation Mortgages (SAMs)

SAMs are a financing device by which the mortgagor purchases a below-market interest rate by agreeing to share any appreciation in the property with the mortgagee when the property is sold. For example, Mortgagor and Mortgagee execute a mortgage with an interest rate of 8%, a rate which is 2% below the market rate. The term of the loan is ten years, although the payments are calculated based on the typical amortization of standard mortgages—thirty years.

The unique feature of the SAM is that the mortgage is granted a contingent interest of, let's say, 5%. The 5% contingent interest is payable to the mortgagee only if the property appreciates in value by a certain percentage compared either to the sales price, if the house is sold within the ten year period, or to an appraisal if the property is not sold within the ten year period and the lender is not obligated to refinance the original mortgage at the end of ten years. In a rising market, the contingent interest in appreciation is supposed to compensate the mortgagee for the lower initial rate. Of course, the mortgagor can offset any improvements to the property that she has made against the increased value of the property. The unique relationship created by the use of a SAM raises many issues involving the status of the relationship between the mortgagor and the mortgagee and its effect on the mortgagor's equity of redemption.

[C]   Shared Equity Mortgages (SEMs)

SEMs are closely related to SAMs. In a SEM, an individual, usually a relative, acts as a private mortgagee by agreeing to become one of the owners of the property. This individual pays a percentage of the mortgage (effectively reducing the interest rate on the mortgage given by the third party mortgagee to the mortgagor) in exchange for a percentage of the equity in the property. Thus, in SEMs there are two owners of the property: one of whom occupies the property, while the other merely makes a passive investment in the property. Obviously, in such an arrangement, the lending bank is not exposed to the same risks presented by a SAM.

For example, suppose that Mortgagor executes a 90% first mortgage SEM with First Bank on a property purchased for $100,000. Pursuant to the SEM, the mortgagor's mother pays 25% of the mortgage amount each month. Since the co-mortgagors' percentage of monthly payments and equity interest must be identical, the mother owns a 25% equity interest in Blackacre (the maximum interest the mother can hold pursuant to a SEM is 45%). Other detailed rules are designed to protect the occupant's interest and regulate the division of proceeds upon resale.[37]

[D]   Reverse Annuity Mortgages (RAMs)

RAMs are typically used by the elderly to get the equity out of their principal residence in order to enable them to be able to live comfortably on the proceeds of the equity that they have built up during their working lives without selling their principal residence.

Assume that Bob and Sue Mortgagor have recently retired and own a home appraised at $100,000 which they own free and clear of any mortgage. Sue has recently retired and they find it difficult to live on their existing income. As a

---

[37] *See also* Iezman, *The Shared Appreciation Mortgage and the Shared Equity Program: A Comprehensive Examination of Equity Participation*, 16 Real Prop., Probate & Trust J. 510 (1981).

result, they trek to First Bank to execute a RAM with a maximum mortgage amount of $80,000, payable on the property's transfer or encumbrance, the death of the survivor of Bob and Sue, or, alternatively, when the maximum amount of the mortgage is incurred. Each month First Bank remits to Bob and Sue $500, which they use for their living expenses. With each monthly payment, the amount of the mortgage is increased not only to reflect the amount of the principal (after the first payment, $500) but also the interest that accrues on the payments they have already received. Upon the death of the survivor of Bob and Sue, the loan in effect reaches maturity and must be paid off by either the heirs to the estate or the intestate takers. If the loan is not paid off, First Bank, like any other mortgagee, has the right to foreclose. If the loan reaches the maximum amount of the mortgage before the death of the survivor, the loan will have to be immediately repaid, usually forcing the mortgagor to sell the property. Actuarially this should never happen since the loan should be structured so as to be in effect upon the surviving mortgagor's death.

[E]   Growing Equity Mortgages (GEMs)

Increasing in popularity, GEMs differ from other types of exotic financing devices in that they call for a fixed level of interest throughout the term of the loan, but an increase in the principal amount of the loan to reflect a shorter than standard maturity period. The interest rate is usually lower than the standard mortgage because of the impact discounting has on the yield of a mortgage[38] and because higher rates are necessary for mortgages with longer maturities due to the increased risk generated by the longer maturity period in the loan.

A GEM is structured like a GPM except that the mortgagor is expected to have sufficient income to make immediate payments to sufficiently amortize a standard mortgage. The increases called for by the GEM are applied to the principal and result in the mortgage being paid off in a much shorter than standard period of time.

For example, a mortgagor executes a GEM with First Bank for $100,000 at a 10% interest rate over a 30-year term. If this were a fixed level standard mortgage, the mortgagor's payments would start and remain constant at approximately $1,028. With a GEM, the mortgagor agrees to increase her payments on a yearly basis by a stated percentage (normally 4-8% per annum), with the extra amount reducing the principal. As a result, the loan may be paid off in as little as 15 years with the initial rate of interest reflecting a below market rate. This note takes into account the effect of discounting and the lessened maturity of the loan.

---

[38] For a discussion of discounting, see *supra* § 6.09[D].

§ 6.07 Junior Mortgages

Junior mortgages arise when there is more than one mortgage of record executed and filed against the same parcel of property. At common law, the priority of mortgages was determined by the first-in-time rule.[39] Today, with the use of recording statutes in all jurisdictions, priority of mortgages is normally determined by the order in which the mortgages were recorded (in the absence of any separate subordination agreement as discussed in § 13.03). In this text, mortgages will be discussed according to their time of recordation.

Let's assume that Mortgagor borrows $80,000 from First Bank to purchase Blackacre for $100,000. First Bank's mortgage is validly recorded and is the only financing encumbrance against the property at the time of recordation. Shortly after the purchase, Mortgagor decides to finish the basement and borrows $10,000 from Second Bank. This loan is also secured by a validly executed mortgage against Blackacre which subsequently is properly recorded. A number of years after Mortgagor's purchase of Blackacre, the property's value has increased to $150,000, while the amount of the principal owing to First Bank is $60,000, and the amount of the principal owed to Second Bank is $7,500. At this point, Mortgagor takes out a home equity loan from Third Bank in the amount of $50,000 to purchase a new Mercedes. This loan is also validly recorded.

If the mortgagor defaults on the loans and the mortgages are foreclosed, First Bank holds a mortgage, which is senior to the other two mortgages, and thus will be the paid first from the foreclosure proceeds. Second Bank holds the second mortgage, which is junior to First Bank's mortgage but senior to Third Bank's mortgage. Hence, following the payment to First Bank, Second Bank will have its mortgage satisfied from the foreclosure proceedings. Lastly, since Third Bank's mortgage is junior to both other mortgages, it will be paid only if there is something left following the satisfaction of the senior mortgages. By extending a loan to Mortgagor that is secured by a third mortgage on the property, Third Bank must take the risk that the funds generated from foreclosure proceedings will be insufficient to satisfy all three mortgages. Since Third Bank's mortgage may not be completely repaid, if repaid at all, Third Bank will likely charge a higher rate of interest on its loan than the other two banks that are senior in priority.

§ 6.08 Wrap-Around Mortgages

Wrap-around mortgages are financing devices originated by mortgagors who wish to preserve an advantageous pre-existing mortgage upon the sale of their property. In effect, mortgagors use wrap-around mortgages in an attempt to evade restrictions upon the transferability of an initial, favorable mortgage.

---

[39] This rule is discussed *infra* in § 10.02.

For example, in 1974, when the interest rates fell to a quarter century low of 6%, Seller entered into a mortgage for $100,000 with First Bank for the purchase of Blackacre. In 2000, the seller wishes to sell Blackacre to Purchaser for $200,000. At this point, the first mortgage on Blackacre is $50,000, giving Seller a net gain of $150,000 (not including the interest paid on the loan to date) on the sale of her residence. However, if Seller does not need all the cash from the sale to purchase her new home, she might offer to structure the transaction as a wrap-around mortgage, which could be advantageous for both parties. First, Seller would require the standard 10% downpayment, or $20,000, upon execution of the real estate purchase and sale contract, which she would pocket upon closing. Instead of requiring Purchaser to go to an institutional lender to finance the remainder of the purchase price ($180,000) at the going rate of 14%, Seller would offer to take a wrap-around mortgage in the amount of $180,000 at a rate of 11%. This mortgage wraps around Seller's original mortgage of $100,000, which has been paid down to $50,000. At an 11% rate, Purchaser pays $1,715 per month on the wrap-around mortgage to Seller instead of paying $2,135 a month to an institutional lender at the going rate of 14%. Upon receipt of said amount, the seller remits her monthly mortgage payment of $514 to First Bank as usual, and pockets the remainder, or $1,201. The seller profits from this arrangement in a few ways. First, by offering the lower interest rate, she is able to raise the sale price of her house.[40] Second, the Seller pockets the difference between the 6% interest rate she is paying out on her original mortgage and the 11% interest she is receiving on the wrap-around mortgage from the purchaser.

The use of a wrap-around mortgage is relatively rare today because lenders are sophisticated enough to place clauses, such as "due-on" clauses[41] and acceleration clauses,[42] in their loans which automatically, or at the option of the lender, cause the entire amount of the loan to become due and payable upon the transfer of any interest by the original mortgagor to a subsequent party. In addition, wrap-around mortgages represent significant risks to both parties, though for different reasons. From the seller's perspective, the device permits amateur lending with all of its attendant risks. From the purchaser's perspective, the same concern arises, but even more important is the question of First Bank's action against the seller, should the seller default. Recall, the first mortgage is still in existence on the property and has priority over the purchaser's later interest in the property. Hence, if the seller-mortgagee does not pay off the first in a timely manner, an event of default may be declared by First Bank requiring the purchaser to amass enough cash to payoff the entire amount of the debt; something that most purchasers cannot do.

---

[40] *See supra* § 6.02[C].

[41] Discussed *infra* § 7.03[B].

[42] Discussed *infra* § 6.09[E].

§ 6.09   Terminology Applicable to All Mortgages

What follows is a definition and discussion of some of the unique terms frequently employed in real estate transactions.

[A]   Points

When a prospective purchaser applies for a mortgage, almost all banks will charge "points" as a condition of making a loan. A "point" is one percent of the face value of the loan. Points are used to raise the effective yields on mortgages. Points represent a one-time transfer from the mortgagor to the mortgagee by which the mortgagee profits in excess of the stated rate of interest on the loan by being paid a certain percentage of the loan (stated in points) up front to make the loan. One discount point will raise the effective yield on a loan by approximately 1/6% to 1/8%, depending on the size of the loan and assuming a 12 year life to payoff.[43]

The borrower may pay points to the lender in one of two ways. First, the borrower-mortgagor can pay the points directly to the lender on the date of closing. Second, the points can be taken directly from the loan proceeds, resulting in a disbursement of loan funds in an amount less than that stated on the face of the note. This process is known as discounting and is discussed below.

Assume that Mortgagor is approved for a first mortgage from First Bank in the amount of $100,000 at 8%, with three points. In the typical transaction, the mortgagor will have to remit 3% of the loan ($3,000) to the mortgagee in order to pay for the points. This can be accomplished if the lender reduces the amount disbursed to $97,000 or if the mortgagor pays the lender $3,000 at the closing. The effective yield on the loan is higher than the 8% stated in the loan because the mortgagee has in reality lent $97,000, but is being paid interest and principal on $100,000. Assuming the normal 12 year payoff, the true interest rate is approximately 8½%.

However, the shorter the payoff period, the higher the lender's yield. This can be demonstrated by assuming that the borrower-mortgagor wins the lottery the month after she closes on the purchase of her home and decides to pay off her mortgage. At 8%, she would owe approximately $100,750, with $750 representing the interest on the loan. However, the mortgagor has really borrowed $97,000, and her payment of $100,750 represents a gain of $3,750 for the lender. This corresponds to an interest rate in excess of 40% per annum, instead of the 8% charged on the face of the loan. Points may also be used where the lender anticipates a rising money market (interest rates are expected to rise) and wishes to limit its risk, because it is using a fixed rate loan by charging the purchaser points ex ante. This admittedly far-fetched example should demonstrate that if the loan is paid off in less than 12 years, the yield or true interest rate will rise.

---

[43] *See* O'Connell, *What is a Point Really Worth?*, Mortgage Banker, Mar. 1981, at 31.

However, if the loan is maintained to maturity, the yield will be lower but will still be in excess of the stated 8%.

Nonetheless, borrowers agree to points for two reasons. First, lack of bargaining power in the face of a unified market causes the borrower to accept the existence of points generally, and to attempt to find a loan with both a low interest rate and the lowest amount of points possible. Second, borrowers may feel comfortable paying points up front since such a loan translates into lower monthly payments over the long haul. If the true interest rate was charged and no points were used, the rate would be higher and hence monthly payments would be higher. A loan with points is a better option for buyers with available cash who intend to hold the property for the length of the mortgage than for buyers who wish to use the property as a short-term investment.

In essence, points should be viewed as a form of interest in excess of the going rate. Thus, the prevailing interest rate should reflect and incorporate the number of points requested by the lender. The higher the number of points charged, the lower the interest rate, and vice versa. Therefore, it is not uncommon to see different interest rates for different mortgage loans from the same lending institution where the only factor creating the differential interest rates is the amount of points paid ex ante. Hence, a cash-rich mortgagor may choose to "pay" points up front and "buy down" the interest rate on a long-term loan if she plans to hold it to maturity. Her decision may be influenced by tax considerations since points are fully deductible in the year in which they are paid.

[1] Veteran's Administration Limitations on Points

Veteran's Administration (VA) rules for granting VA loans limit the number of points that the mortgagee can charge to one point, including the origination fee (described below). Since most banks normally charge more than one point, the seller must pay the additional points required by the lender at closing in order to go forward with the transaction. The seller should and will add the points that must be paid into the total purchase price. When dealing with a veteran using a VA loan, care should be given to take into account the impact of the restrictive regulations of the VA in drafting the financing contingency in the real estate purchase and sale contract.

[B] Origination Fee

Closely related to the concept of points, the origination fee is a fee stated by the lender to cover its cost of originating the loan. In reality, it is a disguised point which raises the effective yield on a loan. In a competitive market, the cost of originating the loan is incorporated into the interest rate.

The origination fee is stated in terms of the points of the loan. Thus, in addition to paying the stated points, the mortgagee may also be required to pay an additional point(s) called for under the guise of an origination fee. In some jurisdictions, the origination fee is synonymous with the lender's points, in others the imposition of an origination fee is distinguished from the charging of points. However, the origination fee is always stated as a percentage of the face amount of the mortgage in the same manner as points.

[C]   Private Mortgage Insurance (PMI)

PMI is an insurance policy that the mortgagee will require if the amount of the loan exceeds a certain loan-to-value ratio, typically 90%. If the loan-to-value ratio exceeds the mortgagee's set level, the risk of default and foreclosure is unacceptable without PMI coverage. A PMI policy insures the lender-mortgagee against a loss generated by foreclosure of the property. The premium for the PMI varies with the type of policy, and the type of coverage, but on average it is approximately 1% of the loan amount initially and .7% of the loan amount thereafter. The PMI charge is paid for by the mortgagor, even though the mortgagee is the beneficiary.

For example, Mortgagor purchases Blackacre for $100,000 by paying 5% down and financing the balance of $95,000 with First Bank. First Bank requires the mortgagor to obtain and pay for PMI as a precondition to making the loan. The premium for the first year must be paid at closing; thus, the mortgagor must come up with close to $1,000 by this time to pay for the PMI policy. The annual cost of the PMI, $60 per month in this case ($720 divided by 12) will be added to the monthly payments of the mortgage. For this amount, the mortgagee will be protected if the mortgagor defaults and the property brings less than the mortgagor's amount of indebtedness at the foreclosure sale.

The limit of PMI protection is normally 20% of the amount of the initial loan, plus the lender's costs at foreclosure. Thus, PMI serves as a very expensive device for the protection of the mortgagee's interest in the premises, insuring that the mortgagor has a loan-to-value ratio of at least 20% upon foreclosure—that amount is guaranteed and protected from loss by the policy. If it suffers a loss, the insured mortgagee will recover the maximum amount of the policy, 20% of the insured value of the premises plus its costs at foreclosure. However, if the insured mortgagee's loss is only 10% of the value of the property (the amount realized upon foreclosure is 90% of the debt), it will recover only 10% of the face amount of the policy, its actual loss.

[D]   Discounting

Closely related to the concept of points discussed above, discounting occurs when the face amount of a loan, either upon disbursement or transfer in the secondary market by the mortgagee-lender, is reduced to raise the true yield of the interest on the mortgage above the amount stated on face of the mortgage.

An example best demonstrates how discounting works. If the mortgagee-bank holds a $100,000 mortgage that is paying an 8% interest when the market rate is 10%, it will have to discount the mortgage in order to sell it because no one will buy a mortgage which pays less than the going rate in the market. In order to give the investor a 10% rate of return parallel the market, the mortgagee must discount its mortgage by $20,000, reducing the price of the mortgage to $80,000 when it is sold. The investor purchasing the mortgage will know that its face amount (the amount of the indebtedness) is $100,000, which pays $8,000 per year if not compounded. However, the investor will receive a 10% return from her discounted mortgage since she has invested $80,000, for a return of $8,000 per annum. Consequently, the original mortgagee will lose $20,000, but will insure itself against a further loss in a rising market.

[E]   Acceleration

Closely related to due-on clauses,[44] acceleration clauses in mortgages are triggered by certain events normally within the control of the mortgagor, such as default, sale, or encumbrancing the property with a junior mortgage without the consent of the mortgagee. When the event triggering the acceleration occurs, the mortgagee has the right to require that the entire remaining balance (the amount of the indebtedness) be paid within a certain time period (usually 30 days), or the loan will be considered in default and subsequently subject to foreclosure.

---

[44] For a discussion of this issue, see *infra* § 7.02[B][1].

CHAPTER

7

VOLUNTARY TRANSFERS OF MORTGAGED PROPERTY

---

§ 7.01   Introduction

This section focuses on the legal issues raised when a party to the standard mortgage desires to transfer her interest in the property to a subsequent party (hereinafter referred to as the transferee). There is no question that each party to the typical mortgage transaction has the unfettered right to transfer its interest in the property. Thus, in the absence of a contractual restriction, the mortgagor has the right to sell his equity of redemption free and clear of any restraint imposed by the mortgagee. Indeed, any attempt to restrict, via the mortgage contract, the mortgagor's right to transfer her equity of redemption in the property is measured in terms of the impact it has on the alienability of the property. An absolute restriction on the mortgagor's right to transfer her equity of redemption would probably be held void as an impermissible restriction on alienability. Similarly, any attempt to wholly restrict the mortgagee's right to transfer his interest in the property—the right to receive the proceeds of the loan as provided in the note—would likewise prove unavailing.

The entire purpose of the exercise that culminates in the execution of the promissory note and mortgage is to create a *negotiable instrument* that is transferrable to one who can assume the exalted and protected status of a "holder in due course" (HIDC) pursuant to the UCC. However, the fact that each interest is freely transferable does not mean that the parties may do so either to the detriment of, or in violation of, the prior mortgage agreement. Transferring the interest is one thing, weakening the other party's rights in ways not expressly permitted by the contract creating the debt is something else.

Thus, if a mortgagor could transfer his interest in the property without the mortgagee's permission, and without paying the mortgage off—thus creating an unsecured debt—there would be no incentive to enter into a mortgage. It would not be worth the effort to document the mortgage transaction if the mortgagor could dissolve the mortgage the day after the transaction by transferring the property to a strawman (one used solely to accomplish the transfer who will then transfer the property back to the original transferee-mortgagor) and having the strawman transfer back to her. This section addresses the unique legal issues that arise when either party to the typical mortgage transfers its interest to a transferee and the effect, if any, such a transfer has on the other party to the original mortgage transaction.

§ 7.02　Transfer by the Mortgagor

When property that has a preexisting mortgage on it is sold or transferred by the mortgagor, two things can occur: first, the sale can generate enough money to enable the original mortgagor to pay the balance due to the mortgagee, thus paying off the mortgage. Second, the mortgagor may attempt to transfer his equity in the premises to the transferor without paying off the existing mortgage, thus leaving the mortgage as a valid encumbrance against the property.

[A]　The Clean Method—Transfer Free of the Mortgage Debt

Although it happens rarely today in the typical transaction, the transferee (the new buyer) may have enough cash available to pay the entire purchase price in cash without outside financing. Assuming this is the case, the transferee will want title free and clear of any encumbrance, including a mortgage, that may impair the value of the property. Thus, the mortgagor (the seller) will pay off his indebtedness in its entirety at the closing and transfer clean title to the transferee. This is known as "the clean method" because the debtor-mortgagor upon payment of the mortgage, no longer owes any obligation to the mortgagor and is considered clean (i.e., debt-free).[1]

Other clean methods of transfer that result in the end of the relationship between the original mortgagor and mortgagee include novation (a contractual doctrine that allows the transferee to be substituted for the original contracting party with the other contracting party's approval; in effect creates a new contract between the transferee and the mortgagee), the mortgagee's cancellation of the original mortgage, with a concomitant release of the original mortgagor, conditioned on the execution of a new mortgage with the transferee, at rates presumably approximating market rates and last, and perhaps most common, the transferee's financing her purchase through the execution of a new mortgage with an outside lender who agrees to pay off or "take out" the existing mortgage. In this situation, since the mortgage is paid off with the new loan, the property is not transferred with the old, preexisting mortgage and the mortgagee is not adversely affected by the transfer.

---

[1] *See* Storke & Sears, *Transfer of Mortgaged Property*, 38 Cornell L.Q. 185 (1953).

[1] Prepayment Clauses

The above transfers assume, of course, that the mortgagor has the right to pay of the mortgage debt in advance or to prepay the mortgage. Because most mortgagees include due-on clauses in the mortgage, which cause acceleration of the debt in the event of a transfer, they grant the mortgagor the right to prepay the mortgage upon transfer. To do otherwise the mortgagee would run the risk of having the contract considered void as an adhesion contract.[2]

[B] The Dirty Method—Mortgagor Transfers the Property With the Encumbrance

The original mortgagor may attempt to transfer the mortgage, along with the real property securing the mortgage, when selling the property to a subsequent purchaser. If the existing mortgage has an interest rate below the current market rate, it is in both the mortgagor and the purchaser's interests to hold onto the old below-market interest rate mortgage on the property. Replacing the rate with a new, higher market rate mortgage would be more expensive for both parties. Because the higher interest rate means higher monthly payments, the seller-mortgagor may be forced to lower the sales price of his property in order to sell it to a buyer who can qualify for a mortgage or, contrarily, a purchaser may be forced to pay more per month for a property he wishes to buy.[3] On the contrary, the lender-mortgagee wants to terminate the old below-market rate loan upon transfer in order to increase his yield on a loan with a shorter maturity rate and in order to reloan the realized proceeds from the old loan at the new, higher market rates to avoid portfolio lag—i.e., in order to keep the bank's portfolio up to current market rates.

In order to demonstrate the impact of interest on the price of a home sold by a mortgagor, and the benefits to the mortgagor of transferring a mortgage with a below-market rate to a subsequent purchaser, assume the subsequent purchaser has a sufficient down payment to purchase the property. Often, however, the most important element of the transaction to the purchaser is the amount of the monthly payment under the highest mortgage for which he can qualify. As the example in § 6.02[B] demonstrates, if the purchaser has income of $4,000+ and wishes to spend the maximum amount of his income on a conventional mortgage, most banks and institutional lenders will allow him to qualify for a loan which requires a monthly payment of approximately 25% of his gross income, or $1,000. If the selling mortgagor has a loan with a balance of $100,000 on his house at 6%, it requires a monthly payment of approximately $500 to amortize it. If the going or market rate is 12% for new mortgages, the borrowing mortgagor can qualify for a loan of $50,000 from a bank or

---

[2] *See* Wellenkamp v. Bank of America, 21 Cal.3d 943, 148 Cal. Rptr. 379, 582 P.2d 970 (1978).

[3] For a discussion of the effect of the interest rate on the market and the price of property, see *supra* § 6.02[B].

institutional lender which will require a monthly payment of $500 a month, for a total of $1000 a month. Notice, the house is sold for $150,000 with the new purchaser taking over the old mortgagor-seller's payments (he has either assumed the first mortgage or taken subject to the old mortgage, discussed *infra*) and the seller receives the $50,000, which is generated by the new mortgage. If, however, the old mortgage cannot be transferred to the new buyer, and the new buyer must finance his purchase by resorting to a traditional lender at market rates, the new buyer will only be able to qualify for and so afford a mortgage of $100,000 because his monthly payments at 12% = $1,000 a month. Thus, by transferring the old mortgage to a subsequent purchaser, the original mortgagor may be able to obtain a higher in price for the property, which reflects the below market interest rate of the first mortgage. *In effect, what the mortgagor-seller is doing is selling the economic value of the old below-market rate by adding it to the purchase price of his house.* This is the reverse of discounting from the mortgagor's perspective. He has made a good deal and would like to transfer the mortgage to the new purchaser for the price of $50,000. Standing in his way is the bank or lender with its battery of lawyers.

[1] Due-on Clauses

One way to prevent the mortgagor from "selling" the advantageous interest rate on the mortgage and requiring the lending mortgagee to keep the below-market loan in its portfolio until maturity (because why would anyone in their right economic mind pay a loan off early unless the market interest rate *drops* below the interest rate in the mortgage?) is through the use of due-on clauses in the mortgage instruments. As succinctly stated in *Wellenkamp*,[4] a due-on clause, which includes a due-on encumbrance as well as a due-on sale clause, "is a device commonly used in real property security transactions to provide at the option of the lender, for acceleration of the maturity of the loan upon the sale, alienation, or further encumbering of the real property security."[5] If the lender could successfully insert and use such a clause in a mortgage, then the lender could forbid an attempt to transfer the economically advantageous mortgage by the mortgagor. Prior to *Wellenkamp*,[6] the lender who incorporated due-on clauses in a mortgage instrument could and frequently did condition his consent to a transfer (without exercising the due-on clause) on an increase in the loan's interest rate to a level close to the market rate. The party's refusal to so raise the rate resulted in acceleration of the loan in accordance with the due-on clause and, if not paid in full, led to foreclosure of the property. The result of the heavy-handed, almost automatic use of due-ons in the mid to late 1970s by lenders during a period of wildly rising interest rates in the real estate market, lead to numerous challenges to the use of due-on clauses, which were

---

[4] Wellenkamp v. Bank of America, 21 Cal.3d 943, 148 Cal. Rptr. 379, 582 P.2d 970 (1978).

[5] *Id.* at 946, n.1.

[6] *Id.*

based on legal theories too numerous to recount herein. Essentially, all of these challenges culminated in the California Supreme Court's decision in *Wellenkamp*.

In *Wellenkamp*, the California Supreme Court, following the lead of numerous other courts, held that institutional leaders (banks and savings and loan associations) may not automatically, upon the transfer of mortgaged property, enforce a due-on-sale clause contained in an otherwise valid mortgage or deed of trust.[7] The court applied a balancing test that measured the "quantum of restraint" imposed from the enforcement of the clause.

The court rejected the lender's argument that it should be allowed to enforce the clause to maintain its loan portfolio at current rates by ruling that the risk of inaccurately projecting interest rates over the term of a mortgage could not be placed on mortgagors.[8]

[a] Garn-St. Germain Depository Institutions Act of 1982

The ability of state courts to rule on the applicability of due-on clauses hampered the development of a national secondary market in mortgages and led to serious constitutional questions regarding the scope of the Commerce Clause and the disparities in the treatment of federally versus state chartered institutions and subsequently prompted Congress to pass the aforementioned act which, in part, preempts state restrictions on due-on clauses. As a result, mortgages today may contain validly enforceable due-on clauses, which give the lender the right to accelerate the debt to maturity should the mortgagor attempt to transfer the property without the mortgagee's consent.

[C] Transfer of a Mortgage by the Mortgagor—Effect on the Mortgagee's Rights vis-a-vis the Mortgagor

In order to make a rational decision to enforce a valid due-on clause when faced with a transfer, the rights of the mortgagee must be examined to determine the scope of its options in the event it fails to enforce the due-on clause and permits the transfer. If the mortgagor and the transferee enter into an agreement pursuant to which the property is transferred with the mortgage still extant on the property, it must be remembered that the mortgagee, in the absence of contractual rights given in the mortgage like the due-on clause, is unaffected by the subsequent agreement between the mortgagor and the transferee. Basic contract law governs and good common sense dictates that the two parties cannot, without the mortgagee's permission, contract for anything that detrimentally affects the mortgagee's interest, without his being party to the contract. Thus, even if the mortgagee fails to exercise his acceleration rights as provided by the

---

[7] *Id.*

[8] Unfortunately, *Wellenkamp* creates certain counterproductive effects that are too detailed to discuss herein but that are discussed in Johnson, *Correctly Interpreting Long-Term Leases Pursuant to Modern Contract Law: Toward A Theory of Relational Leases*, 74 Va. L. Rev. 751, 778-780 (1988).

due-on clause, that failure does not affect the mortgagee's right to enforce other provisions of the mortgage including, but not limited to, suing the original mortgagor if the mortgage is not promptly paid or foreclosing on the property and pursuing the original mortgagor for a deficiency judgment if necessary. As between mortgagor and mortgagee, little has changed; the mortgagor is still liable to the mortgagee for all of the covenants and promises in both the note and the mortgage.

[1]   Transferee's Failure to Make Payments

In the agreement between the transferee and the mortgagor, the transferee will either take "subject to" the mortgage or "assume" the mortgage. In either case, the transferee becomes principally liable for the mortgage debt since he is using the property and the land becomes the primary source of the payment of the mortgage debt. Thus, if the original mortgagor is called to pay the mortgage debt due to the transferee's failure, he may seek reimbursement from the land and if there is a deficiency, he may seek payment from the transferee who is personally liable for any deficiency. The mortgagor's precise rights against the transferee depend primarily upon the agreement made between the mortgagor and the transferor at the time of transfer. Under that agreement, the mortgagor either takes "subject to" or "assumes the mortgage."

[a]   Mortgagor vs. Transferee Who Takes "Subject to" the Mortgage

Ignoring for a moment how the transferee takes subject to the mortgage, the legal effect is that the transferee is not personally bound by the terms of the mortgage, including the obligation to make payments on the mortgage. The transferee, when she takes subject to the mortgage, has made no promises or covenants that she will pay the mortgagor pursuant to the original mortgage and, since she was not privy to the original transaction, she is not bound by that mortgage agreement personally. In this situation, if the transferee refuses to make payments, the mortgagor has no rights against the transferee personally for payment but can look to the land as security for the debt owed to the mortgagee and, as a result, if the mortgagor pays the mortgagee for the debt, the mortgagor may step into the shoes of the mortgagee. That is, the mortgagor is subrogated to the mortgagee's rights and inherits the rights of the mortgagee with regard to the land. Thus, the mortgagor, standing in the shoes of the mortgagee pursuant to the equitable doctrine of subrogation, may foreclose on the property for non-payment of the debt even though the non-assuming transferee is not personally liable for the debt.

For example, suppose that Mortgagor sells Blackacre to a transferee who does not wish to be personally liable for the mortgage on Blackacre. Both agree the fair market value and sales price of Blackacre is $100,000, but it has a first mortgage of $75,000 held by First Bank as mortgagee. As a result, transferee pays mortgagor $25,000 in cash and takes subject to the encumbrance or mortgage. Transferee has an economic incentive to pay the mortgage even though he is not personally liable thereon because his failure to do so will result in First Bank's initiation of foreclosure proceedings against mortgagor that more than likely will result in transferee's loss of the property and the loss of his $25,000 investment in the premises. If, however, transferee does walk away from the property, he is not personally liable to First Bank and mortgagor's only recourse is to pay the mortgage and subsequently bring her own foreclosure action against transferee—thus, reclaiming the property in lieu of the debt owed pursuant to taking subject to the encumbrance.

Students are often mystified as to why the transferee will pay $25,000 for property with an agreed price and fair market value of $100,000. Transferee pays only $25,000 because that is the value of the property with, or if you prefer, reduced by the encumbrance. If transferee paid the mortgagor $100,000 without having the first mortgage removed it would be an extremely stupid transaction because someone would eventually have to pay First Bank $75,000 to have the mortgage removed on the property and the mortgagor would not have a strong economic incentive to do so since he is no longer using the property. Of course, he is still personally liable on the note, but in many states, due to the "one-action rule,"[9] and as a matter of custom and practice in other states, First Bank will bring its foreclosure action first, resulting in the sale of the property, and then pursue the mortgagor only if there is a deficiency. Since the property is worth something to someone, if the mortgagor is paid $100,000 for property in which he has an equity interest of $25,000 and personal liability on the note, he is in a better position by allowing the foreclosure sale to take place and then making up any deficiency—assuming there is one—with part of the $100,000.

[b]   Mortgagor vs. Transferee Who Assumes Mortgage

Ignoring for the moment how the transferee assumes the mortgage, the legal effect is that the transferee has made a promise or covenant to pay off the preexisting mortgage pursuant to its terms and conditions and his failure to do so results in a breach of that promise for which he is personally liable to the mortgagor, to whom the promise was made. However, once again, the land is looked to first as security for the transferee's debt and promise in the event of breach, and it is only if there is a deficiency in the value of the land, when compared to the amount paid by the mortgagor as a result of the transferee's breach, that results in the personal liability of the transferee.

Continuing our hypothetical, if the transferee defaults when the mortgagee is owed $50,000 and the land is worth $125,000 and the original mortgagor is called upon to pay the debt of $50,000, he has the right to seek reimbursement from the assuming transferee. More importantly, the mortgagor "steps into the shoes

---

[9] For a discussion of the one-action rule, see *infra* § 8.07[A][2].

of the mortgagee" after paying the mortgage debt and can therefore exercise the mortgagee's power to foreclose if he is not reimbursed. If he forecloses and the property brings more than his claim for reimbursement—which it should in this fact situation—then he is made whole and has no further recourse against the transferee. However, if the property sells at foreclosure for $40,000, notwithstanding its fair market value of $125,000, the mortgagor can proceed against the transferee who is personally liable for the $10,000 shortfall.

[2] Mortgagee vs. Mortgagor—"Discharge"

Zastrow v. Knight,[10] demonstrates the concept of discharge and how it may impact the mortgagee's rights against the mortgagor when the transferee and the mortgagee have entered into a direct agreement that somehow alters the terms and conditions of the original mortgage. In this situation, once again, a distinction is made between a transferee who has assumed the mortgage and a transferee who has taken subject to the mortgage.

[a] Discharge and the Assuming Grantee

As indicated above, the relationship between the three parties involved in transferring property subject to an existing mortgage is a complex one. When the transferee assumes a mortgage, new rights and new relationships are created. For all intents and purpose, the relationship between the mortgagor and the assuming transferee is likened to a relationship between a guarantor (the transferee) and his principal (the mortgagor), with the mortgagee acting as a creditor. In this tripartite relationship, when the creditor-mortgagee extends the surety-transferee's period for payment by granting him additional time to make monthly payments *without* the consent of the guarantor-mortgagor, the guarantor-mortgagor's rights are negatively affected because the guarantor-mortgagor cannot, at the true instant of default, step in and pay off the debt and proceed against the surety-transferee and the property. Instead, the guarantor-mortgagor must wait until default actually occurs, which may be much later and at a time when the property's value may have declined. In other words, the surety-mortgagor may be harmed by the extension of time granted by the creditor-mortgagee to the surety-transferee. Thus, a duty is placed on the creditor-mortgagee to refrain from doing anything which diminishes the rights of the guarantor-mortgagor against the surety-transferee. For reasons having to do with problems of proof and the burden of proof, if the creditor-mortgagee does anything which is held later to increase the guarantor-mortgagor's risk without that party's permission, the guarantor-mortgagor is completely and totally discharged from the underlying obligation.

[b] Discharge and the Non-Assuming Grantee

When a transferee takes subject to a mortgage, and as discussed above, the land serves as the sole security for the debt, the transferee does not act as surety.

---

[10] 56 S.D. 554, 229 N.W. 925 (1930).

The correct way to think about this is that the land acts as security with the guarantor-mortgagor guaranteeing the debt to the creditor-mortgagee only to the extent that the land is worth less than the debt at the time of default. Hence, if the creditor-mortgagee increases the risk of the surety in this situation, the surety-mortgagor's obligation is discharged to the extent of the value of the surety (the land) at the time the act increasing the guarantor-mortgagor's risk occurred.

For example, let's assume that the mortgagor transfers Blackacre worth, $100,000 with an $80,000 mortgage, to First Bank who transfers it on to a non assuming transferee—meaning the transferee takes subject to the mortgage. Due to the proximity of a newly constructed toxic waste dump, the value of Blackacre plummets to $70,000 on September 1. The transferee misses his September 1 payment, but on that date is given an additional 30 days to make his payment by the mortgagee without the consent of the mortgagor. The transferee makes the payment but ultimately defaults permanently one year later when the property is worth $50,000 and the mortgage has been reduced to $75,000. If the property brings $50,000 at foreclosure, the mortgagee may sue the original mortgagor for only $5,000 because the mortgagor is released to the extent of the value of the property at the time the extension of payment was agreed to between the transferee and the mortgagee—$70,000. Thus, the fact that the value of the property subsequently plummeted to $50,000 is irrelevant. The mortgagor is released to the extent of the security on the date of discharge, $70,000, which is subtracted from the amount of the note, $75,000, at the time of foreclosure, limiting the original mortgagor's liability to $5,000 ($75,000 − 70,000).

In *Zastrow v. Knight,* the defendant, an assuming-transferee in an action brought against him to recover $2,500 due on a promissory note, asserted as a defense to the mortgagee's claim, the lack of a suretyship between the assuming transferee and the mortgagee.[11] The defendant argued that successive transfers of the mortgaged realty destroyed the surety relationship that had once existed because of an extension agreement between the mortgagee and the party in possession (a non-assuming transferee). The Supreme Court of South Dakota held that when a transferee takes subject to a mortgage, while assuming no personal liability, the security in his hands is nonetheless liable for the payment of the mortgage debt. The court therefore held that to the extent of the value of such security, "the original mortgagor and the grantee [transferee] subject to the mortgage stand in a relation to one another, which, while not a true suretyship, is nevertheless equitably analogous therein and subject to the operation of the same principles."[12] Thus, when the mortgagee agreed to extend the time of payment to a non-assuming grantee (the party in possession) without the consent of the original mortgagor or the subsequent assuming transferee, the value of the security measured at the time the extension is granted, is released as to the

[11] 56 S.D. 554, 229 N.W. 925 (1930).

[12] *Id.*

mortgagor and any assuming transferees. In other words, the effect of the extension agreement between the original mortgagee and the non-assuming transferee negates the suretyship relationship (guarantee) established when the property is transferred from the original mortgagor to a subsequent mortgagor. To the extent the debt owed on the mortgage, which is guaranteed by the original mortgagor and any subsequent assuming transferees, exceeds the amount of the released security (the land), the original mortgagor and any subsequent transferees are still liable as sureties (guarantees).

The ruling in this case prohibits the mortgagee and a subsequent non-assuming transferee from altering the rights and responsibilities of the original mortgage by entering into subsequent agreements. Any subsequent agreement that has the effect of increasing the original mortgagor's (and assuming transferors') risk of loss, has the effect of releasing, as a practical matter, the mortgagor to the extent of the value of the land from any claim by the mortgagee. This will deter the mortgagee from entering into any agreements with subsequent transferees without the original mortgagor's (and assuming transferors') consent.

[D]   Transfers of a Mortgage by the Mortgagor—Effect on the Mortgagee's Rights vis-a-vis the Transferee

As noted above in § 7.02[C], the mortgagee's rights vis-a-vis the original mortgagor are essentially unaffected by any transfer made by the mortgagor to a transferee. However, if a transfer is accomplished with or without the consent of the mortgagee, the mortgagee, depending upon the type of transfer agreement between the mortgagor and the transferee, may have new rights against the transferee that place him in a better remedial position than he was in before the transfer should there be a default on the underlying mortgage. The existence or nonexistence of these new rights no doubt have an effect on whether the mortgagee will consent to a transfer of the mortgaged premises with the mortgage (in other words, waive its right to accelerate the debt upon transfer) when that consent is needed to effectuate a transfer.

[1]   Transferee Takes "Subject to" the Mortgage

A transferee who takes subject to the mortgage is one who does *not* expressly agree to be bound by the terms and conditions of the mortgage. As such, the transferee who takes subject to the mortgage has an economic incentive to pay off the debt to protect his investment or equity in the premises but is not personally liable to make the payments under the mortgage agreement. If the transferee takes subject to the mortgage, the mortgagee has no personal rights against the transferee directly but can proceed against the land, which has an indirect impact on the transferee. Alternatively, the mortgagee can proceed directly against the original mortgagor on the promises and covenants contained in the mortgage. Of course, and as discussed above, if the mortgagee pursues his remedies against the mortgagor, the mortgagor is subrogated to the mortgagee's rights against the land, and the mortgagor can then proceed against the land to be reimbursed for his payment. In no event, however, when the transferee takes subject to the mortgage, will the non-assuming transferee be held personally liable for payment of the debt represented by the mortgage.

[2] The Transferee Assumes the Mortgage

The transferee assumes the mortgage by making an express promise or covenant to the original mortgagor—not the mortgagee—that she will pay the mortgage debt. In this situation, where an express promise is made to the mortgagor that the transferee will pay the debt, as discussed above, the mortgagor or beneficiary of the promise may sue the promising transferee personally for damages caused by the subsequent breach of the promise. However, the transferee has not made any express promise to the mortgagee and it would seem that the mortgagee could not gain from the promise. However, pursuant to the third party beneficiary theory, the true beneficiary of the transferee's promise to pay the debt is the mortgagee. Sometimes called the "creditor beneficiary," the "donee beneficiary," or the "incidental beneficiary" theory, the third party beneficiary theory is uniformly used to establish a "fictional" relationship between the transferee and the mortgagee to aid in enforcing the mortgagee's rights under the mortgage.

[a] Mortgagee vs. Transferee Who Assumes the Mortgage

Pursuant to third party beneficiary theory, the mortgagee may proceed directly against the assuming transferee since he is the beneficiary of the transferee's promise to the mortgagor.[13] Moreover, if successive transferees agree to assume the mortgage, all the assuming transferees may be personally liable to pay the mortgage debt should there be a breach by the transferee in possession. In this situation, the mortgagee simply picks the most solvent transferee or the "deepest pocket." Of course, if the assuming transferee sued by the mortgagee is not in possession, the assuming transferee sued by the mortgagee is subrogated, to the extent of his payment, to the rights of the mortgagee and may proceed against the transferee-grantee in possession for reimbursement.

In *Bankers Mortgage Corp. v. Jacobs*,[14] the plaintiff-mortgagee (a bank which had purchased a note secured by a mortgage from the original lender) sought to enforce its rights pursuant to the mortgage by suing the assuming transferees directly instead of first foreclosing on the mortgage and then pursuing a deficiency judgment in equity.[15] The assuming transferees objected, claiming that they could not be sued directly since there was no privity of contract between the assuming transferees and the assignee-mortgagee. The court held in favor of the plaintiff-mortgagee bank relying on a statute that allowed a third party beneficiary to sue directly the promisor of a contract that provided a benefit.

---

[13] *See* Bankers Mortgage Corp. v. Jacobs, 613 F.Supp. 1579 (U.S.D.C. E.D. Va. 1985).

[14] *Id.*

[15] *Id.*

The court's opinion is based on a theory that the mortgagee is the primary beneficiary of the assuming transferees' promise to assume the mortgage. As a result, the technical requirements of privity necessary to bring a direct action at law are superseded by statute. Although a statute was used in this case to allow the mortgagee to sue the transferees directly, one could argue that this result should occur in the absence of an express statute, given the parties' interest and intentions following a transfer in which the transferees have assumed the mortgage as opposed to taking subject to the mortgage.

As an example, suppose that A, the original mortgagor, transfers to assuming transferee B, who transfers to non-assuming transferee C, who transfers to assuming transferee D, who defaults. If the mortgagee wishes to sue D directly he may encounter some archaic, formalistic rules that prohibit him from so doing, notwithstanding D's express promise to assume the mortgage because there has been a break in the chain of promises of assumptions. The better and modern view is that by assuming the mortgage, D intended to benefit the mortgagee and should be held to that promise, irrespective of breaks in the chain of assumptions.

§ 7.03   Transfers by Vendees Who Purchased Pursuant to an ILSC

Transfers by vendees who purchase pursuant to an ILSC raise all sorts of interesting issues, of which only a few can be addressed herein. The important thing to note is that the vendee is transferring his right to possession without transferring the one thing that the mortgagor possesses that the ILSC vendee does not: title. The absence of legal title in the vendee creates unique problems which courts have had a difficult time addressing. The reason for the difficulty however, is the form of the transaction as opposed to its substance. In most states today, the ILSC is treated as nearly as possible like a mortgage and therefore the rules that apply with respect to the transfer of a mortgage by a mortgagor would seem to apply to an ILSC vendee. Thus, any attempt to limit the ILSC vendee's right to transfer her equity in the premises should be treated like a due-on clause is treated in a mortgage. Similarly, any transferee of the ILSC by a vendee should be treated like the transferee of a mortgage and the parties' rights should turn largely upon whether the transferee of the ILSC assumed or took subject to the ILSC.

[A]   Creation of Junior Mortgages by the ILSC Vendee Without the Vendor's Permission

One sort of transfer that can take place with an ILSC is the creation of a junior mortgage by the ILSC vendee. Like a mortgagor, the ILSC vendee should have a similar right to encumber his equity in the premises by placing a junior mortgage on the property. Unlike the mortgagor, the ILSC vendee does not have legal title; a fact that will be known to the junior mortgagee who undertakes a proper title search and discovers that title remains with the vendor. Nevertheless, transfers have been made by ILSC vendees and the issue of how a junior mortgagee should be treated when the ILSC vendee defaults presents significant problems.

In *Fincher v. Miles Homes of Missouri, Inc.*,[16] the Supreme Court of Missouri found that a vendee's interest in property is mortgageable even if that interest arises pursuant to an ILSC.[17] Here, the vendees had only an equitable interest in the property in question (they were in the process of paying off the first note on the property) at the time they executed a note to a third party, giving as security for that note the vendees' interest under the terms of the ILSC. The court went on to state that the third party, holding a note secured by a deed of trust, held only a security interest in the property, and was entitled to collect the amount the lien secured, and no more when the property was foreclosed on by the original vendor-mortgagee.

In *Fincher*, the court took the unorthodox approach of giving the vendor the opportunity to pay the junior mortgagee for the balance due on the mortgage when the ILSC vendee defaulted on both the ILSC and the mortgage to the junior mortgagee (the proceeds were used to build a house on the lot and the vendor and the junior mortgagee were aware at all times of the other's existence). By attempting to protect all of the parties' rights in a situation where the vendee had abandoned the property, the court created a fictional situation in which the ILSC vendor was essentially given the vendee's equity of redemption without giving the junior mortgagee an opportunity to protect his position, by redeeming from the senior mortgagee the interest that a junior mortgagee is normally allowed.[18]

[1] Treating the ILSC Like a Mortgage

If, however, the ILSC is treated like a mortgage it is relatively simple to determine the respective rights of the parties in a situation like that presented in *Fincher*. In other words, the ILSC vendor's position is analogous to and should be treated like a first mortgagee, the ILSC vendee should be treated like a mortgagor and the junior mortgagee who takes a mortgage on the ILSC vendee's equity interest in the property, should be treated like a junior or second mortgagee and their priority upon default should be determined accordingly.[19]

§ 7.04 Transfers by the Mortgagee

As noted above, the typical mortgage transaction results in two documents being executed: the promissory note and the mortgage. The entire purpose of the promissory note is to produce a negotiable instrument, governed by the rules

---

[16] 549 S.W.2d 848 (Sup. Ct. Mo. 1977).

[17] *Id.*

[18] For a discussion of the junior mortgagee's right to redeem the mortgage from a senior mortgagee, see *infra* § 8.04.

[19] For a discussion of priority and the junior lienholder, see *infra* § 8.04.

of the UCC, that is freely and easily transferable to a subsequent purchaser for value who may acquire the preferred status of a holder in due course (HIDC). Thus, quite frequently the mortgagee will transfer his interest in the mortgage, along with other mortgages, on what has come to be known as the secondary mortgage market. Through the process of discounting (discussed above), a price is established for a mortgage based on the interest rate of the mortgage, date of maturity, and current market rate. The mortgagee frequently sells his interest in those mortgages—its right to receive the monthly payments—in order to execute new, more profitable mortgages. Investors or purchasers of the mortgages on the secondary market attempt to protect their interest in the properties and in a mortgagor by purchasing title insurance. The mortgagee normally, but not always, retains the right to service the loan for a fee—usually 1% of the amount of the payment—so that the mortgagor is unaware that the mortgagee has transferred its interest in the property; payments remain payable to the original mortgagee as long as it is servicing the loan.

Assume that First Bank holds a first mortgage on Blackacre in the amount of $100,000 with an interest rate of 10%. Interest rates have risen so that a comparable investment pays 10½% interest. Moreover, First Bank is interested in obtaining additional funds so that it may make new loans at the 10½% rate. First Bank packages the mortgage along with many others and sells them on the secondary market. Since rates have risen, to achieve a yield of 10½% an investor will discount the face amount of the mortgage to reflect a yield of 10½%. To achieve that yield over the life of a typical mortgage, say 8 to 10 years to pay off, such a loan would be discounted by approximately 2½ points or $2,500 so that the loan would be sold for $97,500. Most financial institutions would not lose money on this sort of transaction because they extracted points up front which impacted the mortgagee's yield. In addition, the mortgagee retains the very lucrative right to "service" the loan by collecting the monthly payment.

[A] Federal Intervention: FNMA, GNMA, FHMC and the Secondary Mortgage Market

As a result of this process of buying and selling mortgages, a national secondary market has developed for the purchase and sale of mortgages. This national secondary market is a result of governmental efforts following the Depression of the 1930s "to facilitate the financing of residential housing, enhance the liquidity of the mortgage market and provide direct support to selected types of mortgages." As a result, three organizations were formed to accomplish the objectives noted above.

[1] Federal National Mortgage Association (FNMA)

Although now a private entity, this governmentally created organization maintains a secondary market for residential mortgages by buying and selling mortgages using the auction process.

[2]   Government National Mortgage Association (GNMA)

In addition to its special assistance function of providing housing in disaster and urban areas, GNMA, a wholly owned corporate instrumentality of the federal government, raises money for housing by selling mortgage-backed pass through investments to investors issued in certificates whose minimum denomination is $25,000. The certificates are "backed", i.e., secured, by a pool of mortgages that are insured by the Federal Housing Administration (FHA), and the monthly payment of principal and interest from the mortgages are "passed through" to the investor.

[3]   Federal Home Loan Mortgage Corporation (FHMC)

Created in 1970 as a private corporation, FHMC serves as a central credit facility or intermediary by buying and selling mortgages both on its own behalf and for investors. In addition, as a private corporation, it is supposed to shift the role of establishing a secondary market for mortgages from the government to the private sector.

[B]   Rights of the Transferee vs. the Mortgagor

However accomplished, the transfer of the mortgagee's interest in the property to a subsequent transferee raises interesting problems due to the intervention of the UCC rules and regulations governing the transfer of negotiable interests. The usual issue raised by the transfer of the mortgage from the original mortgagee to a subsequent transferee is the extent of the parties' rights and responsibilities when the mortgagor receives no actual notice of the transfer and therefore continues to pay the original mortgagee. Is the payment to the original mortgagee a defense for a claim for non-payment to the transferee who now holds the note? An answer to that question depends on the legal characterization and status of the transferee.

[1]   Holder in Due Course (HIDC)

A holder in due course is a transferee to whom a negotiable instrument has been negotiated (transferred), who pays value and has no notice of any defects in or defense to the note.[20] If the transferee meets the test, the transferee is a HIDC and takes free of so-called personal defenses, including, most importantly, the personal defense of payment. Thus, the fact that the mortgagor made payment to the original mortgagee because he had no notice of the transfer is irrelevant to a claim by a HIDC that it is entitled to be paid pursuant to the note. Payment is not a personal defense because, pursuant to the rules of the UCC, the obligor-mortgagor has the right to demand from the payee production of the note prior to payment. Failure to do so puts the mortgagor, not the transferee, at risk.

Although these rules seem rather odd when the transferee can easily give actual notice of the transfer to the mortgagor, they reflect a preference for low

---

[20] UCC § 3-302.

transaction costs and easily transferable interests. Moreover, most mortgagor's are not hurt by these business rules because the mortgagee is usually, but not always, the servicing agent of the transferee and payment to the agent of the principal raises a *real* as opposed to a *personal* defense (*real* and *personal* defenses are clearly defined in the UCC) and holders in due course *do* take subject to real defenses. Moreover, when the transferee does not employ the original mortgagee as the servicing agent, it makes good business sense to notify the mortgagor of the transfer instead of relying on a lawsuit and the legal right to payment when the lawsuit can be so easily avoided.

[a] Close-Connectedness

The transferee's status as a HIDC can be destroyed if the party challenging can show that the transferor and transferee were so closely connected or engaged in so many transactions that the knowledge of the transferor should be imputed to the transferee thus destroying its status as a party without notice of personal defenses or defects in or defense to the note.[21]

In *United States Finance Co. v. Jones*,[22] the Supreme Court of Alabama held that the purchaser of a mortgage was not a holder in due course where the original mortgagee secured the note through fraudulent means which were known, or should have been known, to the purchaser as a result of its dealings with the mortgagee.[23] The court held that the purchaser, through its agents, servants or employees had knowledge, or possession of knowledge, of facts at the time of purchase sufficient to impute knowledge of the infirmities, defects, and defenses of the mortgage to the purchaser of the note from the original mortgagee. Therefore, the court held, the purchaser was not a purchaser in good faith.

The court in *Jones* correctly took a functional and instrumentalist approach by looking to the purpose of HIDC status and by refusing to accord that "privileged" status to an entity that, although it technically complied with the requirements of a HIDC, was clearly not entitled to the benefits received by a HIDC due to its own actions.

[2] Transferee Who is Not an HIDC

A transferee who is not an HIDC takes the instrument subject to all of the obligor's defenses, real and personal, including payment to the mortgagee as long as the mortgagor has not received effective notice of the transfer. Although there is some disagreement with respect to this issue, the better view is that notice imparted solely by recording the transfer or assignment is ineffective to provide valid notice to the mortgagor based on the rationale that the cheapest cost avoider in this situation is the transferee who can give written notice to the mortgagor in possession.

---

[21] *See* United States Finance Co. v. Jones, 285 Ala. 105, 229 So.2d 495 (1969).

[22] 229 So.2d 495, 285 Ala. 185 (1969).

[23] *Id.*

As a caveat, note that mortgage notes are negotiable instruments and therefore a subsequent holder, if it qualifies in other respects, can attain the status of an HIDC. However, if the instrument is not negotiable, the holder cannot be an HIDC. One easy way to destroy the note's negotiability when it is secured by a mortgage is to expressly incorporate the terms of the mortgage into the note instead of merely referring to the fact that the note is secured by a mortgage.[24]

[3] Impact of Recording Acts

Throughout this section, we have not discussed the role that the recording acts, which are discussed in more detail in Chapter 10, play with respect to resolution of the issues addressed herein. The reason for this, is that the recording acts are largely irrelevant as a practical and a legal matter. Given the transferability of notes, pursuant to the rules of the UCC, the rules of notice required by the recording acts are largely vitiated and ignored. Similarly, in most contexts, even if notice was required to be imparted by the recording act before a valid transfer was made by the mortgagee to a transferee, such notice imparted by the record would be meaningless since most mortgagors and vendees do not check the record prior to making a payment.

In *Giorgi v. Pioneer Title Insurance Co.,*[25] an assignee of a promissory note secured by a deed of trust sued the title insurance company and the trustee named in the deed for the amount of the note, which had been disbursed to the payee by the title insurance company after the assignment.[26] The assignee alleged that even though the title insurance company did not have actual notice of the assignment of the note, it did have constructive notice because the assignee had duly recorded the transfer. In finding for the title insurance company, the Supreme Court of Nevada held that requiring "an agency. . .to run a title search before making any disbursements to a payer. . .would impose an impractical and crushing burden on such agencies."[27]

Giorgi is one of the few cases that raises the issue of whether the recording acts take priority over the rules of the UCC. In *Giorgi*, the court held that the recording act did not alter the rules of negotiable instruments and did not impart constructive notice to mortgagors that their duty to pay the mortgagee had been obviated because the mortgagee had transferred its interest in the mortgage. The transferee who was not a HIDC, alleged that since he recorded the transfer, the mortgagors' payments to the original mortgagee were ineffective. The transferee argued that mortgagors had constructive notice of the assignment or transfer of

---

[24] *See* Holly Hill Acres, Ltd. v. Charter Bank of Gainesville, 314 So.2d 209 (Fla.Dist.Ct.App. 1975).

[25] 85 Nev. 319, 454 P.2d 104 (1969).

[26] *Id.*

[27] *Id.*

the mortgage to him. The court rejected this argument stating that "the mortgage follows the rules applicable to the negotiable instrument it secures."[28]

[C] Transfers by Vendors in an ILSC

The vendee in an ILSC takes subject to all outstanding mortgages and other interests of record on the date the vendee executes the contract because the vendee should and is required to search title. However, as noted above, the vendee is not entitled to marketable title until the date set for closing, usually some 20 to 30 years later. However, the vendee can protect himself from subsequent transfers of the vendor's interest by taking possession; this imparts actual notice of the vendee's interest to any subsequent transferee. Thus, any subsequent transferee will have inquiry notice of the existence of the vendee and will take subject to the vendee's interest and is required to notify the vendee if there is a change in payment.

---

[28] *Id.*

CHAPTER

8

INVOLUNTARY TRANSFERS OF MORTGAGED PROPERTY

SYNOPSIS

§ 8.01 Introduction

A mortgagor's worst nightmare is the forced sale of her home because she cannot pay the mortgage due to a deterioration in her personal finances. Although much attention is focused on the reasons for mortgagor default, including but not limited to relevant loan-to-value ratios that are discussed *supra*, this section focuses on the mechanics of foreclosure starting with the mortgagor's default and concluding with deficiency judgments which may be awarded to the foreclosing mortgagee following the foreclosure sale.

§ 8.02 Default Prior to Foreclosure

The first step in the mortgagor's loss of her equity or her interest in Blackacre occurs when she is in default of her mortgage obligation. Although there are many ways to be in default of the obligations contained in the mortgage, the simplest and the easiest to understand is a default created by non-payment of the mortgage due to exigent financial circumstances visited upon the mortgagor. (In fact, any breach of any covenant or agreement in the standard FNMA/FHMC Uniform Mortgage gives rise to the mortgagee's default remedies.) If the mortgagor fails to make a payment on the date due in the mortgage, the mortgage is in default and the lender is given certain contractual rights to enforce the default.

[A] Curing Default

The typical mortgage will give the mortgagor a period of time, normally 30 days, within which to cure the default and "reinstate" the mortgage. If the mortgagor cures the default within the stated period, no further action may be taken by the mortgagee.

[B] Failure to Cure Default Within Stated Period—Acceleration

If the thirty days elapse and the mortgagor has not cured the default within the period, the mortgagee has the option to accelerate the debt and in so doing declare all sums immediately due and payable.

[C] Mortgagor's Rights Following Acceleration

Once the mortgagee has accelerated the debt, the mortgagor has the right to cure the default by paying off the mortgage. This will have the effect, of course, of negating the mortgage since there will be no underlying debt.

[1] Prepayment Penalties

Although rarely found in mortgages today, some mortgages contain prepayment penalties that are triggered by the acceleration clause in mortgages if the mortgage is paid off by the mortgagor. Courts have taken a harsh view of such clauses and in some states the amount of the prepayment penalty is limited to either an amount equal to some number of monthly payments (say 6) or a percentage of the amount of the indebtedness at the time it is paid off.

To enforce a prepayment clause at the same time, the lender-mortgagee alleges it has a right to restrict the mortgagor's right to transfer the property and the mortgage though the use of due-on clause strikes most commentators as an adhesion contract allowing the mortgagee to profit at the expense of the mortgagor, no matter what happens in the future. As a result, prepayment penalties have been severely criticized and their use has been curtailed.

[D] Notice of Foreclosure

Also contained in the notice of acceleration received by the defaulting mortgagor is a notice of foreclosure advising the mortgagor that if the default is not cured within the thirty day period, or if the mortgagor is unable to comply with the notice of acceleration, the mortgagor's interest in the property will be foreclosed. The foreclosure will typically be accomplished pursuant to a private power of sale contained in the mortgage.

[E] Failure to Timely Cure—Notice of Foreclosure

Although the statutes vary from state to state, a representative foreclosure process is used in California and will serve as the model for the rest of the discussion in this section. In California, the mortgagee must record a notice of default and intent to sell the property in the County Recorder's office in which the property is located. The filing of the notice of default, triggers a 90-day period during which the mortgagor can cure the default and prevent the foreclosure sale from occurring by paying the amount past due and certain fees or costs of foreclosure to the mortgagee which are designated by the statute. The past due amount, plus the fees, are normally referred to as arrearages and if the mortgagor makes timely payment of the arrearages before foreclosure, the default will be cured and the mortgage will be reinstated.

It is not in the best interests of the mortgagor to repeatedly default and cure by paying the arrearages. Aside and apart from the bad credit history that will be created, it is very costly because the fees that can be charged by the mortgagee when the mortgagor defaults are not de minimis and can be substantial in the case of a large mortgage. Moreover, in some states, the mortgagor's right to cure defaults is limited, i.e., the mortgagor may be allowed to cure defaults twice within any twelve month period. A third default that occurs within a twelve month period cannot be cured by paying arrearages but can only be cured by paying the balance due on the mortgage plus any applicable costs.

§ 8.03 The Equity of Redemption

At common law, the mortgagor and the mortgagee used a mortgage transaction that was very similar to the creation of a defeasible fee. The mortgagor would transfer title to the mortgagee upon the condition that the property would be reconveyed to the mortgagor as long as the mortgagor paid the debt by a date certain (known as "law day"). During the period before the payment of the debt, the mortgagee was entitled to possession (hence, the development of the title theory of mortgages)[1] and use of the property either to reduce the debt owed on the debt depending on how the transaction was structured. If the mortgagor failed to comply with the terms of the deed by failing to pay the debt by law day, title was irrevocably vested in the mortgagee who would be regarded by

---

[1] See supra § 6.02[[D][3].

the judges in the law courts as the absolute owner of Blackacre since the divesting condition could thenceforth never be met. However, the equity chancellor in the courts of equity had the power to allow a defaulting mortgagor to redeem his interest in the property from the mortgagee's foreclosure action by curing his default within a reasonable time after law day, as long as the mortgagor made the mortgagee whole in the process. As a result, many transactions were set aside by the equity courts and the mortgagees could not rely on the state of their title following mortgagor default because some court might later order the mortgagee to accept the mortgagor's late payment after law day to redeem the property from the mortgage. In order to prevent this from happening, mortgagees began to go to the equity court on law day to foreclose the debtor-mortgagor's equity of redemption.

[A]   Foreclosing the Mortgagor's Equity of Redemption

The mortgagor's equity of redemption is the right to cure the default of the mortgage and redeem the property in the hands of the mortgagee. Until the mortgagor's equity of redemption is foreclosed, the mortgagor has the right to cure the default by paying off the mortgage, plus interest and cost thereon. At common law, the mortgagee would bring a suit on law day or shortly thereafter detailing the mortgagor's default and requesting the mortgagor to cure the default. The court would issue a decree ordering the mortgagor to pay the debt, with interest and costs, within a certain amount of time; if the mortgagor failed to do so, the mortgagor's right to redeem was permanently forbidden. This equitable process, canceling the mortgagor's right to redeem, led to the development of the modern foreclosure practices discussed below which have had the effect of canceling the mortgagor's right to redemption and thus the mortgagor's interest in the property.

[1]   Compare Statutory Redemption

Although some speak of the process by which the mortgagor reinstates the mortgage as some form of redemption, the mortgagor's equity of redemption and reinstatement of the mortgage should not be confused with statutory redemption which can occur only *after* there has been a valid foreclosure of the mortgagor's equity of redemption.[2]

§ 8.04   Objective of Foreclosure Action

The modern foreclosure practices detailed below have one common objective: foreclosing the mortgagor's equity of redemption following default. In accomplishing this objective, the mortgagor must be given the right to redeem from the default without unduly prejudicing the rights of other parties. In addition, any system of foreclosure must adequately address and protect the interests of the mortgagee and other entities with an economic interest in the property. The

---

[2] *See infra* § 8.06.

following principle should be used to resolve all disputes involving conflicting interests in foreclosed property: *The foreclosing mortgagee is entitled to transfer, via the foreclosure process, the same quality of title it encumbered when it originally placed its mortgage on Blackacre, absent any consensual or other subsequent contractual obligations. Thus, any purchaser at a valid foreclosure sale—including the mortgagee—is entitled to purchase the title of the mortgagor as it existed the instant before the foreclosing mortgage lien was placed on Blackacre.*

[A] Treatment of Junior Lienholders—An Example

Let's assume that Able purchases Blackacre for $100,000 by paying a $20,000 deposit/downpayment to the seller and arranging for an $80,000 mortgage on First Bank on Blackacre. All prior encumbrances (mortgages) are paid off and title is conveyed to Able subject only to the first mortgage of $80,000. One year later, Able borrows $10,000 from Second Bank, which is secured by a mortgage to build an addition on to the house located on Blackacre. Two years later, Able executes a home equity loan of $15,000, which is secured by a mortgage from Third Bank, in order to purchase a new car. All mortgages are validly executed and promptly recorded. If Able defaults on all the mortgages and First Bank seeks to foreclose its mortgage first, it must properly notify all the parties with an interest in Blackacre, including Second and Third Banks whose interest in Blackacre are validly recorded, in order to give them an opportunity to bid at the foreclosure sale to protect their respective interests in the property. Failure to notify junior lienholders results in a problem known as the "omitted junior lienholder," which is discussed *infra* § 8.04[C]. When First Bank forecloses, what it offers for sale is the state of title it encumbered when it placed its mortgage on Blackacre. Hence, the purchaser at the foreclosure sale is entitled to purchase the property at the foreclosure sale free of First Bank's mortgage which is being foreclosed, and also free of any junior encumbrances including Second and Third Bank's mortgages.

Although it appears the purchaser at First Bank's foreclosure is getting a windfall, she isn't because First Bank is entitled to sell the interest in the property that it secured when it placed its mortgage on the property. First Bank's security on Blackacre was unencumbered by any other mortgage. That is what First Bank is entitled to sell; anything less would result in the ex post diminution of First Bank's security without First Bank's consent. Second and Third Bank aren't "harmed" by this chain of events because when they made their secured loans to Able on Blackacre they did so with the knowledge of First Bank's mortgage and the increased risk involved in such a loan. For this reason, it is virtually certain that each junior lienholder charged a premium in the form of higher interest to reflect the increased risk. In addition, Second and Third Bank have a right to bid in at the sale to protect their interest in the property.

[B]   Bidding at the Sale—Strategy for Junior Lienholders

A junior lienholder can protect his interest by bidding in at the foreclosure sale. As detailed below in § 8.05[A][2][b], the foreclosing mortgagor is entitled to make a credit bid up to the amount of the encumbrance at the time the foreclosure takes place. Hence, in our hypothetical example if all the amounts of the mortgages remain the same, for explanatory ease, First Bank may make a credit bid of $80,000 for the property, which it will probably do in order to protect its interest in the property. Second Bank must bid over $80,000 to obtain the property. In fact, once it comes up with the $80,000 in cash, it can use the amount of its loan to make credit bid of $10,000 for a total bid of $90,000. First Bank has no practical or legal reason to complain if Second Bank bids $90,000 and purchases the property because it had the opportunity to bid higher at the sale, and did not. First Bank has been paid off to the extent of the amount owed, $80,000, the extent of its debt and claim pursuant to the mortgage. However, to protect its interest, Third Bank must bid in excess of $90,000 in order to purchase the property—$80,000 to First Bank and $10,000 to Second Bank. Once again, however, if Third Bank is able to pay the $90,000 in cash to First and Second Bank, it can add the amount of its mortgage as a credit of $15,000 and make a total bid of $105,000. For the same reasons, Second Bank, like First Bank cannot be expected to complain if it is outbid for the property, so long as it is paid off in full.

To complete this rather lengthy hypo, let us assume all have bid as stated above, yet an outsider or stranger to the title outbids them all and pays $110,000 for the property because she believes that the property has a fair market value of $150,000. The parties are paid in the order of priority as long as there is money left to pay them. In this situation, every mortgagee can be paid in full with $5,000 remaining after all the mortgagee's have been paid off. That $5,000 belongs to the mortgagor and represents his equity in the property.

[C]   Problems Created by the Omitted Junior Lienholder

As discussed *supra* in § 8.05[B][1], if a senior lienholder, like First Bank, forecloses its mortgage when there are junior mortgages like Second and Third Bank's mortgages on Blackacre, Second and Third Bank are *necessary* parties who must be notified of the foreclosure sale in order to terminate their respective interests in the property being foreclosed. Failure to properly notify a junior lienholder of the foreclosure action creates a problem commonly referred to as the omitted junior lienholder.

Continuing our hypothetical, if we assume that First Bank is foreclosing its mortgage of $80,000, it must notify Second and Third Banks of the foreclosure sale since their respective interests could be detrimentally affected (wiped out) by the foreclosure sale. If First Bank properly notifies Third Bank but fails to properly notify Second Bank with its $10,000 mortgage of the foreclosure sale,

Second Bank becomes an omitted junior lienholder with certain rights. To clarify the issues we will assume that First Bank made a credit bid at the foreclosure sale of $80,000 and there were no other bids so that First Bank was the purchaser at the foreclosure sale and Third Bank's interest in the property as a secured lien or mortgage was properly terminated by the foreclosure action.

[1]   Third Bank vs. First Bank

In order to analyze the issues presented by the omitted junior lienholder, the parties' rights vis-a-vis each other must be analyzed separately starting with Third Bank's rights against First Bank. Remember, that Third Bank and the mortgagor, who were properly notified of the foreclosure action, no longer have any interest in the property because they each had a chance to bid at the foreclosure sale to protect their respective interests. Hence, their claims are no longer relevant to the problem. More importantly, the goal of the solutions discussed below is to put the parties in the position they would have been in had all parties been properly notified of the sale. The remedies should be judged against that standard.

[a]   Foreclosure

To protect its interest as a junior lienholder, Second Bank is given the right to foreclose its interest in the property when it is improperly or wrongfully omitted from the first sale. This gives Second Bank the right to have a sale and bid on the property. However, in order to protect the rights of all the parties, First Bank's mortgage, *in the amount of the debt at the time of foreclosure as opposed to the amount bid at the foreclosure sale,* is revived in the hands of the purchaser of the property—here, First Bank—so that the sale is made subject to the existence of a first mortgage of $80,000. That means that anyone who purchases at this subsequent foreclosure sale by Second Bank, purchases the property knowing First Bank must be paid off to the tune of $80,000 or First Bank will reforeclose.

[b]   Redemption

Second Bank also has the right to redeem the first mortgage by paying off the amount of the debt in the hands of the mortgagor-purchaser (which was its right prior to foreclosure) and thereby could compel a transfer of the now revived first mortgage to Second Bank to be added to the second mortgage. Subsequently, either or both mortgages could be foreclosed by Second Bank.

As a practical matter, neither of the rights given to Second Bank are very effective since there will probably be no bidders if Second Bank chooses to foreclose and thereby revives the first mortgage of $80,000. Moreover, the redemption right given to Second Bank requires it to come up with $80,000 in order to exercise that right—a daunting task for most second mortgagees. Finally, as discussed below, the purchaser at the foreclosure sale who now stands in two shoes, one as mortgagee of an $80,000 mortgage, the other as the purchaser of the mortgagor's equity of redemption, has rights which effectively counter those given to the omitted junior lienholder (in this case, Second Bank). This may not seem just, but on balance the junior lienholder has very few rights to begin with, even if properly notified of the foreclosure sale.

[2]   First Bank vs. Second Bank

First Bank does not have to sit idly by and allow Second Bank to take the initiative when this problem develops. It can take one of two approaches: First, it can act to eliminate the problem by taking aggressive action before Second Bank acts. Second, it can respond to and deftly counter moves made by Second Bank.

[a]   Redemption

Because First Bank was the purchaser at the foreclosure sale it purchased the mortgagor's equity of redemption. As such, it may redeem the mortgages that were placed on the property by paying them off. Hence, standing in the shoes of the purchaser, First Bank may totally eliminate this problem immediately after it is created by paying off Second Bank's mortgage.

This would be a very stupid and costly move on First Bank's part since it has other, more effective remedies which will eliminate Second Bank's lien at lesser cost. These should be used before redemption unless time is of the essence or the amount of the junior lien that is improperly omitted is de minimis.

[b]   Re-foreclosure

Having failed once to notify Second Bank, First Bank can go through foreclosure again, this time properly notifying Second Bank. If First Bank makes a credit bid of the amount of the mortgage its interest is protected because it will either be the highest bid or if First Bank is outbid for the property, it will receive the $80,000 owed it pursuant to the mortgage.

The remedies of redemption and re-foreclosure may be used by any purchaser at the foreclosure sale as defensive means to counter the actions of the omitted junior lienholder. Although complicated and confusing at first glance, if patiently worked through, problems of the omitted junior lienholder (which are too numerous to address in this text) can be resolved if one remembers and takes into account that the purchaser at the foreclosure sale not only pays off the mortgage lien and therefore stands in the shoes of the mortgagee, that purchaser also has all of the rights of the holder of the equity of redemption—the rights of the mortgagor/owner prior to foreclosure. Thus, the purchaser has two separate and distinct categories of rights which owner must be considered in resolving any problem presented by the omitted junior lienholder.

[D]   What the Purchaser Purchases at the Foreclosure Sale

It is important to recognize that what the purchaser obtains at the foreclosure sale is exactly what is being foreclosed—the mortgagor's equity of redemption.

In other words, the purchaser obtains the mortgagor's equity in the property *as it existed at the time the mortgage that is being foreclosed was executed and placed on the property.* What is being transferred, albeit involuntarily, is what was transferred as a security interest to the foreclosing mortgagee; the state of title ex ante or eo instanti before the execution of the foreclosing mortgage. Thus, in the hypothetical above, the party purchasing at the foreclosure sale obtains the title as it existed the instant before the first mortgage was placed on Blackacre. From the purchaser's prospective it doesn't matter who is paid off or in what order.

[1] Purchaser at Foreclosure Sale of Junior Lienholder

It should be apparent that if, for some strange reason, there is a default on a junior encumbrance, like the second mortgage and not the first, and Second Bank seeks to foreclose without First Bank's participation, Second Bank may do so. However, the purchaser at Second Bank's foreclosure sale gets exactly what the mortgagor had the instant before the second mortgage was placed on the property: property encumbered by a first mortgage of $80,000 but free of any other liens, including Third Bank's mortgage of $15,000.

It is rare that the junior lienholder will be the first party to foreclose for practical as well as legal reasons. Practically speaking, when the mortgagor defaults, she defaults on all the debts, from the top down so to speak. Second, as a practical matter Second Bank will be reluctant to foreclose without First Bank also foreclosing because Second Bank's likelihood of producing others to bid and purchase the property are detrimentally effected by the existence of the first mortgage on the property. Finally, in a well-drafted mortgage security instrument, First Bank will be given the right to declare a default and foreclose its mortgage if the mortgagor is in default on any of the subsequent mortgages on the property. (Moreover, given the uniformity of mortgage documents given the impact of the secondary mortgage market, essentially all mortgages contain such an "acceleration clause" allowing the mortgagee to declare an event of default.)

Although we are examining the process sequentially, it should be noted that the foreclosure process used by the mortgagee in cases of default where the mortgagor fails to cure by paying arrearages, will be governed by both public law—state rules—and, in most states, private laws—provisions set forth in the mortgage. Thus, although we are focusing on the end of the process, it must be remembered that the mortgagee's choice of method of foreclosure is inevitably influenced by its choices for foreclosure as set forth in the mortgage. Hence, the mortgage must be examined to delineate the parties' rights with respect to foreclosure.

§ 8.05 Methods of Foreclosure by Mortgagee

What follows is an analysis of the prevalent methods of foreclosure as they are presently employed in the United States, with an emphasis not only on the process, but on the interests of those effected by the foreclosure sale.

[A] Power of Sale Foreclosure

Used in about half the states, the right to conduct a private power of sale foreclosure may be given to the mortgagee in the mortgage or the deed of trust. Essentially, the mortgagee is given the power to utilize the foreclosure process without resort to the courts or any other official governmental body. Depending on the state and the process used, the property is sold to satisfy the debt owed by the mortgagor to the mortgagee at a public sale conducted by a public official, a third party, or in rare instances the mortgagee (this assumes, of course, that proper notice has been given to interested parties and the sale has been conducted properly).[3] No judge is involved in the sale.

[1] Mortgage vs. Deed of Trust

A reason for the popularity of the Deed of Trust in residential transactions is the ease by which power of sale foreclosure can be accomplished so long as the fiction of the distinction between trustee and beneficiary is maintained. The deed of trust formally interposes an alleged neutral party—the trustee—into the proceeding at the time of default and it is the *neutral trustee* who is to conduct the sale fairly, protecting the rights of both the mortgagor and mortgagee. The fact that the trustee is normally an agent of, or selected by, the mortgagee is conveniently ignored. The fiction of a neutral party convinced many judges and many states to allow power of sale foreclosure in a deed of trust even though power of sale foreclosures were forbidden when mortgages were used because they were allegedly harmful to the rights of mortgagors. This distinction is largely of historical significance and today in the states that allow power of sale foreclosure they can be obtained regardless of whether a mortgage or deed of trust is used by the parties in their transaction.

[2] Conduct of Sale

Because the private power of sale is conducted without judicial supervision it is susceptible to attack by mortgagors who may later claim that the sale was improperly conducted and is therefore void or voidable. Some of the more common challenges include defective notice given to the mortgagor,[4] including improper place of time or sale, failure to comply with statutory publication requirements to satisfy notice requirements, chilled bidding caused by wrongful actions of the mortgagee and, most importantly, inadequacy of price.[5]

---

[3] *See infra* § 8.05[A][2].

[4] *See infra* § 8.05[A][2][c].

[5] Defects in the conduct of sale as they relate to the treatment of junior lienholders, such as the omitted junior lienholder, are discussed *supra* in § 8.04[C].

[a] Inadequacy of Price

At a foreclosure sale, the property is auctioned off to the highest bidder who becomes the purchaser of the property pursuant to the foreclosure sale. Problems may arise when the winning bid for the property is well below the fair market value of the property. The courts have developed two theories to deal with this problem. The first and most prevalent approach is to analyze the process by which the foreclosure takes place and to uphold the sale, no matter what the final sales price, if the procedure or process is not subject to a valid attack. Other courts ignore the procedural niceties and focus on the price realized upon foreclosure to determine if the sales price is a price "that shocks the conscience;" if so, it may be set aside upon proper motion.

[b] The Use of Credit Bids in the Typical Sale and Chilled Bidding

Mortgagor is in default on a mortgage to First Bank which mortgage is in the amount of $75,000. The property has an assessed and fair market value of $100,000. At the foreclosure sale, which has been properly noticed and conducted, the only bidder is First Bank which bids $10.00 for the property, leaving a deficiency of $74,990.[6] Assuming there is no statutory redemption,[7] this sale will be upheld in most states as long as First Bank can prove that it complied properly with all relevant procedures. There may be no other bidders because these sales are akin to distress sales in which the market does not properly function. In addition, the foreclosing mortgagee sets the terms of the sale and normally requires all-cash, a procedure which has the effect of eliminating most non-institutional lenders (consumers) since they do not have the available cash to outbid the mortgagee. Because the mortgagee can make a "credit bid" up to the amount of the debt owed (the mortgagee has already advanced that sum to the mortgagor in the form of the original loan), most non-institutional bidders have a difficult time matching or exceeding the mortgagee's bid. Hence, in this transaction if Pat, the purchaser at the foreclosure sale, bids $11.00, First Bank would bid $12.00 and so on and so forth until it reached $75,000. If Pat bids $75,001, Pat has to pay that amount in cash, with $75,000 remitted to the bank and $1 going to the mortgagor (assuming no other mortgagees and no transaction costs incurred as a result of the sale). Plus, First Bank retains the right to bid above the amount owed, $75,000, but it only has to pay in cash the amount it bids in excess of $75,000; so, it has a "competitive" advantage at the foreclosure sale. However, if Pat doesn't show up at the foreclosure sale and there are no other bidders, First Bank can bid whatever it deems adequate, including $10.00, creating a winning bid and a whopping deficiency judgment.

---

[6] *See infra* § 8.07.

[7] *See infra* § 8.06.

Most courts would uphold the sale discussed above as long as the procedural requirements have been properly complied with and there is no evidence of chilled bidding. Chilled bidding would occur if the mortgagees agreed prior to the sale to allow First Bank to bid $10.00 and later to split the profits that would be realized upon resale of the property to a bona fide purchaser for value. Assuming there is no proof of collusive behavior leading to chilled bidding, courts take an objective view and do not inquire into the adequacy of the price. Such a procedure may provide for more efficient transactions and better bidding at the foreclosure sale because the objective test insures that as long as the parties comply with the requirements imposed by the mortgage and the statute with respect to the conduct of the sale, the purchaser at the foreclosure sale will obtain title free of any encumbrance caused by a challenge to the price.

On the other hand, courts that review the adequacy of the price obtained at the foreclosure sale may actually chill the bidding at the foreclosure sale because of the future possibility that the title received by the foreclosure sales purchaser may be voidable due to the mortgagor's subsequent attack claiming inadequate price. The end result of such a challenge, or of the opportunity to make such a challenge, may force the bid by the mortgagee to be at the amount of the debt in order to thwart any later charge of inadequate price. In this respect, the states that follow the "subjective view" and examine the price received to determine its adequacy may accomplish the same practical result that is obtained through the use of anti-deficiency legislation.[8]

[c]   Notice Requirement

There is some question on whether the mortgagor must be given actual notice of the foreclosure sale as a result of the decision in *Mullane v. Central Hanover Bank and Trust Co.*[9] *Mullane* involved the constitutional requirement that notice be given to beneficiaries of a judicial settlement of account by a trustee of a trust fund established by the banking laws of New York in a method (by mail) calculated to be successful given the information that the trustee had available (address of the beneficiaries) at the time notice was required to be given. Without going into too much detail regarding *Mullane* and its applicability to mortgages and the private power of sale foreclosure, when the address of the mortgagor is known or reasonably susceptible to discovery by the foreclosing party, anything short of notice by mail runs the risk of being constitutionally defective.

[d]   Constitutional Questions—"State Action"

Constitutional law requires that the mortgagor be given constitutionally approved notice of the foreclosure before the equity of redemption may be terminated, which may or may not include actual notice, if *state action* is found.

---

[8] *See infra* § 8.07.

[9] 339 U.S. 306, 70 S.Ct. 652, 94 L.Ed. 865 (1950).

In addition, if *state action* is found, the validity of a private foreclosure sale may be challenged on due process and other constitutional grounds. Thus, the involvement of public officials in the foreclosure process has the potential of supplying *state action*—a constitutional concept that defies coherent description and is thankfully beyond the scope of this text

In *Turner v. Blackburn*,[10] the court invalidated North Carolina's foreclosure process as violative of the constitutional right of due process because state officials were involved in the foreclosure process through the use of "upset bids".[11] A three judge federal court held that the mortgagor must be given a hearing prior to a foreclosure and sale due to the fact that a public official was given statutory authority to set aside foreclosure actions by receiving and enforcing "upset bids" or bids by certain parties identified in the statute. These bids, when made, have the effect of redeeming the property from foreclosure or transferring the property from a foreclosing mortgagee to a third party.

However, this is a rare factual situation which limits the importance of the case. Very few, if any states, have mandated procedures that require a public official to be so intimately involved in the foreclosure process when a private power of sale foreclosure is utilized. The overriding objective to use a private power of sale foreclosure is to avoid entanglement with public entities or bodies.

[3]   Collateral Attacks on the Legitimacy of the Process—Void vs. Voidable

All of the defects discussed above render the purchaser's title at the foreclosure sale voidable; thus, passing title to the purchaser may result in the transfer being set aside later due to a successful attack by the injured party, i.e., the mortgagor. Voidable defects may be cured and therefore beyond challenge, when the property is transferred to a bona fide purchaser for value. On the other hand, some defects in the sale are so significant that they render the transaction void ab initio. Thus, a foreclosure sale held subject to a forged mortgage is void and can never pass good title to a purchaser even a bona fide purchaser for value.

[B]   Judicial Foreclosure

As the name implies, judicial foreclosure is a foreclosure accomplished by resort to the judicial process, with all the attendant benefits and costs of the judicial process. The risk of many of the defects discussed above: notice, adequacy of price, due process, etc., is reduced significantly, if not totally, when judicial foreclosure of the mortgagor's interest is employed. On the other hand, the costs associated with judicial foreclosure leads most mortgagees to avoid its use when legally permissible.

---

[10] 389 F. Supp. 1250 (W.D.N.C. 1975).

[11] *Id.*

[1]   Necessary vs. Proper Parties

The only significant issue raised by judicial foreclosure that differs from private power of sale foreclosure is whether the proper parties have been notified of the foreclosure action. To handle this problem, courts have developed a rule that differentiates *"necessary"* parties, who must be notified of the judicial foreclosure action in order for it to have any validity, from *"proper"* parties who may be notified but the absence of notice to whom does not detrimentally impact the finality of the action. Essentially, a necessary party is a party whose rights will be affected by the foreclosure action. Hence, using the example discussed above in § 8.04[A], if First Bank is the foreclosing party, both Second and Third Bank are necessary parties since their respective interests in the property would be effected (negated probably) by a foreclosure of First Bank's interest. On the other hand, if Second Bank is foreclosing only on its mortgage, First Bank is a proper party which may be joined in the judicial foreclosure action to improve the resolution of the dispute, but it is not necessary to resolve the dispute since First Bank's interest is uneffected by the foreclosure of Second Bank's mortgage.

[a]   Judicial Foreclosure and Deficiency Judgments

One significant advantage to the use of judicial foreclosure over power of sale foreclosure, assuming the mortgagee has a choice, is that in some states a deficiency judgment, discussed in § 8.07, can only be obtained if judicial foreclosure is utilized. Statutes allow deficiency judgments only when judicial foreclosure is used due to a belief that deficiency judgments are appropriate only when the court or some other officer of the court assesses the property's value rather than permitting deficiency judgments when a power of sale foreclosure is used and the property's value is established by a bidder who may or may not be an interested party. In any event, in most states, the grant of a deficiency judgment subject to a judicial foreclosure is one of the advantages of the judicial process. Once the judicial foreclosure action is held, there is no need for another adjudication fixing the amount of the deficiency should a deficiency judgment be entered.

[C]   Strict Foreclosure

Largely of historical significance (it is used currently in only two states: Connecticut and Vermont), strict foreclosure is similar to judicial foreclosure in that the court processes are used to accomplish the foreclosure. However, unlike judicial foreclosure, no sale is held; the court merely grants the mortgagor a period of time to pay the mortgage debt, failure to do so within the stated time period results in the termination of the mortgagor's equity of redemption and the transfer of the property's title to the mortgagee.

[D]   Deed in Lieu of Foreclosure

To avoid the hassles and costs associated with foreclosure, especially in those states in which judicial foreclosure is the only procedure authorized for foreclosure, the mortgagee will often agree to accept a deed transferring fee simple title to Blackacre when the mortgagor is in default and cannot cure the default. The transfer of a "deed in lieu of foreclosure" will normally be upheld by courts if oppressive means are not used by the mortgagee to obtain the deed and if the mortgagor receives some consideration in exchange for the transaction. In the typical transaction, the mortgagor's consideration will be a binding promise by the mortgagee not to pursue a deficiency judgment or any other subsequent action against the mortgagor following execution and transfer of the deed in lieu of foreclosure.

[1] Clogging the Mortgagor's Equity of Redemption

To protect the mortgagor's equity of redemption, courts in equity refused to enforce agreements made contemporaneously with the execution of the mortgage which eliminate the mortgagor's equity of redemption without a foreclosure. This prohibition on the clogging of the mortgagor's equity of redemption is inapplicable to a deed in lieu of foreclosure which takes place subsequent to the execution of the mortgage and, if properly executed, is supported by new consideration.

[2] Merger Doctrine

The merger doctrine is said to apply when two legal interests in one parcel of property are held by the same entity or person. Thus, when the mortgagee obtains a deed in lieu of foreclosure, the mortgagee holds the previously encumbered fee title and concomitantly the lesser interest as a mortgagee. Pursuant to the doctrine, the smaller interest is merged into the larger interest and the mortgagee is now regarded as the owner of the property in fee simple and its mortgage interest is extinguished. Problems arise with the doctrine of merger if the mortgagee accepts a deed in lieu of foreclosure and there are junior lienholders like Second and Third Bank. Pursuant to the doctrine of merger, Second and Third Bank will argue that since First Bank's first mortgage was merged into the fee, and, as a result, Second Bank's second mortgage is now the first mortgage and Third Bank's third is now the second; thus, transforming significantly the priorities and the rights of the parties. Most courts reject the argument for merger stating that it is a doctrine of intent and that the merging mortgagee (First Bank) has no intent to have its concurrent interests work via merger to its detriment in this situation. A better approach would be to view the doctrine of merger as inapplicable when it would provide an unbargained for windfall to the junior lienholders.

[E] Installment Land Sale Contracts

As noted above in the discussion of installment land sale contracts (ILSC) as alternative financing devices in § 6.04[A], the better and emerging view is to treat vendees in ILSCs like mortgagors in all respects, including protecting their equity of redemption by requiring that their interest in the property be foreclosed by the applicable method of foreclosure in the jurisdiction in which the property is located. In those jurisdictions which ignore the practical aspects of ILSCs and treat them as executory contracts, issues raised by foreclosure are irrelevant because the vendee loses her interest in the property, pursuant to the contract, when she defaults on the contract. In this respect, one can analogize the vendee's loss of interest in the property to either strict foreclosure or a deed in lieu of foreclosure. However, unlike other foreclosure processes, no action need be taken by the vendor in order to negate the vendee's interest in the property, except perhaps action taken to remove the vendee from her possession of the property.

§ 8.06   Statutory Redemption

Not to be confused with the mortgagor's equity of redemption, statutory redemption arises, if at all, only after the mortgagor's equity of redemption has been foreclosed pursuant to a valid foreclosure process. Although the details vary from state to state, the basic structure remains the same in those states that have statutory redemption schemes (more than half the states have some sort of statutory redemption scheme): Following foreclosure, the mortgagor or an assignee of the mortgagor is given the right to redeem the foreclosed property from the foreclosure by paying the purchaser (during the redemption period) the amount the purchaser paid and not the amount of the debt. *The redemption sales price is the amount of the purchase price and not the amount of the debt.* Although periods vary, the typical redemption period appears to be one year following the date of foreclosure, although some statutes provide as little as three months and others provide as long as eighteen months. During the redemption period, the mortgagor or her successor is normally allowed to remain in possession of the property. Following the expiration of the redemption period, junior lienholders may be given rights to redeem from the foreclosure sale.

Continuing our hypothetical, if First Bank properly forecloses its mortgage via power of sale, the highest bidder will purchase the property subject to the mortgagor and junior lienholders' statutory redemption rights. If the highest bidder bids $70,000 at the foreclosure sale, the mortgagor has a year to come up with $70,000 to redeem the property from default. The fact that the mortgage was for $80,000 is irrelevant as the statutory redemption price is set by the sales price. If the mortgagor fails to redeem, the junior lienholders are normally given a much shorter period to redeem following the expiration of the mortgagor's redemption right. Thus, Second Bank may have as little as five days after the expiration of the mortgagor's right to redeem, to also redeem. Likewise, Third Bank, following the order of priority, will have the same period—here 5 days—to redeem following the expiration of Second Bank's redemption rights. During the redemption period, the mortgagor is entitled to possession of the property and its rents and profits. If none of the redemption rights are exercised, the purchaser at the foreclosure sale is entitled to remove the mortgagor from possession and the rights of the mortgagor, as well as the junior lienholders, Second and Third Bank are terminated with respect to Blackacre. If the mortgagor or a junior lienholder exercises the statutory redemption rights interesting questions are raised with respect to the effect on junior lienholders.

[A] Effect on Junior Lienholders

Although each statute must be closely examined to determine its precise effect on junior lienholders, statutory redemption may create new rights that impact rights of junior lienholders whose interest have been validly terminated through a foreclosure process. The key question is whether, and to what extent, junior liens are revived when those interests have been extinguished by a valid foreclosure and the mortgagor or a junior lienholder redeems the mortgage. Courts and statutes take varied approaches that are too numerous to detail herein. At one extreme, however, are statutes which provide that no liens are revived when the mortgagor or a junior lienholder redeems. At the other extreme are statutes that provide that all liens are revived, including the lien that was the subject of the foreclosure action to the extent that the amount realized upon foreclosure is less than the debt (the unpaid deficiency), following foreclosure by any party.

[B] Preemption by Federal Government

The Multi-family Foreclosure Act of 1981 exempts from state statutory redemption schemes federally insured mortgages on one-to-four family dwellings that are foreclosed utilizing power of sale foreclosure.[12] By statute, which preempt sale rules, the U.S. government is given statutory redemption rights on the same property when it is a foreclosed junior lienholder

In *United States v. Stadium Apartments,*[13] the court refused to recognize Idaho's post-sale redemption statute as controlling in an FHA foreclosure.[14] The court based its decision on the high cost to the government of holding the property during the redemption period. The court also emphasized the meager (in its view) value of the redemption to the debtor.

[C] Critical Economic Analysis

Statutory redemption has been criticized for a number of different reasons. Taking a very broad view, statutory redemption may raise the cost of foreclosing because it is factored into the purchaser's (i.e., the purchaser at the foreclosure sale) costs ex ante. The purchaser is aware that it may not be able to obtain the property until some period of time after default occurs, which may cause a dead weight loss for the purchaser since it is not receiving either the income, which

---

[12] *See also* United States v. Stadium Apartments, Inc., 425 F.2d 358 (9th Cir. 1970), *cert. denied,* 400 U.S. 926 (1970).

[13] *Id.*

[14] *Id.*

might be generated from the property following default, or the value of the already foreclosed mortgage on the market.

[1]   Chilled Bidding

One of the defects of statutory redemption is its impact on the bidding process that is supposed to take place upon foreclosure to insure an accurate price for the property. Statutory redemption may have the effect of chilling the bidding given that the interest purchased at a foreclosure sale subject to statutory redemption is akin to a defeasible title which is worth less than a fee simple absolute.

[2]   Waste

Although protection from waste is subject to an injunction if discovered by one with an interest in the property, including the mortgagee, the monitoring costs may be too high to allow the mortgagee to adequately protect its interest in a post-foreclosure situation with a mortgagor in possession who possesses redemption rights. On the other hand, the mortgagor who is in possession and has no intention to exercise her redemption rights, even though she may have notified the mortgagee of her election to redeem (there is no punitive sanction if the mortgagor fails to redeem as previously noticed), has little economic incentive to protect or improve the property. In fact, the mortgagor may have the opposite incentive—to remove as much value as possible during the redemption period since that value may accrue to the mortgagee.

The use of statutory redemption appears to insure that the foreclosing mortgagee bids up to the amount of the debt at the time of foreclosure, nothing more and nothing less, where the value of the property is greater than the mortgage, thus eliminating the prospect of a deficiency judgment. This is so because if the mortgagee bids less than the amount of its debt it runs the risk of losing the property and a portion of the value of the property upon foreclosure, with no, or limited, recourse against the mortgagor. There is limited incentive to bid above the amount of the debt for the reasons discussed above having to do with the mortgagor's continued possession of the premises during the redemption period. If the goal is to protect the mortgagor from the effects of inadequate bidding at the foreclosure sale, statutory redemption may promote the proper incentives.

§ 8.07   Deficiency Judgments

To understand the concept of deficiency judgment, reference must be made to the basic mortgage transaction in which both a note and a mortgage securing the debt are executed by the mortgagor. A mortgage may be foreclosed in order to pay the debt represented by the note, however, if the foreclosure action does not bring enough to satisfy the amount of the debt at the time of foreclosure, a deficiency results. Thus, if First Bank has a mortgage for $80,000 and is owed that amount at the time of foreclosure and realizes only $70,000 upon foreclosure, it is still owed $10,000 on the original debt. It may attempt to obtain this shortfall or deficiency by obtaining a deficiency judgment against the mortgagor.

[A] How Acquired

Theoretically, a mortgagee seeking a deficiency judgment should be treated similar to a judgment creditor seeking satisfaction on a debt owed to it by a debtor. In fact, in some states, how one goes about obtaining a judgment and executing that judgment against the mortgagor is a matter of debtor-creditor law. However, because of the problems created by foreclosure, and the perceived inequities of the entire foreclosure process, state legislatures have placed limits on how and when a mortgagee may obtain a deficiency judgment against a defaulting mortgagor. In many states a mortgagee can only obtain a deficiency judgment if it complies with very specific requirements. These requirements, which when satisfied entitle the mortgagee to a deficiency judgment, are listed below. The requirements are listed separately from the section on anti-deficiency legislation[15] because although these requirements make it harder to obtain a deficiency judgment, and therefore can be considered "anti-deficiency" to some degree, they do not bar deficiency judgments entirely as do some anti-deficiency legislative schemes.

[1] Procedural Limitations

Many states limit the use of deficiency judgments by placing strict procedural limits on when they may be obtained. One such limit includes allowing deficiency judgments only when a certain type of foreclosure process, typically judicial foreclosure, is used. Moreover, strict notice and time limits may be enforced to limit the applicability of deficiency judgments.

[2] One-Action Rules

Related to procedural limitations on foreclosure actions, most one-action rules require the mortgagee to obtain its deficiency judgment, if applicable, in the same action foreclosing the mortgagor's equity of redemption, thus requiring the mortgagee to use judicial foreclosure if a deficiency judgment is sought. If the deficiency judgment is not sought in the initial foreclosure action, the mortgagee waives his right to a deficiency judgment.

[3] Fair-Value Legislation

Some states limit the mortgagee's right to a deficiency judgment by limiting the amount that the mortgagee can obtain in a deficiency judgment to an amount arrived at by an independent third party based on the fair market value of the property at the time of default and foreclosure. Hence, the price realized upon foreclosure is irrelevant (actually, it is only one piece of evidence of the

---

[15] *See infra* § 8.07[B].

property's fair market value), and the only deficiency judgment which is permitted is the difference between the fair market value at the time of the foreclosure and the amount of the debt as independently determined by the judge, jury, or some other third party authorized by statute.

[B] Anti-Deficiency Legislation

Closely related to the methods discussed above, anti-deficiency legislation has been enacted in about half of the states to bar or severely limit the mortgagee's right to obtain a deficiency judgment in certain or all situations. As by-products of the Great Depression, statutory redemption and anti-deficiency legislation are reactions to the inequities of foreclosure proceedings. In passing these pro-mortgagor or debtor protection type statutes, state legislatures were concerned with what they perceived to be the plight of the defaulting mortgagor who, through no fault of his own, was losing the family homestead. As a result, the rationale supporting these statutes is premised on the view that the foreclosure rights granted the mortgagee, including the right to receive a deficiency judgment, are too oppressive and must be curtailed in certain situations. Given this goal, the California anti-deficiency judgment scheme is one of the most pervasive and analyzed anti-deficiency schemes in the country.

[1] California

The California anti-deficiency regulatory scheme has evolved over a number of years and represents the culmination of attempts to protect the mortgagor by limiting the mortgagee's foreclosure rights.[16] Although California had a one-action rule prior to 1933 requiring the mortgagee to exhaust his security before seeking a deficiency judgment against the mortgagor, that rule was largely an ineffective means of stemming the tide of deficiency judgments sought during the Depression. As a result, in 1933 California enacted fair-value legislation that limited the mortgagee's right to obtain a deficiency judgment. Concurrently, the state legislature enacted a law which barred deficiency judgments on purchase money mortgages in order to discourage sellers who financed the sale from overvaluing the security. Finally, in 1940, the legislature prohibited deficiency judgments following private power of sale foreclosures. This represented an attempt to steer mortgagees toward the use of judicial foreclosure pursuant to which a deficiency judgment can be obtained, assuming the transaction involved is not a purchase money mortgage in which the right to obtain a deficiency judgment is barred by separate legislation.

[C] Economic Analysis

Attempts to protect the mortgagor's interest in her property—her equity of redemption—from what are often perceived to be overreaching, rapacious financial institutions may seem laudable as a normative goal. However, it should

---

[16] Cornelison v. Kornbluth, 15 Cal.3d 590, 125 Cal.Rptr. 557, 542 P.2d 981 (1975).

(Matthew Bender & Co., Inc.)

be remembered that attempts to protect the mortgagor are not made without incurring a cost, and these costs must necessarily be balanced against the resulting benefits. Many studies demonstrate that the use of anti-deficiency legislation may be counterproductive, harming the very class of individuals it is designed to protect. While anti-deficiency legislation may raise the mortgagees' cost of doing business, these costs are in turn passed on to new mortgagors as part of the price of obtaining a mortgage. In addition, unduly harsh restrictions on deficiency judgments in one state may cause the mortgagors in that state to be at a "competitive disadvantage" with mortgagors in other more "mortgagee-oriented" states which raises even more complicated incentive dilemmas (i.e., mortgage funds may be more easily or cheaply available in states that freely allow deficiency judgments).

CHAPTER

9

PRIVATE TECHNIQUES OF TITLE GUARANTEE

---

§ 9.01 Introduction

The unique legal issues raised by the transfer of real property are readily apparent in the methods used to assure the status of title and ownership to individuals interested in acquiring an interest in the real property. Two different systems have developed to address the issues raised by securing title to an asset, land, that, unlike personal property, has an infinite useful life. The infinite life of real property is one aspect which gives rise to the potential for a panoply of ancient legal claims to the land which cannot be solved by recourse to simple rules to determine ownership such as the default rule in personal property that possession equals ownership. Also, the fact that real property is immobile leads to title problems that are addressed by different methods of title assurance. This section addresses one of the two private methods of title assurance which are based on agreements or contracts between the parties to a transaction. The private methods of title assurance are distinguished from public methods addressed in Chapter 10 in that no governmental body or authority is employed to guarantee title. Instead, private contractual agreements made between parties must be analyzed to determine what, if any, guarantees or assurances are given to the vendee by the vendor (or perhaps some third party) regarding the status and quality of the title of the real property being conveyed.

§ 9.02 Warranties of Title

Warranties of title are promises or covenants contained in the deed that is delivered from the vendor to the vendee on the closing date set forth in the Real Estate Purchase and Sale Contract regarding the status or quality of title being conveyed in the transaction. The contract in the typical transaction sets forth what type of deed and quality of title the vendor must convey to the vendee on the date set for closing. The type of deed will by and large determine the warranties or promises contained therein. The vendor's failure to deliver the deed called for in the contract is *nonconforming tender* which the vendee can reject depending on the rights given by the contract. If the vendee accepts the nonconforming tender, pursuant to the doctrine of merger, previously discussed in § 4.04[A], the vendee waives her rights to quality of title or the type of deed called for in the contract.

[A] Full or General Warranty Deeds

Language in the contract requiring the vendor to convey via a full or general warranty deed (or requiring the vendor to convey with full English covenants of title; used in a few Northeastern states) requires a deed containing the six covenants defined below (although in a few states the Covenants of Quiet Enjoyment and General Warranty are regarded as one, single covenant).

[1] Present Covenants That Do Not Run (The First Triad)

The first three covenants contained in the general warranty deed are the so-called present covenants which may only be breached at the instant of the conveyance from the vendor to the vendee. Since these covenants are breached at that instant, the benefits of the covenants do not run to (cannot be used by) remote grantees.

By stating that a covenant does not run to remote grantees, that is the benefit of the covenant is not impliedly transferred to a transferee of the original vendee, remote grantees or transferees cannot sue on present covenants benefitting immediate grantees or vendees even if the statute of limitations has not run to bar the cause of action.

As an example, assume that Vendor transfers fee simple title (absolute ownership) to Blackacre to vendee by full warranty deed even though the vendor has only a life estate (an estate limited to the life of the vendor). At the instant of the transfer, the vendor has breached the covenant of seisin (defined below) and the vendee may sue on that breach. However, if the vendee remains in undisturbed possession for three years and does not check the record state of title to Blackacre she may never know that she received less than she bargained for. As a result, she may transfer Blackacre to a transferee via a full warranty deed. The transferee cannot sue the original vendor on the present covenants since they are personal to the first or original vendee and are not impliedly transferred by the deed conveying title to the transferee. However, the transferee may be able to sue the original vendee on the present covenants, if any, contained in the subsequent deed from the vendee to the transferee.

[a] Covenant of Seisin

The covenant of seisin is a promise by the vendor that she is seised of (owns) the estate that she is purportedly conveying in the deed. In the example above, although the vendor has an interest in Blackacre, the covenant would be breached because she does not own a fee simple interest in Blackacre but instead owns only a life estate.

[b] Covenant of the Right to Convey

Simply stated, the covenant of the right to convey is a promise by the vendor that she has the right to convey the estate indicated in the deed. In other words, there are no legal or other impediments to the vendor's transfer of title that would later cause an otherwise effective transaction to be negated. This covenant would be breached, for example, if the vendor was a minor or subject to a guardianship with no legal power to convey her ownership interest to a buyer.

[c] Covenant Against Encumbrances

The most commonly litigated and breached covenant, a covenant against encumbrances with no exceptions limiting the vendor's promise, guarantees that there are no valid outstanding interests in Blackacre at the time of the conveyance that limit or financially diminish the value of Blackacre. Mortgages, liens, easements, and other recorded and valid unrecorded restrictions all have the effect of reducing Blackacre's value by creating an interest in someone other than the vendee and therefore cause the covenant to be breached. Municipal regulations, such as zoning, do not violate the covenant against encumbrances, but violations of applicable public regulations, like zoning, do violate the covenant against encumbrances because violations of zoning ordinances cost money to remedy.

[2] Future Covenants That Do Run (The Second Triad)

Future covenants are called future covenants because they are not breached at the instant of transfer like present covenants but they are breached, if at all, at some undetermined point in the future following the transfer. Since these future covenants touch and concern Blackacre, it is intended that they run to benefit remote grantees. Because there is privity between the vendee and her transferee, these promises "run with the land" to benefit remote grantees-transferees and therefore are transferred to remote transferees by the vendee when she transfers the property.

Although the reasons are largely historical and beyond the purview of this guide, covenants which have not been breached and which "attach to the land," are impliedly transferred with the land when the property is transferred from the vendee to the transferee. Since the promise benefits the land, it makes good sense to transfer the promise along with the land. On the other hand, if the present covenant of the remote grantor-vendor was breached at the instant of conveyance, the vendee did not have the benefit of a promise but rather a *cause of action* against the vendor which, at common law, could not be impliedly transferred from the vendee to the transferee. Hence, the largely historical distinction between present covenants that do not run and future covenants that do run with the land.

If in our above hypothetical the vendee transfers to the transferee, the transferee cannot sue on the present covenants. However, if the transferee is subsequently evicted by the remainderman 2 years after she takes possession because the life tenant-vendor has died thus terminating his life estate (and the transferee's life estate pur autre vie), the transferee may sue the vendor (actually the vendor's estate since he is dead) for breach of the covenant of quiet enjoyment—the future covenant (*see below*), as long as the action is brought within the period prescribed by the statute of limitations.

In *Brown v. Lober*,[1] plaintiffs purchased property from defendant who conveyed the property via a general warranty deed. When plaintiffs attempted to sell the subsurface rights to the property they learned that a prior-grantor had reserved a two-thirds interest in the mineral rights on the property, and so sued defendants for breach of covenant of seisin for the difference between the price plaintiffs would have received for full subsurface rights, and the price they in fact received for one-third of the subsurface rights.

The Supreme Court of Illinois found that the cause of action for breach of the covenant of seisin was barred by a ten year statute of limitations. The court held that the present covenant was breached at the moment of the conveyance of the property and not the moment the harm was discovered.

On the other hand, the court held that the covenant of quiet enjoyment—the future covenant— could not be breached until some point after the conveyance of the property. Here, however, the covenant of quiet enjoyment was found not to have been breached because no one had, as of the date of the suit, attempted to mine the property or take any other action that would effectively amount to constructive eviction.

This case demonstrates the difference between covenants that do not run and are breached, if at all, at the instant of conveyance, and covenants which can only be breached *in futuro*. Here, also, the plaintiffs bore the loss caused by their failure to search title at the time of purchase to disclose the outstanding encumbrance.

As a caveat, note that Iowa, as represented in the famous case of *Rockafellor v. Gray*,[2] has eliminated the artificial distinction between present and future covenants and hold that all covenants run with the land and are transferred to remote grantees unless expressly negated by words of the transfer.

[a]   Covenant of Quiet Enjoyment

The covenant of quiet enjoyment represents the vendor's promise that the vendee or a transferee of the vendee will not be disturbed with respect to the possession and use of Blackacre by someone with superior title.

---

[1] 389 N.E.2d 1188, 75 Ill.2d 547 (1979).

[2] 194 Iowa 1280, 191 N.W. 107 (1922).

[b]   Covenant of General Warranty

The covenant of general warranty represents the vendor's promise that the vendor will defend the vendee against claims made by anyone asserting superior title to Blackacre and will compensate the vendee for any loss suffered as a result of the assertion of superior title in a third party.

[c]   Covenant of Further Assurances

The covenant of further assurances represents the vendor's promise that subsequent to the transfer of title, he will execute any documents or do anything within his power to perfect the title conveyed to the vendee.

[B]   Special Warranty Deed

Although in a few states a Special Warranty Deed is any deed that contains some covenants but not all of the six covenants in a General Warranty Deed, as a *term of art*, a Special Warranty Deed is a deed that conveys title to Blackacre with all of the covenants, but the covenants relate only to the vendor-grantor's actions with respect to the property. In other words, the grantor-vendor is only warranting that *she* has done nothing to detrimentally affect title to Blackacre. She is not making any promises or warranties with respect to any predecessor in the chain of title.

Let's assume that a vendee discovers that the vendor of the property in question had only a life estate to convey and not the fee simple as warranted in the original deed. Assuming she chooses not to sue the vendor (perhaps he is judgment proof or in the Bahamas), she may make a transfer limiting her liability to subsequent transferees by using a special warranty deed. Pursuant to that special warranty deed, the vendee is promising that she has done nothing to detrimentally impact title and therefore cannot be sued when and if the transferee is evicted by the remainderman.

[C]   Quitclaim Deed

A Quitclaim Deed contains no warranties of title and basically transfers whatever interest the grantor-vendor owns at the time of the transfer.

If a vendor who has a life interest in Blackacre conveys his interest by using a quitclaim deed, the vendee would receive the vendor's life estate in Blackacre and would not be able to sue based on any breach of warranty because none are contained in the deed.

[D]   Practical Limitations on Effectiveness of Warranty Deeds

Although warranty deeds are widely used in most locales, their effectiveness is limited by a number of factors so that although a warranty deed provides the vendee with some rights vis-a-vis the vendor, those rights are normally regarded as secondary protection only to be used if the problem that develops is not covered by title insurance (*see below*) or other methods of title assurance.

[1] Statute of Limitations

Like any cause of action, breaches of covenants that give rise to a cause of action are limited by the applicable statute of limitations. As a result, when present covenants are breached at the time of conveyance the statute of limitations begins to run on the cause of action and may later bar the vendee's cause of action if the action is not brought within the period prescribed by statute (normally four or six years). The problem may be exacerbated if the vendee is unaware of the breach of a present covenant until the statute of limitations has expired.

[2] Damages Are Limited

The effectiveness of warranties are limited by the archaic rules that govern the maximum amount that may be recovered in the event of the breach. Generally, the vendor's liability pursuant to a warranty deed is the amount she receives from her vendee, notwithstanding the amount of damages incurred by the vendee as a result of the vendor's breach.

For example, if a vendor receives $100,000 for Blackacre and the vendee is evicted following the vendor's death when Blackacre was worth $200,000 and it would take $200,000 to buy similar property, the vendee is limited to a recovery of $100,000 even though she can show damages of $200,000. Thus, in some situations the damage amount provided by warranty deed is akin to the amount realized when the vendee seeks rescission of the agreement.

[3] The Limited Value of the Guarantee

Because in most residential transactions the warranty or guarantee is made by an individual, with limited assets and a "limited useful life" (if the warrantor dies, a claim against the testator's estate must be made within a certain time—6 months typically—to preserve the claim), the warranty or guarantee is said to be only as good as the guarantor. Thus, if the warrantor dies, goes bankrupt, or flees the jurisdiction, the value of the warranty may be nominal.

[4] The Impact of the Growth of the National Secondary Market

As discussed in Chapter 7, a national market for the sale and transfer of mortgages has developed, supported in large part by the United States government. These purchaser-investors on the secondary market care little about personal guarantees of vendees who they have never met or never will meet, and who are located in far off locales that they will never see. Thus, these investors demand guarantees of property title from institutions that they feel comfortable dealing with—title insurers. As a result, financial institutions that wish to transfer their mortgages on the national market must use title insurers even if it is not customary in the locale.[3]

Although warranty deeds are subject to denigration, they are still used in most transactions as a sort of bonding and information sharing vehicle by which the

---

[3] Johnstone, *Title Insurance*, 66 Yale L.J. 492, 502-505 (1957).

vendor conveys to the vendee relevant information about what the vendor believes to be the state of the title at the time of transfer. The vendee may not necessarily receive much when the vendor makes a transfer via a General Warranty Deed, but the vendee receives some valuable information if the vendor refuses to transfer by any device except a Quitclaim Deed (unless, of course, it is the custom of the locale).

§ 9.03 Title Insurance

The term title insurance is something of a misnomer in that title insurance is not truly insurance of the type predicated on actuarial risks of loss arising from unpredictable (in the micro sense) future events. Instead, studies show that only a small percentage of the amount of premiums received is paid out in losses (estimated to be anywhere from 4% to 10%). Furthermore, while true insurance acts prospectively protecting the insured from future harms, title insurance operates retroactively protecting the insured from events that occurred before the policy was issued. "Thus, the practical effect of a title insurance policy is to protect the insured against the effect of a title searcher's negligence. However, since the policy relieves the insured of the burden of establishing this negligence and since it relieves him of the expense of defending against claims attacking his ownership, title insurance is more advantageous than other methods of securing title."[4]

[A] Mechanics of Operation

Title insurers are normally contacted by the vendee, or the vendee's attorney, well in advance of closing in order to prepare a *preliminary title report* (PTR) which contains an opinion of the insurer as to the status of the title and an offer to insure that title for a sum stated therein. The amount of the policy depends on the face amount of the insurance. If the offer is accepted, the title insurer will issue a policy of title insurance effective the date of closing, insuring the title of the insured-vendee as described in the policy with the promise that if the title is found to be less than is represented and warranted in the policy and should a loss ensue, the insurer will make good the loss.

[B] Types of Policies

Although the policy is a matter of contract between the insurer and the insured and can take any form, exogenous pressures from institutional lenders and from the government has precipitated the use of standardized national forms promulgated by the American Land Title Association (ALTA). There are two basic types of policies issued by title insurers.

---

[4] Note, *The Title Insurance Industry and Governmental Regulation*, 53 Va.L.Rev. 1523, 1525-25 (1967).

[1]   Mortgagee or Lender Policy

The mortgagee or lender policy is purchased by the vendee, and is usually required by the lending institution as a precondition to making the loan to finance the purchase of the premises. The policy insures the lender *alone* against any losses that might occur if the quality of title should be less than that insured in the policy. As the amount of the mortgage decreases, the actual coverage provided by the policy also decreases so that if and when the mortgage is paid off, the insurance policy is also nullified.

[2]   Owner's Policy

The standard owner's policy protects both the vendee's interest in the premises and the mortgagee's interest up to the amount of the policy if a loss should occur as a result of the status of the title being less than that warranted in the policy. There are two types of owner's policies: Form A and Form B. The two policies are identical except that Form A does not insure against unmarketability of title and excludes from coverage, "[t]he refusal of any person to purchase, lease or lend money on the estate or interest covered hereby in the and described in Schedule A."

In most states, the bulk of the premium paid to purchase the policy goes toward the title-searching function of the title insurer. As a result, the portion that is actually used to fund the actuarial risk of loss is quite small. Hence, increasing the coverage of the policy to cover not only the mortgagee but the vendee's interest usually involves only an incremental amount. Thus, the owner's policy, which protects both the mortgagee and the vendee, is usually a better buy given the circumstances.

[C]   Scope of Coverage—Exceptions

Using the preferred ALTA Form B policy, title insurers state that the title insured is vested in _____ (name of vendee), subject to certain standard and enumerated exceptions, and, should title fail or be defective for reasons not excepted in the standard and enumerated exceptions and covered by the policy, the insurer will be held liable for the amount of the loss occasioned by the defective title. Thus, to understand the scope of coverage one must first start with the exceptions to coverage.

[1]   Government Regulations

All governmental regulations (which are a matter of public record) that affect the title to Blackacre are excluded from coverage. Also excluded from coverage (although set out separately as paragraph 2 of the policy) are claims arising from eminent domain or other exercise of the governmental rights of police power, unless the notice of the exercise of such rights is validly recorded. In other words, the actions of governmental entities that affect the value of the property are not covered by title insurance except unless the notice has been filed of record and the title insurer negligently fails to disclose the prior recorded interest.

[2]   Paragraph 3 Exceptions

Paragraph 3 of the standard policy excepts from coverage defects: (i) created by the vendee; (ii) known to the vendee but not known to the insurer; (iii) that occur or attach to title after the issue date of the policy (mechanics liens); and (iv) that would not have created a loss if the vendee had paid value for the property (thus, eliminating from coverage any claims that arise if the vendee, as a donee, is not entitled to protection pursuant to the state's recording act because the donee-vendee did not pay value).[5]

[3]   Standard Exceptions

In addition to the exceptions discussed above, there are four standard exceptions that void coverage. No coverage is provided if a loss occurs as a result of: (i) superior rights of parties in possession; (ii) easement rights not shown by public records; (iii) anything that an accurate survey or inspection would reveal; and (iv) any lien for services not shown by the public record (liens that arise as matter of law like mechanics liens).

[4]   Special Exceptions

This is the most important paragraph to the vendee because it lists all the matters of record that may make title defective which the title insurer discovered during its title search. Thus, if the title insurer discovered an ancient mortgage or easement on Blackacre that is validly filed in the record, the title insurer will list this as a special exception which the policy does not insure against loss or damage. All other matters of record that affect title to Blackacre should similarly be listed in the "Special Exceptions" section of the policy. Thus, if a matter affecting title that causes loss or damage is validly recorded and is not covered by one of the exceptions, the title insurer is liable for that loss and damage. It is in the title insurers best interest therefore to list as many of these special exceptions as needed to narrow the applicable coverage.

[D]   Title Plant

The title insurer insures based on its search of the public records of instruments filed in the County Recorder's Office and elsewhere that effect the title to the property being searched. Although title insurers initially searched the public records mechanically at the archives or other depositories of the documents, in most large cities today title insurers have either pooled their resources or have independently established their own title plants. These private title plants duplicate, to a degree, the functions of public records by copying, reorganizing, and filing the instruments that affect title to property within the title plant itself.

---

[5] For a discussion of the donee exception to recording acts, see *infra* § 10.04[A].

[1] Efficiency

Private title plants are maintained by title insurers because they provide the insurer with efficient access to the documents affecting title to the property which is not the case when the archives are maintained by the public fisc. Also, private title plants are frequently computerized by tract and lot number where public records are usually not so efficiently organized.

[E] Scope of Coverage—Analysis

It may seem odd to pay for a policy which lists exceptions to coverage in an effort to preclude paying on the policy, but such is the basis for the multi-billion dollar business that is title insurance. (Can you imagine paying for automobile insurance that pays only if you don't get into an accident?) The nature of title insurance is such that what the insured is really purchasing is reliable and guaranteed information about the status of the title to the property. The vendee-insured gets what he pays the bulk of his policy amount for: a title search disclosing all of the information regarding record title to the property. Hence, if there exists an encumbrance effecting title to the property that is validly recorded but not shown as an exception in the policy in the "Special Exceptions" section, the odds are more than likely that a loss will ensue and a claim will be filed by, and paid to, the vendee. If you analyze the exceptions closely, a pattern develops: those facts within the purview or knowledge of the insured-vendee, which are not covered, are listed as exceptions to coverage, those things that are covered by the recording acts, i.e., must be filed in the County Recorder's Office in order to affect title to Blackacre, are not listed as exceptions and are covered by the typical policy unless otherwise specially excepted. Once that information is disclosed to the vendee, either in the PTR or the Final Title Report, the vendee can determine whether the vendor is delivering the quality of title required by the contract and act accordingly.

[F] Insurer's Liability for Negligent Search

One of the interesting issues raised by title insurance is whether the insurer is liable when it conducts a negligent search which the insured relies on in purchasing the property, causing a loss due to a defect which is not covered by the policy because it falls within one of the enumerated exceptions. For example in *Horn v. Lawyers Title Insurance Corp.*,[6] the title insurer searched title and failed to discover a validly recorded deed vesting a portion of the land in a third party. As a result, the vendee purchased the property and only discovered later that a portion of the property was owned by a third party. When the insured sued the insurer, the insurer defended on the ground that the third party was in possession of the property (the property was an 116,000 acre tract and the third party was occupying a small portion of the tract and his occupancy was not easily

---

[6] 89 N.M. 709, 557 P.2d 206, 94 A.L.R.3d 1182 (1976).

apparent), and therefore the claim arising from the third party was not covered by the policy because occupancy was listed in the policy as an exception to coverage.[7] The insurer prevailed based on his defense that the policy did not impose a duty on the insurer to provide the insured with a perfect or negligence-free search. The court strictly construed the policy and held that the exception provision controlled.

In *Horn v. Lawyers Title Insurance Corp.*,[8] the Supreme Court of New Mexico held that a title insurer was not liable to its insured where the terms of the insurance agreement explicitly excluded from coverage damage caused by occupancies of parties in actual possession. Here, a third party, unknown to the insurer and the insured, was in possession of a minuscule portion of the property (in relation to the size of the entire parcel) which the insured had purchased. A search of the records by the insurance company failed to discover the adverse title, although the instruments showing title had been duly recorded and would have been discovered by a non-negligent search. The court held that any search undertaken by the title insurance company was solely for its own protection as indemnitor against losses covered by its policy and therefore it could not be held liable for damage done to the insured.

Horn has been severely criticized for narrowly construing the function of title insurance and ignoring the realities of the business. A negligent search of the records, it is alleged, should *not* be excused merely because the title insurance company is fortunate enough to have an exception in the policy that "covers" its negligent actions when the primary purpose of purchasing title insurance is obtaining a valid, non-negligent title search. What the insured is normally understood to be purchasing is the insurer's search of the record and a listing of those matters that affect title. The opinion in *Horn* does not reflect the parties' intention as such.

[G] Transferability

Title insurance policies are not transferable to subsequent vendees of the property thereby necessitating a new policy for each subsequent transfer of the property no matter how soon the subsequent transfer occurs following the initial issuance of the policy. As a practical matter, most policies terminate when the insured transfers her interest in the property to a subsequent vendee.

Although the policy is not transferable to a subsequent vendee, it is incorrect to consider the policy terminated upon the vendee-insured transfer of the subject property. Pursuant to the terms of the policy, the insurer must defend the insured against any claims that arise as a result of defects in title covered by the policy—including claims that may be brought by a subsequent purchaser against the vendee for defects of title as long as they are brought within the period allowed

---

[7] *See supra* § 9.03[C][3].

[8] 557 P.2d 206, 89 N.M. 709 (1976).

by the statute of limitations. In this limited respect, the vendee is protected for a period of time following her transfer of property from claims brought against her as a result of covered defects.

§ 9.04   Abstracts and Abstracter Liability

Abstracts are title reports prepared by a title examiner (who may or may not be an attorney) following a search of the public records which summarizes the transfers made of the subject property and all other matters or interests that effect title to the property. The abstract will also contain the abstracter's certification regarding the period of coverage and the records searched by the abstracter. An attorney will then examine the abstract and render a written opinion regarding the status of title. Most importantly, the attorney guarantees the status of title.

[A]   Use of Abstracts

In certain locales, abstracts are used in conjunction with title insurance when the title insurer does not have a title plant, or the resources to search the record personally and relies on the abstracter's opinion in issuing a title policy. However, because of the nationalization of the secondary market for mortgages and the need for title insurance, the use of abstracts is subsiding.

[B]   Abstract vs. Title Insurance

The major negative involved in using an abstract as compared to a title insurance policy is that the abstracter's liability and the attorney's liability, if applicable, are limited to the extent of the abstracter's solvency. In other words, like warranties of title,[9] the abstracter's guarantee is only as good as the abstracter. The major advantage of an abstract is that it may be cheaper than a title insurance policy if what is being purchased by the vendee is information regarding the status of title and not the insignificant (statistically) actuarial risk of loss that is provided by a title insurance policy. In addition, unlike title insurance policies, abstracts can be used again and again when the property is transferred by the vendee to subsequent vendees. Usually the abstracter will charge a nominal fee to update the abstract to reflect transfers and interest that occurred subsequent to the issuance of the initial abstract.

[C]   Abstracter Liability

It is customary in many states for the abstract to be paid for by the seller of the property and to be provided to the buying vendee. Hence, there is a privity problem should a defective abstract result in the injured vendee suing the abstracter. Because no contractual relationship exists between the vendee and the abstracter, contract based claims are normally denied even though it is apparent that the vendee is the party relying on the abstract. As a result, a number of courts have allowed abstracter liability in tort for negligent misrepresentation

---

[9] *See supra* § 9.02.

to avoid the problems created by the artificial privity requirement. [10] Similarly, courts have avoided the statute of limitations bar by holding that the statute begins to run when the injury occurs and not when the abstract is prepared and issued. [11]

In *Williams v. Polgar*, [12] the Supreme Court of Michigan faced the question of whether a faulty abstracter should be liable to a buyer whom the abstracter should have foreseen would rely on the abstract. As is the custom and norm in most communities, the seller here contracted with the abstracter for the policy and provided the policy and abstract of title to the buyer. The abstract failed to include a prior, duly recorded deed. The plaintiff did not learn of the prior deed, which conveyed the property to the county board of road commissioners, until after the execution of the land contract with the defendants.

The court found in favor of the buyers, affirming the elimination of the privity requirement in Michigan. Further, the court held that a title abstracter may be found liable in cases where a third party relies to his detriment on the services of the abstracter, regardless of whether the abstracter had actual knowledge of the reliance. Unlike *Horn*, [13] the court here looked beyond the form of the transaction to its substance to correctly decide the issue.

[D]   Attorney Liability

Attorneys who search title and provide abstracts or opinion letters regarding the status of title are held to the traditional negligence standard of reasonable care and skill in the performance of their duties. Reasonable care in this situation is measured against the custom and practices of the attorneys in the locale in which the property is located. In addition, Title Standards have developed to assist attorneys in the preparation of the abstract or title opinion and a violation of those standards may be prima facie evidence of a negligent search. [14]

---

[10] *See* Williams v. Polgar, 391 Mich. 6, 215 N.W.2d 149 (1974).

[11] *Id.*

[12] *Id.*

[13] 557 P.2d 206, 89 N.M. 709 (1976)

[14] For a discussion of Title Standards, see *infra* § 10.07[C].

CHAPTER

10

PUBLIC TECHNIQUES OF TITLE GUARANTEE

---

§ 10.01 Introduction

In order to be able to transfer title and ownership of real property to a vendee the vendor must establish his ownership interest in the subject parcel with some degree of certainty. Numerous methods of title assurance have developed to provide the purchaser with some evidence that the vendor selling the real property is actually the true owner. This section describes the "public" techniques of title guarantee or assurance. Public techniques of title assurance differ from private techniques in that a governmental entity or body is relied upon to determine the ownership interest of real property and statutes are consulted to verify the status of the title being transferred.

§ 10.02 The Recording Acts—English View

In England at common law, the "first-in-time rule" operated to determine the ownership of land. Each landowner kept in a secure location documents or muniments of title designed to prove that he was the owner of the parcel being sold. If such proof was satisfactory to the vendee, the real estate and the documents evidencing title were transferred to the vendee by the vendor. Public records were not consulted to determine the actual owner of the real property sold. Once the land was transferred by the vendor, he had nothing left to convey to a subsequent purchaser-vendee, having previously conveyed his interest to the first purchaser-vendee. Therefore, no subsequent vendee could take an interest in the property from the original vendor via a subsequent transfer. According to the "first-in-time" rule, the first purchaser from the true owner of the property takes title to the property and can successfully defend his title against any subsequent purchaser-vendee.

§ 10.03 The Recording Acts—American Developments

Relying on muniments of title presented by the vendor proved to be unsatisfactory to American vendees. As a result, every jurisdiction has enacted a statute that allows all documents affecting title to property to be recorded in the county in which the property is located (if the property is located in two or more counties, the documents must also be recorded in multiple counties). In a typical transaction, before purchasing the property, the vendee verifies the seller's ownership interest in the property, by undertaking a title search.[1] More importantly, if the title search is done correctly, the vendee can rely on the state of the title as revealed in the County Recorder's Office (where documents are filed and archived) and prevail against a prior vendee who at common law, under the common law first-in-time rule, would be recognized as the owner of the property. To change the priorities established by the first-in-time doctrine, the vendee seeking to avoid the operation of the first-in-time rule must strictly comply with the recording act recognized in the jurisdiction in which the property is located. There are three different types of statutes used to protect vendees who rely on the record state of title: race, notice, and race-notice statutes.

[A] Race Statutes

In the two remaining Race jurisdictions, North Carolina and Louisiana, the putative vendee can rely entirely on the record state of title to establish his ownership in the property. In other words, if the record shows title is held by A, free and clear of any prior recorded claims, B can purchase the property even if he is aware of the fact (has "actual knowledge") that A had previously sold the property to X. If X failed to record the proper documentation to prove his interest in the property, X will lose to B even if B has actual knowledge of X's claim *as long as B records his interest in the property first.* (How can B have actual knowledge of X's claim? Perhaps he is told of X's claim by A or, better yet, X is in possession of the property.) The priority of X and B's claim to the property will be determined by who wins the "race" to record documentation of interest in the property. If X loses the race to the County Recorder's Office, X may have a claim of unjust enrichment against A.[2] Thus, B must record first to protect his interest against prior vendees of the property *and* subsequent vendees of the property from A. If both B and X fail to record their interest in the property, A remains the record owner and may make other transfers jeopardizing both B and X's interest in the property. If B loses the race, he may have a claim against A based on the covenants of title contained in the deed from A to B.[3]

[1] Rationale

Although the Race statute seems somewhat unfair, its value lies in its efficiency. Because it limits inquiry to matters of record only and does not require the subsequent purchaser to establish that he took title without notice or in good faith, some commentators feel that it is the most efficient and preferable statute.

---

[1] *See infra* § 10.05.

[2] *See* Patterson v. Bryant, 216 N.C. 550, 5 S.E. 2d 849 (1939).

[3] *See supra* § 9.02.

Moreover, X in our example is not viewed as the "innocent" purchaser, but the party who could have prevented the harm (the cheapest cost-avoider) by recording his interest in the property immediately upon acquisition. As a practical matter, note that a race statute can be distinguished from other types of statutes because nowhere does it mention the word "notice."

[B]   Notice Statutes

On the other hand, Notice statutes, utilized in about half the remaining states (more than twenty jurisdictions), focus on the record notice imparted to the punitive vendee by the filing of documents in the County Recorder's Office, *and the subjective actual knowledge of the prospective vendee* in determining the owner of property. In Notice jurisdictions, the vendee claiming protection pursuant to the Recording Act (in other words, attempting to avoid the result created by the common law's first-in-time rule) must show that he relied on the record state of title *and had no notice, actual or inquiry, of any other ownership claim at the time the subsequent vendee purchased the interest in the property.*

In our hypothetical, in order for B to prevail against X in a Notice jurisdiction, all B must do is prove that he had no notice of X's claim at the time he purchased or gave value for A's interest. If X had properly recorded his claim before B paid A, B would have record or constructive (synonymous terms) notice of X's claim. If A told B of X's claim, B would have actual notice. If X was living on the property at the time that B gave value, B would have inquiry notice (B would be charged with the knowledge of X's interest in the property). In all three cases of notice, B cannot take protection pursuant to the Recording Act and will lose to X.

Take notice that B does not have to record first to prevail against X. The only salient fact in a Notice jurisdiction is that B had no notice of X's adverse claim at the time he purchased or gave value for his interest in the property. However, B does have some practical incentive to record and should be advised to do so as quickly as possible. If B fails to record, he empowers A to make a subsequent transfer to a subsequent bona fide purchaser without notice of B's claim. B will prevail against X because B is a subsequent purchaser for value without notice of X's claim, however, he can lose to a subsequent vendee—C—if C can prove that he was a subsequent purchaser without notice of B's claim.

Notice statutes are preferred over Race statutes because they reward the good faith purchaser-vendee and penalize the knowing wrongdoer instead of allowing a knowing wrongdoer to profit by winning the race to record first.

[1]   Short Comings of Notice Systems

Notice statutes are frequently criticized because they make the recording system less efficient by requiring the parties to resort to off-the-record matters to establish their claims to the property. In addition, unlike Race-Notice statutes, the subsequent purchaser-vendee does not have to record in order to prevail against a prior purchaser-vendee who failed to record timely. As a practical matter, note that notice statutes are easy to spot because the statute will contain language focusing on the actual notice of the claimant and will not require the claimant's claim to be "first duly recorded."

[C]   Race-Notice Statutes

These hybrid statutes, combining the attractive features of the Race and Notice statutes, are used in about half the jurisdictions. In order to prevail in Race-Notice jurisdictions, B must have no notice of X's claim *and must first duly record his interest to prevail against X.* That is, B must satisfy *both* requirements to avoid the common law rule of first-in-time.

[1]   Inquiry Notice

Inquiry notice is defined as that notice imparted by a given state of facts that would put a reasonable person on notice that further inquiry is warranted. The subsequent purchaser will be charged with notice of facts that are revealed had the purchaser-vendee undertaken the inquiry. As with actual notice, the standard is not totally subjective. Instead, the appropriate standard is what the reasonable hypothetical purchaser knew, or should have known, from the state of affairs that gave rise to the controversy. Race-Notice statutes are easily identified because they discuss the state of knowledge of the claimant and require that his interest in the property be first duly recorded.

§ 10.04   Caveats Applicable to All Recording Statutes

Although there are three different types of recording acts used in the United States, the fact that they all derive from the same source does provide some common problems and uniform rules.

[A]   Purchaser for Value

To qualify for protection pursuant to most, if not all, recording acts, the vendee must show that he gave value/consideration for the property that is the subject of the dispute. That is, donees are not protected by recording acts.

[1]   Measuring Value

What constitutes "value" is an extremely difficult determination and is a question of fact handled differently by different jurisdictions. Some jurisdictions inquire into the adequacy of consideration by comparing the sales price to the fair market value of the property. Other jurisdictions, make no inquiry into the adequacy of consideration as long as some consideration, even a nominal amount—a dollar or ten dollars in some cases—is paid and stated in the deed transferring the property.

[2]   Timing of Value

Whatever standard the jurisdiction uses, all jurisdictions agree that the value must be transferred contemporaneously with the transaction in order for it to count as consideration. A new mortgage or other interest in real property given to Baker by Abel to secure a pre-existing debt owed to Baker by Abel is not considered valuable consideration. Instead of giving up something of value to receive an interest in the property in this case, Baker has improved his position by taking a security interest in property for an unsecured debt that has already been incurred.[4] However, compare the situation where Baker takes a deed in full satisfaction of a preexisting debt. By cancelling the debt and by foregoing any collection processes available, including but not limited to, reducing the debt to a judgment through litigation, Baker has changed his position—given value—by foregoing valuable legal rights and by accepting the deed in full satisfaction of the debt.[5]

In *Gabel v. Drewrys Limited, U.S.A., Inc.,* the plaintiff held a prior duly executed (but unrecorded) mortgage on a third party's property which it failed to record until after the defendant in the case recorded its mortgage on the same property.[6] Hence, the plaintiff was second in priority according to the recording acts, but first in priority under the common law first-in-time-rule. Thus, the only way plaintiff could prevail would be to preclude the defendant from taking protection pursuant to the Recording Act—Race Notice—in this case. Because the defendant, at the time it executed the subsequent mortgage, agreed to forebear suit against the third party, the defendant claimed it was a bona fide purchaser for value and as such held a superior claim to the property than the plaintiff (should be protected under the Recording Act). The Supreme Court of Florida, however, held that because the defendant did not fix a definite period of forbearance at the time it executed the mortgage ("there was no specific date fixed"), the defendant had extended no consideration and as such was not considered a bona fide purchaser (not protected under the Recording Act), but merely a debtor whose rights were secondary to those of the plaintiff.

[B]   Forgery

The Recording Acts do not protect a purchaser if his title is based on a forgery in the chain of title. Thus, if Abel acquires his interest in the property by forging his name as grantee to a deed from Owen, the true owner, any subsequent transfer from Abel to a bona fide purchaser for value is invalid. Even if Abel records his deed and appears to be the record owner, as long as Owen has done nothing to assist or aid in his scheme to forge Owen's signature to the deed and is in no way party to the transaction, a purchaser in these circumstances cannot acquire

---

[4] *See* Gabel v. Drewrys Ltd., U.S.A., Inc., 68 So. 2d 373 (Fla. 1953).

[5] *See* R. Cunningham, Stoebuck & Whitman, The Law of Property § 11.10, at 786 (1984).

[6] 68 So.2d 372 (1953).

title to the property. Professor Rabin has described it as follows: The recording acts protect vendors from unrecorded deeds that are good without resort to the recording act. Recording acts do *not* make a prior bad act good, i.e. a forged deed, although they will make good a subsequent deed which is considered bad only because it occurs later.

[1]   Rationale

In the above situation where Owen is blameless, there is nothing Owen can do to prevent the harm from occurring in a subsequent transfer. If Owen is not in possession, which would provide inquiry notice in Notice and Race-Notice jurisdictions, there is nothing short of Owen's checking the record periodically to prevent the perpetration of the forgery. Clearly, this is a heavy burden to place on Owen and one which creates an inefficient result. On the other hand, Baker, our purchaser from Abel, has in some sense selected Abel and chosen to deal with Abel voluntarily and is in the best position to police or monitor both Abel and the transaction to insure that he is not defrauded. Hence, as between two relatively innocent parties, it is best to place the risk of loss due to forgery on Baker who has chosen to deal with Abel voluntarily.

[a]   Title Insurance

As a practical matter, Baker or any purchaser can protect his interest from loss due to forged instruments by purchasing Title Insurance.[7]

[C]   Fraud

Deeds fraudulently procured from the true owner, Owen, by the miscreant, Abel, and subsequently introduced into the stream of commerce by Abel through a sale of the property to a bona fide purchaser for value without notice of the fraud, present a slightly more vexing problem. Although a forged deed is *void ab initio* and is not capable of transferring an interest to anyone, a deed procured by fraud is only *voidable*. Hence, if title is acquired to a voidable deed by a bona fide purchaser for value, it is valid against the owner and a court will not honor the true owner's request to nullify the transaction.

[1]   Rationale

This rule makes sense when compared to forged deeds because deeds are introduced into the stream of commerce by the owner and it is the owner who is capable of being diligent either in the selection of a vendee or in policing the transaction. Complicating matters slightly is the distinction that some courts make between fraud in the inducement and fraud in factum. Taking the former first, almost all jurisdictions hold that when the owner is induced to part with title based on misrepresentations made by the defrauder—such as if the defrauder promises to pay the purchase price later—the deed is voidable and so can

---

[7] *See supra* § 9.03.

(Matthew Bender & Co., Inc.)

ultimately pass good title if transferred to a bona fide purchaser for value. Proving the maxim that hard cases make bad law, a number of courts have held, however, that in certain situations, involving what is termed "fraud in factum"—e.g., an illiterate owner signs a piece of paper deeding the property to the defrauder while believing he is signing something else—the deed is void because the deed is considered forged and therefore cannot pass good title to a bona fide purchaser for value.[8] The key problem is deciding into which category cases fall and where one draws the line between the categories.

In *Houston v. Mentelos*,[9] the defendant acquired property from the elderly plaintiff through fraud and misrepresentation. The defendant then executed a promissory note and a mortgage deed on the property to a third party. At all times the plaintiff remained in possession. The third party, before disbursing money to the defendant in exchange for the instruments, paid monies to various parties to release existing liens on the property. The court decided that the warranty deed from the plaintiff to the defendant was void, and not voidable, as the trial court concluded. The court held that because the defendant obtained the property through fraud and because there was no negligence or inattention on the part of the plaintiff, the transaction did not operate to pass title to the defendant and, subsequently, the third party. As a result, the third party mortgagee acquired no lien on the property executed by the defendant and title to the property remained with the plaintiff. The court did, however, grant the third party an equitable lien for the amount of plaintiff's property equal to the amount the third party had paid to release the prior liens on the land.

This case demonstrates the inherent difficulty in determining whether a transferred deed is void or voidable once in the hands of a bona fide purchaser for value. Here, the court equated misrepresentations inducing the grantor to sign the deed with fraud and treated the fraudulently induced deed as a forged deed.

One rule of thumb used to determine whether the deed is considered void or voidable is the extent of the harm to the defrauded owner. The harder the case, the more likely it appears that the court will rule that the deed should be treated like a forged deed—fraud in factum—and therefore void. A balancing of the equities to protect the defrauded owner may appeal to the courts' equitable instincts but at a cost to bona fide purchasers and the efficient functioning of the recording system.

§ 10.05   Title Search

To comprehend how a record chain of title is constructed and how the recording acts work, a basic understanding of the process by which title is searched is mandatory. There are two methods used to search title which depend on the

---

[8] *See* Houston v. Mentelos, 318 So. 2d 427 (Fla. App. 1975).

[9] 318 So.2d 427 (1975).

method used to record documents in the public office in which land records are kept and maintained (normally the County Recorder). The first and by far most prevalent method of maintaining these records for inspection is the grantor-grantee index which reveals a chain of title to the property being searched. The second and more efficient method is the tract index, which includes a list of all documents related to a particular tract of land, and is normally computerized.

[A] Grantor-Grantee Index

As noted above, the safest method for securing one's title to property, irrespective of the recording act that is in place, is to first search the record to determine that the vendor is the record owner of the property and then to record promptly the deed transferred from that vendor in order to ensure that the vendee is the record owner of the property. This procedure protects the vendee's interest in the property from prior and subsequent claimants to the property. In order to search the record, the vendee must be able to find the precise documents that affect title to the property that the vendee is purchasing. In states without a tract index, the Grantor-Grantee Index is used to file the documents in a fashion so that they are retrievable by one interested in the status of title to a particular piece of property. Unlike the tract index, however, the documents are not organized by reference to the parcel or land. Instead, the index is organized by grantors and grantees who have previously owned or allegedly owned some interest in the subject property.

[1] Mechanics

When an instrument affecting title to property is taken to the County Recorder's Office for recordation, it is filed away pursuant to a system which varies widely (some of the states now use microfiche, others use drawers and have a system like a library). The thing to remember is that whatever the filing system, the individual searching title cannot physically look through or examine all of the documents filed of record to discover only those documents that affect title to the vendor's land. Thus, the documents are indexed in large volumes or folios that the searcher uses to identify those documents she needs to examine to search title. Once the documents are identified, either original documents or copies are extracted from the files and examined by the searcher. To identify the document, a summary is placed in two indexes or indices: the Grantor Index and the Grantee Index. The Grantor Index is organized alphabetically by the name of the grantor, lists the grantee, the type of instrument or interest created in the property by the document and, finally, where the actual document can be found in the files. The volumes are maintained chronologically and periodically the volumes are consolidated into decennial volumes. For example, there may be an A-C volume for the year 1988, 1987, 1986, etc., and A-C, January 1, 1970-December 31, 1979. Conversely, the Grantee Index is organized alphabetically by the name of the grantee and contains the same descriptive information as the Grantor index.

[2] Objective of Search

The objective of a search of title is to prove that the vendor is the owner of the property or interest she is attempting to convey. In order to do that, it is necessary to show the manner in which that individual purchased or acquired title. After that has been established, the title searchers must continue to search title under the applicable owner's name to insure that the putative vendor has made no detrimental transfers or created any unacceptable encumbrances on Blackacre.

[3] Using the Grantor Index

The searcher starts with the assumption that the vendor is the owner of the land and possesses an interest that can be granted or transferred to another. Hence, the vendor's name will be searched in the Grantor's Index to insure that during the period of her ownership she has made no transfer of the type described above.

[4] Using the Grantee Index

Having discovered no disqualifying transfers that would defeat the vendor's ownership interest or that would impede the sale, the searcher must next ascertain how the vendor acquired her title. Since the searcher does not know the vendor's seller (and would have to verify the transfer in any event), she must examine the Grantee Index to discover the time at which the vendor was the grantee and who was the vendor in that transaction.

[5] Constructing a Chain of Title

Having discovered when and from whom the vendor took legal title and the fact that the vendor has not made any questionable or disqualifying transfers, the title searcher can rest assured that the vendor "apparently" owns title to Blackacre. The vendor apparently owns Blackacre because her title is derivative through her seller who may or may not be the true owner of Blackacre. In other words, our assertion of the present vendor's title rests on an assumption that the vendor received a valid title from her previous vendor-seller. To verify this fact, the title searcher must verify the vendor's seller's state of title by searching the vendor's seller's title under the Grantor-Grantee Index as described above. This process is repeated for every vendor in the chain of title to the property as far back as the original owner, usually called the root of title. The original owner is usually either the government or one claiming title through a land grant by one of the European royal families that divided up the colonies following colonization of North America. (Unfortunately, pursuant to the doctrine of conquest set forth in *Johnson v. M'Intosh*,[10] the claims of the people indigenous to the United States—Native Americans—have been usurped and largely ignored.) Thus, in order to perfect a title search, a searcher must construct a chain of title by using the Grantor-Grantee Index that shows how title devolved from

---

[10] 21 U.S. 543 (1823).

the root of title to the present by searching each and every vendor's name under both the Grantor and the Grantee Index.

[B] Tract Indexes

A tract index is a much simpler proposition. A tract index can be used only when each parcel of land in the county for which the index is viable has a unique number or identifying symbol assigned to it. Every document affecting that parcel is then filed according to that number or symbol and an index is maintained, which includes reference to the parcel number or symbol and not to the grantor or grantee's name. Thus, the tract index will contain lists or pages of identification numbers that identify each instrument that is properly recorded for a tract of land. As a result, all of the documents that affect title to Blackacre will be indexed in one easy to find place.

Tract indexes, where used, are clearly superior to inefficient Grantor-Grantee Indexes. This fact can be easily demonstrated when the title searcher is searching title for a vendor named Karen Anderson or Alex Johnson in Los Angeles County. There may be hundreds of individuals with the same names who have transferred property in the last fifty or sixty years and theoretically each document, at least as represented in the index, must be examined to determine if it is the right Karen Anderson or Alex Johnson. Unfortunately, tract indexes are not used more widely because the adoption or start-up costs are prohibitive.

[C] Length of Search

Although a perfect chain of title would be one that stretches back to the sovereign or the government, a satisfactory root of title is a matter of custom or local practice. Thus, in some jurisdictions, the title searched need only search the record for a sixty year period. Other jurisdictions have a shorter search period. Some states have title standards (*see below*) that establish the applicable search period.

§ 10.06 Priority and the Junior Lienholder

The other major function served by the Recording Acts is to establish the priority of lienholders (mortgagees) to property. Pursuant to the doctrine of first-in-time, the first party who takes a mortgage on Blackacre is considered the first mortgagee and is entitled to all the protection that that status entails, including but not limited to, extinguishing the rights of junior mortgagees at the time of foreclosure.[11] However, failure to properly record a mortgage results in the same problems created by a failure to record a deed transferring title to property. The mortgagee can lose his interest or priority in the property by failure to timely record if a subsequent mortgagee makes a mortgage to the owner of Blackacre and thereafter properly records the mortgage.

---

[11] *See supra* § 8.04[A].

For example, assume that First Bank lends $100,000 to the vendee so that the vendee can purchase Blackacre, but fails to properly record its mortgage in the County Recorder's Office. Subsequently, the vendee executes a mortgage to Second Bank for $50,000 for home improvement purposes. This mortgage is validly recorded by Second Bank following its search of the record which reveals no other interests in Blackacre. If Second Bank has no actual, inquiry or constructive notice of the existence of First Bank's mortgage, its mortgage, which is second in terms of time, will have priority over First Bank's unrecorded mortgage in a Notice, Race, or Race-Notice jurisdiction. Of course, as between the vendee and First Bank, the mortgage debt remains valid and enforceable.

[A]   Circular Priority

A popular problem is one based on circular priority or lienholders. In a Notice or a Race-Notice jurisdiction it is possible to have three parties with mortgages in Blackacre, but to have uncertainty with respect to the order of priority. For example, First Bank may execute a mortgage of $20,000 on Blackacre and fail to record its mortgage. Second Bank may subsequently execute and validly record a $15,000 mortgage on Blackacre *with actual notice* of First Bank's mortgage, thus negating its claim to superiority over First Bank and causing the parties' priority to be determined by the first-in-time rule. Third Bank may then execute and validly record its mortgage of $10,000 with constructive or record notice of Second Bank's mortgage, but no knowledge whatsoever of First Bank's unrecorded mortgage. As a result, Third Bank's interest will be superior to First Bank's and inferior to Second Bank's in terms of priority. Second Bank will be superior to Third Bank, yet inferior to First Bank. Finally, First Bank will be superior to Second Bank and inferior to Third Bank. Hence, circular priority. The priority problems are academic if upon foreclosure enough money is raised to pay off the three mortgages totaling $45,000. The real issue is raised when the amount realized upon foreclosure is less than $45,000, say $30,000, how is that amount to be divided between the three parties?

Although there are many ways to resolve the circular priority problem including pro rata distribution, the use of a contractual subordination doctrine, the employment of an expectations theory and so on, the most efficient way to analyze the problem is from the position of who is at fault, who is blameless, and how to prevent the problem from occurring again through use of a rule that gives the parties an incentive to record properly in the future. Pursuing such ends, one should keep in mind that Third Bank, which did everything it should have done, and so is the least blameworthy of the three parties. Second Bank is next in terms of blamelessness because it knew of First Bank's omission yet still made the loan. And finally, First Bank is the obvious culprit because it failed to record. Lastly, this problem would not occur in a Race jurisdiction where notice is irrelevant.

§ 10.07   Improving the Public Method of Title Assurance

The recording system has been criticized frequently for being inefficient, too costly, and often leading to erroneous results. As a result, theories abound which attempt to replace or abolish the recording act. What follows is a brief synopsis of some of the leading theories put forth addressing alternative methods of assuring title to land by public methods, some of which have been put into practice.

[A]   Title Registration: The Torrens System

Simply put, this method of perfecting title to real property is based on the system used to register ships. Under this method, an adversary judicial process is begun to establish title to the subject property, with notice given to everyone and anyone connected to the property. The judge adjudicates title and issues a certificate of title setting forth the ownership interests in the property. After the initial lawsuit establishing the title to the property, title is transferred via a certificate with the vendor signing off his ownership interest at the time of sale and the vendee obtaining a new certificate from the County Registrar reflecting his ownership interest in the property. All ownership interests are reflected on the Certificate of Title (except for federal government interests) so no search of the records has to take place. The owner of the property is charged with a duty of reasonable care towards the certificate and any encumbrancing mortgagee should require a notarized acknowledgment of its mortgage before expending sums on a mortgage to Blackacre.

Although this may work in theory, it is rarely used in practice because of the initial costs associated with registering the property. The litigation costs associated with obtaining the first certificate are prohibitive when compared to a single search under the recording acts. Hence, many vendors and vendees shy away from its initial use due to cost. Also the method's reliability is not certain and fraudulent schemes and transfers can be employed when using the Torrens System which relies, in part, on the certificate holder protecting his interest in the property from all others.[12] In addition, errors in the registration process in the Torrens System have a disproportionate impact since the certificate is conclusive indicia of ownership interest in the property.

In *Echols v. Olsen*,[13] the husband of the petitioner conveyed his interest in a jointly-owned piece of property to his former wife. The former wife's attorney filed a quitclaim deed in the office of the county recorder but failed to register the deed with the county registrar of titles. Subsequently, a bank obtained an ex parte judgment against the husband and had the judgment memorialized on the certificate maintained in the registrar's office. The certificate showed both

---

[12] *See* Echols v. Olsen, 63 Ill.2d 270, 347 N.E.2d 720 (1976).

[13] 347 N.E.2d 720, 63 Ill.2d 270 (1976).

the husband and the wife as owners of the property. The bank and the respondent (the registrar) contended that under the Torrens Act a judgment creditor who has registered his judgment after the judgment debtor has conveyed his interest, acquires an interest superior to that of a prior grantee from the debtor who did not register his deed in the County Registrar's office.

The Supreme Court of Illinois held that the Torrens Act must be construed in light of the established law of property and that the registry of title with the registrar is not always conclusive. Accordingly, the court found that the bank could not attach its judgment to the legal interest that remained in the husband's name simply because the wife had failed to register the quitclaim deed. In effect, the husband had no interest in the property to which the judgment against him could attach.

Although there are facts in the case indicating that it would not be "fair" to allow the bank to perfect its lien on the wife's property because it didn't rely on the husband's interest in the property in making the debt, this case destroys one of the essential purposes of the Torrens System: reliance on the certificate and not off-record items to prove title.

[B]   Marketable Title Acts

Marketable Title Acts have been adopted in approximately eighteen states (mostly Midwestern) as a vehicle to reduce the time expended on a title examiner's search. This shorter search period is achieved by voiding all interests in the land that appear before an established root of title unless reference is made to the prior interest in the root of title or in special instruments recorded after the root of title which are used solely to perfect and maintain the validity of documents or interests predating the root of title. The root of title is established by the Marketable Title Act and is normally the most recent deed to be of record for a period of years, usually 30 or 40 years. All interests created and recorded before that root of title can be ignored unless a document perfecting the interest has been recorded after the root of title. Thus, the title examiner's main function is to find a root of title and to search instruments affecting title after that root of title was filed of record.

For example, suppose that Owen is the owner of Blackacre in 1900. In 1920, Owen transfers to Abel who validly records his interest in the property. In 1943, when Abel is in Europe fighting in World War II, Yancey a wrongdoer, forges Abel's signature and files a deed which shows a transfer to Yancey. In 1945, Yancey transfers to Zeb. In 1988, Abel brings a quiet title action to clear title to Blackacre. If the jurisdiction has a Marketable Title Act with a 40 year root of title requirement, Zeb will prevail because his title has been of record for the minimum time period and any interests that predate it, including Abel's interest in the property are terminated. In order to prevent his interest from being terminated Abel has to file a document perfecting and maintaining his interest in the property at least once every 40 years.

Marketable Title Acts have been criticized because unlike recording acts, a forged deed, if it serves as a root of title, can eventually transfer title to property.[14] In addition, there are numerous exceptions engrafted on the statute, including the rights of those in possession or those that have paid taxes, that are exempt from the operation of the Marketable Title Act and therefore limit the efficiency of the statutes.

In *Marshall v. Hollywood*,[15] the Supreme Court of Florida upheld a decision conferring marketability to a claim of title arising out of a forged deed, so long as the strict requirements of the recording act of the state were met. Here, where the marketability of title was to be determined more than 30 years after a forged deed created a root of title pursuant to the Marketable Title Act, the court found that notwithstanding the forgery, a claim arising out of a transaction which occurred more than 30 years prior to the claim (the period set by the state recording statute), i.e. before the root of title, was void. The court held that the Marketable Record Title Act provides a marketable title in claimants who can trace their ownership interest to a record claim of title from a root of title more than 30 years old. All interests preceding the root are considered void regardless of whether the actual root of title is a forged deed.

This decision gives full effect to the purposes supporting a marketable title act; i.e., it limits the scope of the title search to some period—30 or 40 years—thus eliminating reliance and off-the-record matters occurring before that date.

[C] Title Standards

Title standards are typically promulgated by the local bar association to guide the attorney in his examination of title by establishing a standard against which title is to be measured. Thus, a title standard may establish the length of a search and presumptions of facts, i.e., that Mike Smith who signed as grantor in a previous deed in the chain of title is the same person as Michael Smith who signed as grantee in the immediately preceding deed, and other common matters of concern that attorneys may encounter in their search of the record. These are normally compiled in a book and distributed by the bar association.

Title standards have been criticized because even though they appear to establish a rule, they cannot change or abolish a rule of law set forth by the legislature or the courts. Thus, while the standards may be used to resolve ambiguities that might arise in the title search, that resolution is not binding on the courts when they decide the issue. Hence, the standards may retroactively be determined to be wrong and cause a client's loss of title. Title standards have

---

[14] *See* Marshall v. Hollywood, 236 So.2d 114 (Sup.Ct. Fla. 1970), *cert. denied,* 400 U.S. 964, 91 S.Ct. 366, 27 L.Ed 2d 384 (1970).

[15] 236 So.2d 114 (Sup. Ct. Fla. 1970), *cert. denied,* 400 U.S. 964, 91 S.Ct. 366 27 L.Ed.2d 384 (1970).

also been criticized because they allow the attorney searching title to shield his actions from a malpractice claim by defending on the basis of the title standard.

[D]   Miscellaneous Acts

There are three other methods used to improve the efficiency of the recording acts either by eliminating stale claims or by limiting the search process. Statute of limitations have been passed by many legislatures to cut off stale claims. In addition, curative acts have been adopted to solve technical defects of documents that have otherwise been validly recorded, i.e., documents that have been of record a certain number of years are deemed valid even if they are not validly notarized or acknowledged," thus, removing technical objections to title that arise out of these defective documents. Finally, adverse possession periods are shortened if the claimant is claiming under color of title, i.e., via a defective deed, which has the effect of clearing title when the adverse possessor is claiming pursuant to a defective deed.

PART 2: CONDOMINIUMS AND COMMUNAL OWNERSHIP

CHAPTER

11

FORMS OF COMMUNAL OWNERSHIP

SYNOPSIS

_____

§ 11.01   Introduction

The last twenty years has witnessed an explosion in the number of types of ownership interests available to purchasers of residential real property. While most people are familiar with traditional idea and legalities associated with ownership and occupancy by one family of a single family detached dwelling, the new forms of communal ownership require a separate explanation. A recurrent feature of these new types of property interests is a common or communal area that is accessible by all those dwelling on the entirety of the property. With the addition of the common areas, the new property interests combine elements of individual and communal living, which were heretofore lacking in the traditional notion of a single family detached dwelling.

§ 11.02   Condominiums

Although they have been used for centuries in Europe, condominiums, derived from a Latin term meaning co-ownership, are a relatively recent development in the United States. Among a set of condominiums, each owner owns the space within the walls of his unit in fee simple absolute (all walls contained exclusively in the common area are part of the common area; walls that are contained totally within the individual's unit are considered part of the owner's unit; and finally, walls that divide common area from private space are viewed as part common area—the exterior half of the wall—and part private space—the interior half within the owner's unit). The owner also owns an undivided fractional interest in the exterior walls, roof, land, common areas, etc., that comprise the rest of the development not owned in fee simple by another owner. Thus, each owner in the unit has two very separate and distinguishable interests: (i) her fee simple interest in her unit, which entitles her to exclusive ownership of the unit, very much like the owner of a single family detached dwelling and (ii) her communal interest in the so-called common areas of the condominium complex, which includes the right to use those common areas, much like the arrangement found in apartments.

[A]   Creation

Each of the fifty states has a law regulating the creation and operation of condominiums in that state. Suffice it to say, a summary of those statutes is beyond the purview of this outline. The FHA, however, has promulgated a "Model Statute for Creation of Apartment Ownership" which has been employed in numerous states as a basis for a statute and is used as the model throughout this section. Under the model statue, two documents are needed to create a condominium: a declaration and the operating by-laws.

[1] Declaration

The Declaration is the most important document because it sets out the physical and legal description of the project by providing a description of the land and the building, specifying the number of units, the common areas and, most importantly, each owner's fractional share of the common areas and the corresponding rights and relationships that derive from that fractional interest.[1]

[2] Operating By-Laws

The operating by-laws pick up where the declaration ends by regulating the day-to-day affairs of the condominium complex. In particular, the by-laws are used to govern the administration of the property and to provide for the election of a Board of Directors, who are responsible for the management of the daily affairs of the complex and who adopt regulations regarding use of the common areas.

[B] Financing

Because the individual vendee purchases a fee simple interest, her property is completely and separately mortgageable from the other owners' interests in their respective units. That is, the owner of a condominium, like the owner of the single family detached dwelling, may finance the purchase of a condominium or obtain a loan against her equity in the condominium by obtaining a mortgage.

[1] Initial Blanket Encumbrance

The fact that the individual vendee may mortgage his interest to finance the purchase of the unit should not obscure the fact that most condominiums, like other commercial or apartment buildings, are typically financed with a blanket mortgage or encumbrance that is secured by the entirety of the project. However, as each unit is sold, and money is paid to the builder-owner of the unit, the unit is released from the blanket encumbrance because a portion of the sales price is paid to the builder-seller's mortgagee to release that unit from the mortgage. Following the release of the unit from the mortgage, even if the developer goes bankrupt and the blanket mortgage is foreclosed, the released units are unaffected.

As an example, assume that Developer constructs a 10 unit condominium complex with the proceeds of a 1 million dollar loan from Construction Loan Bank that is secured by a blanket mortgage on all 10 units. When Developer sells the first unit for $150,000 to the vendee, financed by the vendee's obtaining

---

[1] *See* Berger, *Condominium: Shelter on a Statutory Foundation,* 63 Colum. L. Rev. 987 (1963) ("[t]he declaration serves roughly the same function for the condominium as the subdivision map and restrictive covenant serve in a tract development.").

a mortgage of $135,000 from First Bank (the remaining $15,000 was paid as the vendee's deposit/down payment when the purchase contract was signed), First Bank will take a first mortgage only on Unit #1 and will be the first mortgagee on that unit. In the underlying contract between Developer and Construction Loan Bank, Construction Loan Bank agreed to release each individual unit from the blanket encumbrance once it received a $100,000 incremental payment from Developer. Hence, following this rather simple transaction, vendee owns Unit #1 in fee simple subject to a first mortgage of $135,000, Developer has $50,000 in cash, Construction Loan Bank has a $900,000 first mortgage on the remaining nine units and $100,000 in cash.

[C] Taxation

According to the form of ownership, each unit is taxed separately for property tax purposes. The unit's fractional share of the value of the common area (in our hypothetical, assuming the units are the same size and are valued equally, the fractional share is 1/10) is added to the value of the fee simple owned, resulting in each owner being taxed on a single value representing both the fee simple interest and the interest in the common areas.

[1] Deductibility of Interest

Like owners of single family detached dwellings, the owner of a condominium unit receives a significant tax advantage due to the deductibility of both mortgage interest and the unit owner's property tax.[2]

[D] Transferability

Many condominium by-laws contain restrictions upon the transfer of the owner's interest. There are normally two types of restrictions: first, absolute restrictions forbidding the unit owner from fractionalizing her interest and thus increasing the burden on the condominium's common area. Second, and more problematical is the restriction on the unit owner's freedom to transfer the unit without the other owners' approval of the prospective vendee.

Not unsurprisingly, it is the second restriction which most often leads to litigation. Assuming the putative vendee is not rejected for constitutionally impermissible reasons—race, sex, religion, etc.—[3] these restrictions are judged by the rather subjective standard of whether they impermissibly restrict the alienation (sale) of the fee simple to a class of potential buyers that is too small or too narrow. If so, the restrictions are deemed invalid.

Basically, the courts employ a test, weighing the rights of the unit owner to sell her unit against the collective rights of the other owners to maintain the character and value of the development.[4] It should be noted, however, that great

---

[2] Compare the tax treatment accorded to owners of cooperatives discussed *infra* § 11.05[C].

[3] *See* Robinson v. 12 Lofts Realty, Inc., 610 F.2d 1032 (2nd Cir. 1979).

[4] *See* Johnson, *Correctly Interpreting Long-Term Leases Pursuant to Modern Contract Law: Toward A Theory of Relational Leases*, 74 Va. L. Rev. 751, 771-774 (1988).

weight is given to the rights of the other unit owners because of the fact that the selling unit owner purchased with notice of the restrictions on transferability. Even more importantly, judicial deference is given to the rights of the preexisting owners because they are required to live in close proximity to the new owner, enduring close quarters and the joint use of common areas.[5]

[1]   Rights of First Refusal

Related to restraints on alienation, rights of first refusal, also called preemptive options, grant the other condominium owners (through the condominium owners' association or other collective action), the right to purchase the selling owner's unit at some predetermined or impartially determined (usually by appraisal) price. A clause permitting a right of first refusal is rarely challenged successfully in court given the fact that the exercise of the right results in a sale and not a restriction on the alienability of the property.[6]

[E]   Tort Liability

Because unit owners own an undivided share of the common area, interesting legal issues arise concerning the apportionment of liability for torts that occur as a result of the use of the common area. Traditional tort theory provides that *any* unit owner as a tenant in common with respect to her ownership interest in the common areas is jointly and severally liable for torts occurring in the common area. The unsatisfactory results reached by adhering to this doctrine have been addressed by a number of public and private arrangements. Often, a condominium unit owners' association will take out a private policy to insure the unit owners. In addition, some states have passed laws limiting the unit owner's liability to a pro rata share of the damages based on the percentage of the owner's interest in the common area. Courts have also applied a pro rata formula to apportion damages.[7]

Care should be taken to ensure that the unit owner's interest in the condominium is adequately protected and that the owner is not exposed to liability for torts occurring in the common area should the judgment exceed the amount of the association's policy or should the association declare bankruptcy. Usually an addendum called a rider can be obtained at nominal cost to insure the unit owner individually against any claims of liability arising from torts occurring in the common area.

§ 11.03   Townhouses

Townhouses or townhomes share many attributes with condominiums that differentiate the two from a single family detached dwelling. While condominium

---

[5] *See* Jones v. O'Connell, 189 Conn. 648, 458 A.2d 355 (1983).

[6] *See* Browder, *Restraints on the Alienation of Condominium Units (The Right of First Refusal),* 1970 U.Ill.L.Forum 231, 240-243.

[7] *See* Dutcher v. Owens, 647 S.W.2d 948 (Sup. Ct. Tex. 1983).

units are normally physically contained in one larger unit or building and are frequently built or converted from apartments or other rental arrangements, however, townhouses are constructed as adjoining houses. Thus, condominiums are described as vertical sharing arrangements because units are stacked on top of each other. Townhouses, on the other hand, are described as horizontal sharing arrangements because although the units may share a common wall, each unit occupies a separate vertical space. In all other legal respects, however, townhouses are treated like condominiums.

§ 11.04 Subdivisions

A subdivision, technically speaking, is not a form of communal ownership of real property. One lives in a subdivision, but one does not own a fractional undivided share of the subdivision like a unit owner in a condominium. On the other hand, the legal structure of subdivisions has changed over the last score of years to reflect the advantages gained by communal living arrangements while attempting to minimize the potential disadvantages (externalities—costs imposed on others that are not taken into account by the actor taking the action—associated with common ownership). Thus, many subdivisions are developed along the following model: Traditional single family detached dwellings are constructed on individual units within the subdivision. Upon sale, the vendee receives a standard deed and is regarded legally as the sole owner of Blackacre, a single family detached dwelling. In addition, however, the developer, Don, sets aside and dedicates to the homeowners' association certain common areas, private roads, parks, recreational facilities, etc., that are external to the individual lots being sold (not part of any vendee's property), but contained within the geographic area of the subdivision. The subdivision is structured so that the use of the dedicated land—the common area owned by the homeowners' association—runs with the land in the subdivision. Therefore, the subsequent purchaser of any lot in the subdivision has the right to use the dedicated land and is automatically a member of the homeowners' association. Concomitant with the right to benefit from the common areas is a charge or assessment of dues or fees used to fund the homeowners' association and to maintain the common area.

[A] Compare Condominiums

Besides using a different physical layout, the subdivision scheme avoids many of the problems associated with condominiums. In many states, the homeowners' association is regarded as the owner of the land, much like a corporate entity with each individual owner owning a pro rata share of the corporate share. Hence, if a tort is committed on land owned by the homeowners' association, the most the individual owner stands to lose is her share in the corporate entity, that is the homeowners' association and not a portion of that individual's home or equity therein.

[1]   Regulation, Transferability, etc.

Since the structure of subdivision arrangements is more akin to the traditional single family detached dwelling, there is less attempt to regulate internally matters such as use, transferability, etc., as is the case with condominiums and cooperatives where the owners are in close proximity to one another. Most attempts aimed at regulation relate to aesthetic matters which may impose adverse external costs on neighboring owners by affecting a loss in value to the subdivision. An example of a situation which may warrant regulation is where one owner wants to paint his house chartreuse with vertical black stripes.

§ 11.05   Cooperatives

Cooperatives are radically different from condominiums and other forms of communal ownership arrangements discussed above and require an in-depth explanation. A cooperative or co-op must be thought of as two distinct, albeit related entities: a corporation, which owns an apartment or building, and a landlord, which leases the units to the tenants who are collectively the owners of the corporation that owns the building. Thus, each occupant-owner of the co-op has two legal roles: first, she is the owner of a share or shares of the non-profit entity that owns the building, and second, she is the tenant who leases an apartment from the corporation. Usually, the ratio of ownership in the co-op corresponds to the amount of space or value occupied by the tenant vis-a-vis the other owner-tenants.

[A]   Creation

In order to create a cooperative, three legal instruments must be properly established: First, a corporation must be formed with a valid corporate charter in the state in which the realty is located. Second, corporate by-laws must be established to govern the operation of the corporation. Third, a proprietary lease must be drafted pursuant to which the holder of the share(s) of stock of the corporation is allowed to occupy the apartment in perpetuity as long as the cooperator complies with the responsibilities set forth in the proprietary lease.

For example, if Don Developer builds a 10 unit co-op in New York instead of a condominium, it may be structured as follows: After completing construction on the building with a $10 million mortgage from Construction Loan Bank, Don forms a non-profit cooperation and transfers his ownership interest in the building in exchange for 10 shares of stock. If someone wants to occupy a unit in the building they must purchase a share of stock at the price he sets, here $50,000 (Don wants to make the same $500,000 profit he anticipates making on a condominium as in the example above). The purchaser receives a share of stock and a perpetually renewable proprietary lease to her unit that is a derivative of her ownership of the one stock (the stock and the lease cannot be separated— caveat, a purchaser can, of course, sublease her premises if it does not violate a restriction on transferability). Pursuant to her lease, the purchaser has to pay "rent," which, here, includes her pro rata share to reduce the mortgage on the building, along with taxes, insurance, and the fees to maintain the building and the corporation. When all 10 units are sold, there will be ten owners of corporate stock holding ten leases to ten apartments in the building. They will all pay rent to the corporation that owns the building (the corporation has the usual corporate structure, a President, Treasurer, etc.) who will use the money to pay off the mortgage and maintain the building. Don will walk away with the $500,000 in cash, his profit on the venture.

[B]   Financing

Unlike condominiums, the co-op is financed with a blanket mortgage on the entire apartment building creating substantial problems for the individual cooperator. If each individual cooperator pays his "rent" promptly, the mortgage can be paid off in a timely fashion. On the other hand, if one cooperator defaults in the payment of her obligation, it jeopardizes the other owners in the co-op because they must increase their payments to cover the percentage of the mortgage not being paid by the defaulting cooperator. Thus, each member of the co-op is relying on the other members of the co-op to promptly pay his or her portion of the mortgage and other costs associated with the ownership of the co-op. Failure to so do places the entire co-op at risk and requires the other cooperators to cure the default.

[1]   Lien to Enforce Payment

If a cooperator defaults on any of her payment obligations required by the by-laws or the proprietary lease, the co-op is authorized to make the payment and seek reimbursement from the defaulting cooperator by way of placing a lien on the defaulting cooperator's share(s) of stock. The lien can then be foreclosed resulting in the sale of the stock to satisfy the lien.

[C]   Taxation

Since 1942, cooperators have been allowed to deduct the mortgage interest and property tax attributable to their pro rata share ownership of the co-op.

[D]   Transferability

Because of the close legal relationships cooperators find themselves in, and the trust each member must afford the other members of the co-op, courts uphold rather stringent, even arbitrary limits on the transferability of co-op interests to others.[8]

---

[8] *See* Weisner v. 791 Park Avenue Corp., 6 N.Y.2d 426, 190 N.Y.S.2d 70, 160 N.E.2d 720 (1969).

§ 11.06 Disadvantages Created by Co-op Ownership

Although co-ops are used in New York and other urban areas, there are significant problems which limit their use in other settings. For example, transferability is impeded even if a suitable transferee can be found because institutional lenders cannot grant a mortgage (i.e. take a second mortgage) on the purchasing transferee's interest. Hence, the transferee may have to pay cash for her purchase or the selling cooperator may have to take back a mortgage in order to finance the sale. Also, the fact that each cooperator owns an interest in stock(s) and not in realty raises considerable technical issues about the treatment of the cooperator's interest upon voluntary or involuntary transfer (death or divorce). Whether the interest is to be treated as personalty or realty may greatly affect its transferability.

§ 11.07 Time Share Estates

Time sharing estates are better defined as time-span or an interval estates. Instead of dividing the condominium by space, the condominium or the realty is divided by time allocating to each co-tenant a specified interval of time during which the co-tenant may use the premises. The interval of time, say the month of June, may be limited to a number of years or it may last forever giving the owner a recurring fee simple.[9] Thus, several owners may have the right to exclusive possession of Blackacre for successive periods of time during each year.

[A] Critique

Time-sharing, once widely applauded as the perfect vehicle to structure ownership of a vacation or recreational ownership interest, has fallen into disfavor recently and has been criticized severely. The difficulty with time-sharing appears to be related to the externality problem associated with communal ownership. These externalities are amplified with time-shares because no single owner may have a sufficient economic interest in the premises to monitor the behavior of others. Therefore, the maintenance and operating costs associated with these ventures are said to be very high and the deterioration of the physical structures rapid because of the heavy use to which the properties are put.

§ 11.08 Planned Unit Developments

A Planned Unit Development (PUD) may contain a combination of land use arrangements and can include each and every one of the forms of home ownership discussed above, including single family detached dwellings. The idea supporting the use of PUDs is quite simple: a planned community of mixed uses and housing types results in a better, more varied neighborhood than that provided by traditional methods. Ex ante planning for a complete community that internalizes all of the uses to which the land is to be put, is designed to lead to an economy

---

[9] *See* Dukeminier & Krier, Property 406-408 (1981).

of scale that may not be present with other developments which are designed by different groups who often in competition with one another. Thus, for example, lots near heavily traveled intersections can be used as apartments or co-ops, lots adjacent to these can be put to their optimal use as condominiums or townhouses, and finally, larger, interior lots can be put to their best use as single family detached dwellings.

12

THE HOMEOWNERS' ASSOCIATION

§ 12.01   Introduction

One thing that all of the communal ownership interests share is the fact that the management of communal resources occur through a recognized legal entity best characterized as a Homeowners' Association (also known as Condominium Owners' Association). And, although the type and structure of the Homeowners' Association may vary depending upon the precise nature of the ownership interest being regulated, this section will discuss the issues raised by Homeowners'

Associations as they apply to the regulation of condominium communal owner-ship interests.

§ 12.02 Creation

Most statutes provide for the existence of the Homeowners' Association before the sale of the first unit by filing a declaration in the appropriate form with the appropriate body. Once the declaration is filed, it immediately brings into existence the Homeowners' Association. In addition, other documents such as the bylaws must be filed contemporaneous with the execution of the declaration or shortly thereafter, setting forth rules for governing the day-to-day operation of the Homeowners' Association. State laws and statutes that regulate the creation and organization of these associations must be examined carefully to determine the prerequisites for the creation of a valid association.

§ 12.03 Form and Ownership Structure

By and large, each member of the applicable residential sharing unit automati-cally becomes a member of the Homeowners' Association upon the purchase of the individual's unit. This gives the unit owner certain rights, e.g., voting, and certain responsibilities, e.g., paying assessments, both of which are inherent in the unit owner's status position as the owner of the unit. The Homeowners' Association will itself be organized in one of two ways: If the residential sharing form is a condominium, each unit owner owns an undivided fractional interest in the common areas which corresponds to that owner's fractional ownership in the property. Management, rather than ownership of the common areas, as well as a more limited role managing and regulating the use of the units, is then delegated to the Homeowners' Association. By comparison, other forms of residential sharing arrangements like co-ops and townhouses result in the common area being deeded to the Homeowners' Association which regulates the common areas in its capacity as owner of the common area. The Homeowners' Associations for condominiums also have limited, by comparison, regulatory power over the use to which individual units can be put.

§ 12.04 Role of Homeowners' Association

The Homeowners' Association's role can be divided into two phases. First, it acts like a "private" municipal government providing services or benefits to its members like refuse removal, street maintenance, etc. The costs of these services are paid for by the homeowners themselves in the form of general or special assessments, which are likened to taxes and which are provided by the charter, declaration or by-laws of the Homeowners' Association. On the other hand, once the Homeowners' Association is formed, its primary task is of a regulatory nature and can be divided into two functions: maintaining the common area over which it has exclusive control, and regulating the individual unit owner's occupancy, use, and transferability of his respective unit. This regulatory task can be differentiated from the provision of services in that the regulations set forth by the Homeowners' Association normally restrict otherwise lawful uses and are judged differently—more strictly—from the provision of services.

§ 12.05 Judicial Review of Association Regulations

Although the Homeowners' Association has vast power to regulate the day-to-day affairs of its members as they pertain to the ownership of the units and the uses to which the units can be put, that power is not unlimited and is frequently the subject of litigation. By and large, the courts determine whether the exercise or failure to exercise power is valid by reference to the "reasonableness standard of review." In other words, if the regulatory act, or failure to act, is determined to be "reasonable," it will be upheld by the courts. Conversely, if the act or failure to act is held to be "unreasonable" it will be invalidated. This requires a case-by-case determination.[1] This rather nebulous, indeterminate test has been modified by certain rules that have developed to determine if the challenged regulatory act or inaction is valid.

[A] Within Delegated Power

The court first examines whether the challenged action is within the power delegated to the Homeowners' Association by the charter, declaration, by-laws or by a statute. A regulation is prima facie invalid if it exceeds the power or authority given to the Homeowners' Association.

[B] Rational Relation

The courts closely examine the substance of a regulation to determine if it bears a rational relationship to the "health, happiness and enjoyment of life of various unit owners."[2]

[C] Disproportionate Impact

The regulation is also examined to determine if it has a disproportionate or unfair impact on any one unit owner or group of owners.

[D] Process Fairness

Finally, courts examine the procedure by which the regulation was enacted to be sure that affected individuals received notice and to make certain that the Homeowners' Association complied with its procedures in enacting the regulation.

[E] Arbitrariness

As with most private law matters, if the court determines that the challenged action is arbitrary, capricious, or taken in bad faith, it is invalidated.

---

[1] *See* Note, *Judicial Review of Condominium Rulemaking*, 94 Harv.L.Rev. 647 (1981).

[2] Hidden Harbour Estates, Inc. v. Norman, 309 So.2d 180 (Fla. Dist. Ct. App. 1975).

§ 12.06   Taxation of Homeowners' Associations

Like individual taxpayers, the tax treatment accorded to the Homeowners' Association depends on the organization's structure of the underlying residential sharing unit. In other words, Homeowners' Associations for co-ops are treated differently than those set up for condominiums and other forms of communal ownership.

[A]   Condominiums, etc.

The Association, as a separate taxable entity, must file a return and pay taxes on its taxable income. It is not regarded as a charitable entity, even though some of its interest may qualify as charitable, because its exclusive purpose is not charitable as determined by the Internal Revenue Code (IRC). The Tax Reform Act of 1978 in § 528 provides for so-called exempt function income. Although the rule is very complicated, essentially income derived from dues, fees and assessments from members of the Homeowners' Association, as long as it's a residential development, is exempt from taxation. However, investment income or earnings received from the reserves maintained by the Association or fees received from non-Association members are taxed to the Association.

[1]   Corporate Tax

Irrespective of the form or structure of the organization, the income taxed to the Homeowners' Association is taxed to it at the corporate rate. The Homeowners' Association is mandatorily treated as a corporation for tax purposes.

[B]   Cooperatives

Unlike other Homeowners' Associations, Homeowners' Associations formed to manage and regulate co-ops are not subject to § 528. Hence, all the income attributable to the Association is taxed to the Association at the corporate rate.

[1]   Depreciation of Buildings

Section 216 (c) of the IRC, also adopted in 1976, provides a benefit to cooperative Homeowner Associations not available to other Homeowner Associations. Section 216 (c) allows the Homeowners' Association to offset against its income the depreciation on the entire cooperative project, a substantial benefit that in most situations will allow the co-op Homeowners' Association to offset all income received.

PART 3: THE BASIC COMMERCIAL REAL ESTATE TRANSACTION

Although most of the legal issues raised by the creation and operation of commercial real estate projects are discussed in courses and seminars on Advanced Real Estate Planning and Finance, this brief section is designed to introduce the reader to the terminology employed in standard (simple) commercial transactions and the mechanics of simpler transactions, including some selected legal issues raised by these transactions. The basic purpose of this section is to provide information about the "commercial" transactions that take place before residential real estate is sold to vendees; in effect, a primer on how developers finance and operate the development of their projects, including residential subdivisions. Thus, although much of the fuel that drives the engine of real estate investment is tax oriented, it is also necessary to educate the reader in the basics of commercial development in order to place in perspective the finished commercial projects—the residential development, with associated shopping malls and commercial businesses that service the residents of the subdivision.

However, as any lawyer, developer, or investor is aware, a key factor, if not the key factor, in determining the viability of a commercial real estate venture is the tax ramifications of the venture. Hence, to completely understand any commercial real estate venture, one must be familiar with the farrago of tax laws that could positively and negatively impact the venture. Those tax laws and their impact on commercial real estate ventures are the subject of another course and another review. However, the reader should not lose sight of the fact that the information provided below must be filtered through the tax prism to determine its applicability in the "real world" where tax effects play such an important role.

CHAPTER

13

FINANCING

---

[1] Nondisturbance Clauses

---

§ 13.01 Construction Loans

As the name intimates, the construction loan is used to finance the construction of improvements on land owned by the mortgagor. The basic purpose of a construction loan is to finance the physical development of the land for its ultimate market use. Unlike the conventional mortgage, the construction loan is a short-term loan typically in effect only so long as it takes the owner-mortgagor who is building the improvement (hereinafter Don Developer) to finish the construction of the improvement. Similar to a conventional lender, the lender who lends pursuant to a construction loan normally requires that its mortgage receive first priority, i.e., be a first mortgage, as a condition of making the loan. Thus, the Construction Lender may require other mortgages to subordinate[1] their interests before making the loan. More importantly, construction loans are inherently riskier than conventional loans because the Construction Lender is not able to appraise the value of its security before making the loan to insure that the value of the improvements is in excess of the value of the mortgage. Moreover, there is increased risk that Don Developer may pocket or siphon some of the loan proceeds to other projects that are not secured by the Construction Lender's mortgage. Hence, a specialized industry has evolved to satisfy the needs of the developer who wants to borrow funds to construct an improvement that will ultimately be sold or leased to yet another party (rarely are these types of developments held by developers as a long-term investment). The Construction Lender charges a much higher rate of interest than a conventional lender to reflect the increased risk that is created because there is no tangible asset and also to incorporate its specialized or unique transaction costs associated with its monitoring role as the Construction Lender.

For example, Don Developer purchases a 100-acre tract of land that he plans to develop as a suburban mall. Unfortunately, Don does not have the $12,000,000 it will take to construct the mall per the architect's plans. (We will assume for the sake of simplicity that all the relevant market studies have been accomplished and that the anchor tenants and others have agreed to enter long term leases of one sort or another to occupy and use the mall.) Don executes a short-term construction mortgage with the Construction Lender pursuant to which the lender agrees to loan Don $12,000,000. Of course, prior to making the loan, Construction Lender expended considerable sums verifying the underlying leases, the market study, and the architect's plan, paying particular attention to matters of cost. Moreover, it goes without saying that Construction Lender will not want to give Don the entire $12,000,000 up front, ex ante so to speak, because Don could (i) skip to the Bahamas leaving property worth less than the amount of the

---

[1] *See infra* § 13.03.

mortgage or (ii) (and more likely) construct a mall that is not worth $12,000,000 with the result that tenants will refuse to occupy the mall leading to a default and foreclosure on security (the poorly constructed mall) worth less than the mortgage. The Construction Lender solves this problem by monitoring the project through the disbursement process (*see below*). For these services, the Construction Lender receives interest on the $12,000,000 at 3 percentage points above the prime rate of 8%, or 11% from the date of the first disbursement until it is paid in full by the permanent or take out lender.[2]

[A]   Monitoring Through Disbursement Practices

In order to monitor the project through successful completion (measured by the construction project's value in excess of the amount of the debt), the Construction Lender will disburse funds according to a preset schedule laid out in the loan agreement. The schedule is tied both to the value of constructing the improvements and the value of the improvement following construction. In other words, the Construction Lender uses the disbursement process to insure that the money disbursed is properly spent on the improvement to be constructed on the land. If the project goes sour, the Construction Lender can cut its losses by refusing to make further disbursements. Conversely, Don may sue for specific performance of the agreement in order to receive further disbursements called for by the agreement if he is spending the loan proceeds properly.

As long as the interests of intervening lienors are not involved,[3] it is in the Construction Lender's best interest to draft the loan to provide maximum flexibility for the Construction Lender with regard to future decisions concerning disbursement of funds. This provides the Construction Lender with control and leverage over Don and the project which could lead to architectural changes in the project that might benefit the Construction Lender and not Don. Don, on the other hand, should attempt to limit the Construction Lender's involvement by requiring automatic disbursements at timely intervals, irrespective of the value of construction or the completion rate of the project. As with most things, neither party usually gets all it wants and an industry and accompanying terminology has developed to facilitate and monitor disbursements.[4]

[1]   Draw Inspector

The Draw Inspector represents the lender and her specific role is spelled out in the construction loan. This professional engineer is hired as an independent contractor by the Construction Lender to inspect the building site at regular intervals to ascertain the value of the improvements constructed on the project since her latest visit. Most contracts are structured so that Don Developer will

---

[2] *See infra* § 13.01[B].

[3] *See infra* § 13.01[A][3].

[4] *See* Hall, *How to Build Lender Protection Into Construction Agreements*, 6 Real Estate L.J. 21 (1977).

receive a disbursement equal to a percentage of the increased value of the premises as a result of the improvements constructed on the premises. If the work is inadequate, normally the Draw Inspector has the power to withhold funds.

[2] Retainage

This is the process by which the Construction Lender retains a certain percentage (5-10%) of the money estimated to be needed in order to provide a cushion of funds. These retained funds protect the Construction Lender's interest in case of a minor cost overrun or unexpected additional costs or deficiencies in the construction project.

[3] Lien Waivers

Constructing most commercial projects is a complicated process involving many parties. In particular, if Don Developer is acting as the general contractor in the construction process, even if an independent builder-contractor is used, there will be many subcontractors working on the project whose failure to be timely paid will result in the filing of annoying and costly mechanics' liens against the property. To prevent this from occurring the Construction Lender, through the Draw Inspector, may require the subcontractors to execute Lien Waivers at the time that funds are disbursed.

[B] Optional vs. Obligatory Advances and Priority Problems

A Construction Lender, in order to protect its security interest in the property, may require both that its lien be the first mortgage or lien against the property and that the Construction Lender retain its priority position throughout the construction process. Problems arise, however, because of the manner in which the funds are disbursed. Although Don Developer signs a note and a mortgage for $12,000,000, and the mortgage clearly spells out that the funds will be disbursed at predetermined intervals as construction is completed; a question may arise concerning the priority of lienors whose interests are perfected after the mortgage and the note of the Construction Lender have been filed of record and some, but not all funds have been disbursed.

For example, let's assume that Don Developer receives $1,000,000 upon the recordation of the Construction Lender's mortgage of $12,000.000. Normal progress disbursements are made so that six months after the commencement of the project, $8,000,000 has been properly disbursed to Don Developer pursuant to the construction loan. Unfortunately, notwithstanding the Construction Lender's efforts, certain subcontractors have not been paid and have subsequently filed mechanics' liens totaling $1,000,000. The remaining $4,000,000 is disbursed and the project is completed. Immediately following completion Don Developer defaults because he is unable to obtain a permanent or take out financing[5] and

---

[5] *See infra* § 13.02.

he cannot afford the onerous debt service required by the interest rate called for by the construction loan. The development is sold for $12,000,000 and the mechanics lienholders claim that they are entitled to $1,000,000 because at the time their lien was created and filed of record the mortgage and lien of the Construction Lender was only $8,000,000 and the $4,000,000 disbursed after the mechanics' liens were filed is secondary to those liens. The subcontractors (mechanics lienholders) argue that a security interest is created only when and to the extent of the underlying debt—which was $8,000,000 in the case of the Construction Lender—at the time the intervening lienholders filed their liens. The Construction Lender claims priority or first status for the entire amount disbursed based on the principle that the intervening lienholders had notice of the amount of the debt of $12,000,000—the face amount of the mortgage and the note recorded. The priority of liens will be determined by ascertaining whether the disbursement of the $4,000,000 was an obligatory versus an optional advance per the terms of the mortgage instrument.

[1] Obligatory Advances

Obligatory advances are those advances that *must* be made according to the terms and conditions of the mortgage. In other words, where the lender has no discretion regarding the disbursement of funds, for example the funds must be disbursed on a monthly basis irrespective of the value of the improvements completed at that time, an obligatory advance is created.

[a] Advances to Preserve Collateral

If the Construction Lender is called upon to advance funds that are not required by the loan, but the funds are necessary to protect the Construction Lender's interest in the security, e.g., unpaid taxes or maintenance expenses, the advances are regarded as obligatory, not optional, given the Construction Lender's lack of an effective choice.[6]

[2] Optional Advances

Optional advances are those advances not required by the terms and provisions of the loan instrument, but nevertheless made by the Construction Lender in the exercise of its discretion.

[3] Defining Optional and Obligatory Advances

Unfortunately, there is no current doctrine or theory which neatly and conveniently defines each category. All that can be said is the greater the Construction Lender's subjective discretion regarding the disbursement of funds, the more likely a court will later determine the advance to have been optional. Conversely, if the disbursement is conditioned upon the developer's meeting

---

[6] *See* Cal.Civ.Code § 3136. *See also* Note, *Mortgages—Advance Money Provisions—Effect on Preference and Recording Acts,* 29 N.Y.U. L.Rev. 733 (1958).

some objective requirement, the more likely it is that the disbursement will be considered to have been obligatory. There are no hard and fast rules in an environment in which the Construction Lender wishes to retain control over the funds until it is content with the progress of the construction. The only insightful comment that can be made is that the courts may attempt to distinguish between disbursements triggered by events controlled by the developer and events controlled by the Construction Lender.

Once the definitional hurdle is overcome, the rule granting priority to obligatory advances makes sense if the intervening mechanic lienholders have actual or constructive knowledge of the previously recorded mortgages. One way to perhaps characterize optional versus obligatory advances is by using a third party as a predictor of the probability that an advance will be made in any given situation, based on an objective reading of the mortgagor's rights and options given the requisite fact situation.

[4] Optional Advances and Notice—The Majority and Minority View

Once it is determined that the advance is optional, a second question must be resolved before the priorities of the parties can be definitively ascertained: Did the Construction Lender have notice of the intervening lienors at the time it made the optional advances? If the answer is yes, the intervening lienor is bestowed priority over the optional advance. Unfortunately, "notice" and the manner in which it is imparted by intervening lienholders to the Construction Lender making the optional advance, depends on which rule a particular state follows. In the majority of states the intervening lienor must provide the Construction Lender with *actual notice* in order to gain priority over subsequent optional advances. In other words, constructive notice provided by the record is ineffective for this purpose. A minority of states follow the view that constructive notice to the Construction Lender caused by the intervening lienor's recordation of its lien is sufficient notice to confer priority vis-a-vis later optional advances. In these states, then, the Construction Lender must check the record before making any subsequent optional advances in order to ascertain and maintain priority.

Although the issue of which view is better or more efficient given the roles of the parties, is normally answered by referring to the obligation of the intervening lienor to search the record prior to perfecting its lien. It must be remembered that most of the disputes involving intervening lienors involve mechanics' liens and other liens that arise by operation of law. Hence, most lienors do not "search" the record before providing work and services to the developer. Thus, non-payment by the developer to subcontractors results in an intervening lien that in most instances arises on the date of performance or the date of delivery of goods and for services. Consequently, although it may be burdensome to the Construction Lender to search the record prior to making optional disbursements, if optional disbursements are analogized to new obligations or loans, perhaps the Construction Lender should shoulder the burden.

§ 13.02 Permanent or Take-Out Mortgages

Normally arranged contemporaneously with the construction loan, the Permanent or Take-Out Loan is a loan arranged to replace the temporary Construction Loan after construction is completed. The Permanent Loan is used by the parties because the risks associated with the Construction Loan, and the justification for higher interest rates, disappear when construction of the improvements are completed. Only then can a conventional lender use conventional methods to assess the value of the security. The Permanent Loan is arranged, in most instances through a Buy-Sell Agreement (discussed *infra*) because Don Developer and the Construction Lender need to know from the beginning that financing will be available upon completion of the project in case Don Developer does not have the funds to pay off the Construction Loan immediately upon completion of construction.

[A] Mechanics of Operation

Although Permanent Loans can take many different forms, there are three typical types.

[1] Conventional Mortgage

The Permanent Loan may be structured as a conventional loan especially if Don Developer is planning to hold on to the project for a lengthy period of time. Even if Don Developer is planning to sell the development immediately after completion, the property may be more attractive to a buyer if financing is in place and the buyer need only pay Don Developer his equity in the project. This latter scenario assumes, of course, that the mortgage is assumable or transferable by its terms and conditions to a subsequent purchaser.[7]

[2] Hybrid Conventional Mortgage

In this situation a conventional mortgage is used but Don Developer has no intention of maintaining his entire ownership interest, but wants to sell off the project piecemeal to maximize his profitability. In this situation, Developer and mortgagee normally have an agreement where Don releases the pieces of the project as they are sold in exchange for a concomitant reduction of his mortgage indebtedness. In effect, the mortgagee agrees to finance the project while it is being sold to others and the cost of the interest is internalized by Don Developer as a cost of doing business until the entire project is sold.

[3] Residential Subdivisions

If Don Developer is constructing a residential subdivision with houses to be sold to individual consumers, the permanent financing would be structured at

---

[7] For a discussion of transferability and due-on clauses limiting same, see *supra* § 7.02.

two levels: the first level includes the financing for the entire project and the second encompasses the financing made available to the purchasers of the homes. Thus, there may be something akin to a blanket mortgage or an encumbrance on the entirety of the subdivision prior to the first sale. As the units are sold, the encumbrance is removed only as to the unit being sold, much like the hybrid mortgage discussed above. On the other hand, the mortgagee may be required to offer purchasers first mortgages at predetermined rates that may be better than the market rate in order to assist in the marketing of the subdivision. Hence, such a tie-in may be advantageous to all parties. Don Developer and the purchasers receive the financing they need and the financial institution gains a steady stream of customers, obtained at a cheaper cost. The financial institution does not have to compete with other lending institutions for customers and, more importantly, the loans may have less expensive transaction costs because of the financial institution's familiarity with the title and other aspects of the project.

[B] Buy-Sell or Tri-Party Agreements

The mechanics of the Construction Loan and the Permanent Loan are typically arranged in a Buy-Sell Agreement negotiated by and between Don Developer, the Construction Lender and the Permanent Lender (sometimes referred to as a Tri-Party Agreement). It is normally a very complex agreement by which the funding for the project is transferred from the Construction Lender to the Permanent Lender while constantly insuring that Don Developer adheres to his promise with respect to the construction of a valuable, saleable improvement.[8] In effect, the Agreement binds the developer-builder, construction lender and permanent lender to an agreement that can be subsequently enforced through specific performance. The agreement sets forth as many conditions as possible and sets forth the standards for the Permanent Lender's approval of conditions so that the project is certain to be financed by the Permanent Lender following completion of construction if the developer-builder's completed project meets or exceeds the standards of conditions set forth in the Tri-Party Agreement. Of course, the Construction Lender will press the developer-builder to build a project that meets the Permanent Lender's standards because the Construction Lender does not wish to be stuck with a completed building if the developer-builder subsequently defaults.

In these Buy-Sell Agreements, the interests of Don Developer and the Construction Lender are normally aligned at the inception of the project and in negotiation of the Agreement. Neither the Construction Lender nor the builder/developer is interested in holding on to a project that cannot obtain permanent financing. On the other hand, the Permanent Lender who assumes the mortgage much later in the game does not want to be compelled by a specific performance action to finance a project that is not worth the amount of the indebtedness.

---

[8] *See* Smith & Lubell, *The Buy-Sell Agreement*, 9 Real Est. Rev. 13.

Hence, the Construction Lender attempts to gain the confidence of the Permanent Lender by promising to monitor Don Developer. The promise also eliminates, as much as feasible, any discretion on the part of the Permanent Lender with respect to conditions of construction affecting the Permanent Lender's obligation to execute the permanent loan. The Permanent Lender, in most cases, attempts to retain as much discretion as possible over the project and over its own ultimate decision to finance the project.

§ 13.03   Subordination

Subordination Agreements are best defined as agreements between mortgagees altering the priority of their respective mortgages to accurately reflect the parties' intentions. Thus, subordination occurs when a mortgagee with priority—normally a first mortgage—agrees to release his priority, subordinating his interest to another lender who, in the absence of the agreement, would be junior in priority to the holder of the first mortgage.

[A]   Mechanics of Subordination Agreements

Subordination Agreements normally arise because institutional and other lenders refuse to make certain loans, including developmental loans like Construction Loans and Permanent Loans, unless they have priority as first mortgagee on the land securing the debt in order to maximize their security interest in the event of default. The lender's refusal to make loans unless given priority is based either on existing law or the lender's own policy decision.[9]

Subordination is easily accomplished if the person or entity requesting the developmental or other loan owns the property free and clear with no encumbrancing mortgages. Unfortunately, many, if not all, developers are "cash-poor" or hesitant to pay cash for property if it is not absolutely required (putting more cash into the project may not affect the profitability of the project but it may adversely affect the developer's return on his cash investment in the project; plus, the less cash in this project, the more projects the developer can operate simultaneously). As a result, when most developers purchase a large tract of land from a seller they would rather lay out a small down payment and have the seller take back a mortgage for the remainder of the purchase price, thereby creating a purchase money mortgagee in the vendor who sells the property to the developer.[10] Moreover, the developer would like to pay off that mortgage with someone else's funds—usually the ultimate purchaser of the completed project. (Most of these deals are struck so that the developer may not have to pay interest and definitely will not pay any principal until the project is completed and sold, thereby placing the risk of loss for the failure of the project on the selling vendor

---

[9] For a discussion of the "weak" position of a junior lienholder when a senior lienholder is foreclosing, see *supra* § 8.04.

[10] For a discussion of purchase money mortgagees, see *supra* § 1.06[A].

who has taken back a purchase money mortgage.) The obvious problem created by this type of financing occurs when the developer attempts to arrange a developmental or construction loan to construct the improvements on the project and the original vendor is the first mortgagee either because she recorded prior to the construction lender or because the existing statutory scheme accords priority to the purchase money mortgagee (vendor) or for both reasons. This problem can be resolved if the developer extracts from the selling vendor, at the time the property is sold from the vendor to the developer, an agreement to subordinate her mortgage to subsequent development or construction lenders.

[1] Open Subordination Agreement

In a truly open agreement there is no agreement or mention of a subordination agreement between the parties. In this situation, the developer relies on the vendor-mortgagee, recognizing that if there is no subordination there will be no project and, more importantly, the vendor-mortgagee may not be paid.

[2] Qualified Subordination Agreement

Of slightly more protection than the Open Subordination Agreement, is the Qualified Subordination Agreement in which both parties agree to negotiate in good faith at a later time in order to agree on a subordination agreement when required by the developmental lender. The enforceability of such an agreement remains questionable.

[3] Automatic Subordination

The easiest to understand, the automatic Subordination Agreement is an ex ante agreement between the parties in which the vendor-mortgagee agrees to subordinate its interest to a developmental mortgage. In a truly Automatic Subordination Agreement, the maximum amount and the type of mortgage is spelled out. In certain Automatic Subordination Agreements (often called "Open" Automatic Subordination Agreements), the vendor-mortgagor may unknowingly agree to subordinate its interest to that of any mortgagee used by the purchasing developer.

[B] Judicial Treatment of Subordination Agreements

Courts, especially California courts, have scrutinized Automatic Subordination Agreements because of the possible negative impact on those perceived to be relatively unsophisticated parties. Because most subordination agreements will relegate the vendor to a junior lienholder, the vendor is in a precarious position if the senior lienholder, the first mortgagee, forecloses and the land does not bring enough at foreclosure to satisfy the first mortgagee's debt. In this situation, the vendor's recourse will be against the developer who is normally cash poor or who has formed a cash poor corporation or limited partnership to take title to the realty and so often is judgment proof. Thus, courts have stepped in to protect vendors by holding that "an enforceable subordination clause must contain terms that will define and minimize the risk that the subordinating lien will impair or destroy the seller's security."[11]

In *Handy v. Gordon*, the vendor agreed to an Automatic Subordination Agreement which he later refused to honor.[12] In his defense to the developer's claim for specific enforcement, the vendor claimed the agreement was unenforceable because it was indefinite (the terms of the loans to which the vendor's mortgage would be subordinated weren't spelled out) and it was unfair, i.e., not just and reasonable. The Supreme Court of California held that the action for specific performance did not lie because the Subordination Agreement did not limit the vendor's risk by insuring that any loans to which he was required to subordinate would actually be used to improve the value of the land.[13] Thus, if the agreement had been found valid, the developer could have required the vendor to subordinate to a loan executed by the developer for his personal use and then the developer could have foreclosed, wiping out the vendor's equity in the property.

The case is obviously correct from an anterior perspective if one assumes that a reasonable subordination agreement is premised on the vendor's expectation that the lien to which he is subordinating does not increase his risk of loss of equity. On the other hand, the decision introduces a degree of uncertainty into a consensual transaction which could increase transaction costs. By applying ex post judgment (especially one based on a "just and reasonable" standard) to agreements, the courts could be creating extra drafting costs, uncertainty costs, etc. Instead one could argue that the court should focus on allegations of bargaining process unfairness (unconscionability) that take place ex ante.

[C]   Subordination to Leases

Unlike a mortgage, a lease is not a lien on property but an encumbrance affected by the priority of mortgages. Any lease that is subordinate to a pre-exiting mortgage, including ground leases,[14] is wiped out if a senior mortgage is foreclosed because the mortgagee at the foreclosure sale is entitled to transfer the state of title it secured when it originally placed the lien on the property, i.e., a title free of the "junior" interest represented by the lease. Thus, many long-term lessees require the mortgagee to subordinate to its lease. Conversely, many mortgagees who view long-term lease encumbrances as being just as harmful as senior mortgages require long-term lessees to subordinate to their mortgage.

[1]   Nondisturbance Clauses

If the lessee executes a subordination agreement with the mortgagee or finds herself in a position junior to a mortgagee, she can protect her interest from being

---

[11] Handy v. Gordon, 65 Cal.2d 578, 55 Cal. Rptr. 769, 422 P.2d 329 (1967).

[12] *Id.*

[13] *Id.*

[14] *See infra* § 14.02 for further discussion.

foreclosed by having the senior interest agree to a Nondisturbance Clause pursuant to which the lessee's right to possession and other rights spelled out in the lease are protected in the event of default by the mortgagor so long as the lessee is not in default on any of the terms of the lease.

CHAPTER

14

LONG-TERM LEASES

SYNOPSIS

§ 14.01   Introduction

Although thinking of long-term leases as financing vehicles for the use and development of real estate seems rather odd at first glance, tax and other practical advantages associated with leasing have recently created a boom in the use of long-term leases as alternatives to conventional fee ownership for the use and development of commercial realty.

§ 14.02   The Ground Lease

A Ground Lease is a lease of only the land owned by the lessor-fee owner. The improvements on the land, which the Ground Lessee will use, are constructed by the Ground Lessee and owned by the Ground Lessee. The improvements may or may not revert to the Ground Lessor upon termination of the Ground Lease; if not, the Ground Lessee normally must remove the improvements from the land at the termination of the lease and return the premises to the Ground Lessor in as good a condition as when received, normal wear and tear excepted. Thus, Ground Leases are typically "net leases" with the Ground Lessee paying rent to the Ground Lessor and also paying for the maintenance, taxes, insurance, and any other costs associated with the lease. Thus, the Ground Lessor does not have to offset against the rent any costs typically associated with the ownership and lease of real property to a tenant the funds he receives "net."

[A]   Ground Lease as a Financing Vehicle

In commercial projects, the Ground Lease serves as a financing vehicle for minimizing the Ground Lessee's (often a developer) investment (often a capital outlay) in the project in order to maximum his rate of return.[1]

[B]   Mechanics of Operation of Ground Lease

In a typical Ground Lease, the developer will use the Ground Lease as a financing device because it is a substitute for a purchase money mortgage and requires very little cash investment from the developer except the security deposit associated with a lease.

In a simple example, the developer approaches the owner of vacant land that is suitable for a subdivision. Instead of purchasing the fee and constructing the subdivision, which would require a significant amount of cash or a purchase money mortgage retained by the seller (a mortgage would later have to be subordinated to a Construction Loan and a Permanent Loan), the developer leases the ground and pays rent (which, by the way, is fully deductible as a business expense). The rent associated with the lease is analogous to a mortgage payment but it is fully deductible and the lease does not require a 10% or 20% down payment. The Developer constructs the improvements with a Construction Loan or her own funds and, if a Construction Loan is used a Permanent Loan is arranged. The interest on the loans, if used, is deductible and the developer will take deductions for depreciation on the improvements. At the end of the term, anywhere from 30 to 99 years, the land will revert to the owner of the fee unless other arrangements are made in the lease.

[1]   Valuing the Reversion

From the developer's perspective, although this seems counterfactual, the fact that the lease will revert to the fee owner at the end of the lease is largely irrelevant given the length of the term of the lease because the longer the lease, the smaller the *present value* of the reversion from an accounting perspective.[2]

---

[1] *See* Grenert, Ground Lease Practice (1971).

[2] *See* Johnson, *Correctly Interpreting Long-Term Leases Pursuant to Modern Contract Law: Toward A Theory of Relational Leases*, 74 Va.L.Rev. 751, 776-778 (1988).

[2]   Subordination

Frequently, the Ground Lessor's interest in the premises must be subordinated to the Construction and Permanent Loans arranged to finance the construction of the improvements. The problems associated with subordinating a purchase money mortgage, discussed in § 13.03, are not applicable to the subordination of a ground lease because the Ground Lessor still owns the fee simple in the land.

[C]   Mortgaging the Ground Lease or the Leasehold Mortgage

The tenant-developer pursuant to a long-term Ground Lease, has an interest in land (the leasehold) that is capable of securitization. In other words, a leasehold can be and frequently is mortgaged to lenders. The tenant-developer receives funds from the lender which it may use to construct improvements or simply pocket as a way to get its cash out of the premises immediately following completion of construction. The money received is not taxable since the transaction is a loan and not a sale. The developer pays the mortgage note with the income it receives from tenants occupying the improvements and is allowed to deduct the mortgage payment as a business expense. If the mortgage term runs as long as the Ground Lease, the last payment will be made on the mortgage at the same time that the tenant-developer receives the last payment from her tenants. The mortgagee secures its mortgage by, in effect, securing the stream of income or rents that the tenant obtains as a result of her Ground Lease. In other words, if the tenant-developer defaults, the mortgagee steps in to collect the rent and act as the new tenant-developer of the improvement.

[1]   Protecting the Mortgagee's Interest

The one unique risk taken by the mortgagee securing a tenant's interest in a Ground Lease is the possibility that the tenant will default on the underlying lease and the tenant's interest will be terminated and the holder of the reversionary interest, the Ground Lessor, will take possession. As a result, the mortgagee must protect its position via an agreement with the Ground Lessor to be notified of any default and be given the opportunity to cure those defaults.

[a]   Subordination

One way to avoid the problem is to have the Ground Lessor subordinate its interest to that of the mortgagee.

§ 14.03   Sale-Leaseback

The Sale-Leaseback is a financing arrangement similar to a Ground Lease which limits the developer's equity or investment in the premises.[3]

---

[3] *See* Smith and Lubell, *Reflection on the Sale-Leaseback*, 7 Real Estate Rev. 11-13 (Winter 1978).

[A] Mechanics of Operation

The Sale-Leaseback arrangement is not very complicated: The Sale-Leaseback starts with a developer, Donna Developer, whom we will assume for simplicity's sake purchases a fee simple interest in a piece of property and constructs a shopping center improvement thereon. Following completion of construction, Donna sells the entire development (or alternatively the ground and not the improvements creating a ground lease) to an institutional investor—that is the *sale*. Contemporaneously, the same parties execute a lease pursuant to which the premises are leased to Donna (the prior owner) using a long-term net lease, requiring the lessee to maintain the premises and pay and do all of the obligations normally associated with an owner or landlord.

[B] Purpose of Sale-Leaseback

Although there are certain tax advantages to a Sale-Leaseback, which are beyond the scope of this guide, the institutional investor in a Sale-Leaseback gets a steady stream of income or return on its investment and a manager (Donna Developer) of its property while the lease is in effect. In addition, the institutional investor who purchases and leases the property back to Donna also benefits from any appreciation on the land and the improvements when the land reverts to the investor following expiration of the term of the lease. Donna receives cash and the right to operate the shopping center as sub-lessor, which hopefully result in rents received in excess of the monthly lease payment.

[1] Repurchase Option Caveat

A Sale-Leaseback may be structured so that Donna has the right to repurchase the fee simple of the development at the expiration of the term for some predetermined amount. If so, there is a possibility that courts will construe the Sale-Leaseback as a mortgage substitute.[4] Hence, any attempt by the institutional investor to abrogate Donna's interest in the premises by declaring a default of the lease, may be construed by the courts as an attempt by the institutional lender to clog Donna's equity of redemption. As a result, the investor may be required to foreclose Donna's interest through a foreclosure sale.[5]

---

[4] Discussed *supra* in § 6.04.

[5] *See supra* Chapter 8.

TABLE OF CASES

[References are to Pages and Notes.]

INDEX

[References are to pages.]

[References are to pages.]

[References are to pages.]

[References are to pages.]

[References are to pages.]

[References are to pages.]

[References are to pages.]

[References are to pages.]

[References are to pages.]

[References are to pages.]

Q

R

[References are to pages.]

[References are to pages.]

[References are to pages.]

[References are to pages.]